LATIN

FOR THE ILLITERATI

LATIN

FOR THE ILLITERATI

Exorcizing the Ghosts of a Dead Language

Jon R. Stone

ROUTLEDGE
New York & London

Published in 1996 by

Routledge
29 West 35th Street
New York, NY 10001

Published in Great Britain in 1996 by

Routledge
11 New Fetter Lane
London EC4P 4EE

Printed in the United States of America
Design: Mary Neal Meador
Typography: Jack Donner

Library of Congress Cataloging-in-Publication Data

Stone, Jon R., 1959–
    Latin for the illiterati : exorcizing the ghosts of a dead language / Jon R. Stone.
        p.   cm.
    Includes bibliographical references (p.   ).
    ISBN 0–415–91774–3 (alk. paper). — ISBN 0–415–91775–1 (pbk. : alk. paper)
    1. Latin language—Dictionaries—English: 2. Latin language—Terms and phrases. I. Title.
PA2365.E5S76   1996
473'.21—dc20   95–47985
                                                                            CIP

CONTENTS

To my mother
Bobbie Jean Stone
who taught me my first Latin words:
Amo, Amas, Amat

PREFACE

A decade ago, while in my first years of graduate study, I was taking a seminar in which my fellow graduate students and I were required to read standard theoretical works in the History of Religions. Among the books on that long list of dry academic tomes were several titles in the philosophy of religion, including Rudolf Otto's neo-Kantian work, *The Idea of the Holy* (or *Das Heilige*). It was here that I came face-to-face with the ghosts of a dead language: Latin.

Though as an undergraduate I had encountered the usual "i.e.s" and "e.g.s," along with the periodic "cogito ergo sums" and "et tu, Brutes," Otto presented a nearly insurmountable challenge to a boy who had studied German and Greek. Indeed, the proliferation of Latin words and quotations began to haunt me as I struggled through Otto's work. What was one to make of such things as the "numinous" experience (from the word "numen") with its characteristic religious feelings of awful dread and awe-inspiring fascination that Otto called "mysterium tremendum" and "mysterium fascinosum?" Worse still were the seemingly innumerable phrases that came with no corresponding English translation, leaving me to ward off these menacing spirits as best I could with a moldy old Latin dictionary I had found for half a dollar in a downtown used book store.

To help exorcize these daemons, I began keeping lists of the Latin words and phrases I continuously encountered in my reading. These lists began to grow over my several years of graduate study to the point that they filled a section of the weather-worn notebook I had used during my college days. It was at that point that I decided to type these lists into a handy reference book, not simply for my use but for the use of others likewise haunted. While I would not claim to have rid myself of these ghosts altogether—I still keep lists—I have become fairly comfortable with their presence in my life. What is more, one happy and incidental result of the struggle to deliver myself from my ignorance was a genuine love of Latin and an appreciation of its remarkable influence in the development of Western philosophical and cultural thought. But of greater importance, what I have learned over the past ten years is that one need not be haunted by the specter of Latin.

Latin forms an integral part of our daily lives and its use is foundational to our major branches of knowledge from law and medicine to literature and commerce. To deal adequately with its ubiquitous presence, it is necessary to have access to helpful reference tools. Unfortunately, few reference works exist that focus on remedying the challenges faced by the modern reader whose educational experience—even at the college level—is not firmly grounded in the so-called Classical tradition. Sadly, most of the books that are available to the general reader, while sometimes amusing, are really of no practical value (for instance, few of us have the occasion—or the inclination—to give a toast or recite the Gettysburg Address in Latin; and fewer still have an audience of relatives or interested business associates willing to endure such novelty). This book seeks to correct this deficiency by giving the student and general reader a helpful and practical reference guide. Here, then, is a fairly comprehensive compendium of nearly 6,000 Latin words, phrases, and standard abbreviations taken from the world of art, music, law, philosophy, theology, medicine and the theater as well as miscellaneous remarks and sagely advice from ancient writers such as Virgil, Ovid, Cicero, Terence, Juvenal, Seneca, and others, a *vade mecum* of sorts, that is meant to guide its users as well as instruct them.

Because the specific aim of this book is not to teach Latin but to help the modern reader exorcize the ghosts of this ancient and influential tongue, the various sections are arranged in alphabetical order, giving first the Latin word or phrase and then its common or usual meaning. In some cases, a literal translation of the word or phrase in brackets [   ] is given, followed by its more specialized meaning. An explanation of its origins or usage is sometimes given in parentheses. While most of the translations are not mine *per se*, having been culled from reference books and dictionaries over the years, many of the bracketed translations and most of the parenthetical remarks are my own, with the aid, that is, of *Cassell's Concise Latin Dictionary*. Although I have carefully checked and rechecked both the spellings and tenses of words, I fear that inadvertent errors may still have crept into this text. If mistakes exist beyond the rare editorial lapses, they are my own fault (*mea culpa, mea culpa, mea culpa*).

In addition, I have attempted to be gender-inclusive and gender-neutral wherever possible and whenever such modifications did not compromise grammatical integrity too greatly or run counter to the spirit of a word's or phrase's meaning. I must also point out that on occasion the reader may spot a Greek word or two. As with most languages, foreign words also crept into Latin as the Roman Empire began to expand its territories through conquest. Many of those listed in this work became fairly standard by the Christian era, including such words as logos (word), sophia (wisdom), soter (savior), hippodromos (race track), margarita (pearl), and sarcophagus (coffin).

Finally, let me say a word or two about the insensitive or prejudicial sayings that occasionally appear in this work. In truth, I cringe at some of the phrases in the popular Roman "body of knowledge" that reveal a flagrant disregard of and disrespect for human cultural differences. However, in partial defense of the Romans, I think it is foolish for us moderns, with our greater historical and cultural perspective, to condemn a people who could not escape their own peculiar world with its illiberal views of women and its hostility towards all things foreign. We moderns certainly "know better" than the ancients did, though it did take us nearly two millennia to liberate ourselves from our unenlightened view of the world. Having said this, it must be remembered that, in the end, this book is a reference work, not an apology for Western Roman culture. Though we cannot erase our cruel and ignorantly insensitive past, we can certainly learn from it and endeavor to live above and beyond it.

Valeat Quantum Valere Potest.

Jon R. Stone
University of California, Santa Barbara
February 1995

REFERENCES

Angeles, Peter A. *Dictionary of Christian Theology*. NY: Harper & Row, 1985.

———. *Dictionary of Philosophy*. NY: Barnes & Noble Books, 1981.

Anon. *Latin for Lawyers* (2nd ed.). London: Sweet and Maxwell, LTD, 1937.

Cassell's Concise Latin-English/English-Latin Dictionary (compiled by D.P. Simpson). NY: MacMillan Publishing Co., 1977.

Hines, Sister Therese and Rev. Edward J. Welch, S.J. *Our Latin Heritage*. NY: Harcourt, Brace & World, 1966.

Horn, Annabel, John F. Gummere, and Margaret M. Forbes. *Using Latin*. Glenview, IL: Scott, Foresman and Co., 1961.

Koller, Hermann. *Orbis Pictus Latinus* (3rd ed.). Zürich: Artemis Verlag, 1983.

Mawson, C.O. Sylvester and Charles Berlitz (eds.). *Dictionary of Foreign Terms* (2nd ed.). NY: Barnes & Noble Books, 1979.

Meissner, C. *Latin Phrase-Book* (H.W. Auden, trans.). London: McMillan & Co., 1938.

Moreland, Floyd L. and Rita M. Fleischer. *Latin: An Intensive Course*. Berkeley: University of California Press, 1977.

Novum Testamentum Latine: Textum Vaticanum (11th edition, Eberhard Nestle, ed.). Stuttgart: Württembergische Bibelanstalt, 1971.

Reese, W. L. (ed.). *Dictionary of Philosophy and Religion: Eastern and Western Thought*. Atlantic Highlands, NJ: Humanities Press, 1980.

Webster's II: New Riverside University Dictionary. Boston: Houghton Mifflin Co., 1984.

Webster's New World Dictionary (3rd College Edition). NY: Prentice Hall, 1988.

Wheelock, Frederick M. *Latin* (College Outline Series). NY: Barnes & Noble Books, 1962.

PRONUNCIATION GUIDE

Pronouncing Latin words can seem mystifying at first, even daunting, but one need not utter Latin words and phrases with such tongue-tied trepidation. Most Latin sounds have corresponding English sounds, following the same rules for short and long pronunciation of vowels. For example, the long *a* in *father* is the same sound as the long *a* in the Latin word *pater*. The short *a* in the English words *par* and *far* are very similar in sound to that of the Latin words *pax* and *fax*. The short *e* in *pet* is similar in sound to the Latin *et*, as is the short *i* in *twig* the same as the *i* in the Latin word *signum*. The long *o* in *Ohio* sounds very much like the *o* in the Latin word *dolor*. In the same way, the short *o* in *pot* is pronounced similarly to the short *o* in *populas*. Likewise, the Latin *u* in *runa* and *pudicus*, one long and the other short, sound the same as the long and short *u* vowels in *rude* and *put*.

With respect to Latin consonants, one should nearly always pronounce them as those in English (e.g., **b** = b, **d** = d, **f** = f, **l** = l, **m** = m, **n** = n, **p** = p, **r** = r, **s** = s, **t** = t, etc.), with the exception of **c**, **g**, **h**, **i-j**, and **v**, which are always pronounced like **k** (as in kirk), **g** (as in give, gave, and go), **h** (as in hard), **y** (as in you, yam, and use), and **w** (as in we and was) respectively (though, I must confess, I have never heard William F. Buckley, Jr., quote Julius Caesar as having declared before the Roman Senate: "weenie, weedie, weekie" [i.e., "I came, I saw, I conquered"]. I suspect that most *literati* shy away from such ridiculous and silly sounding pronunciations as this one).

Vowel diphthongs are another matter. Most Classical Latin linguists prefer to pronounce **ae** as if it were a long *i* (as in pine), **oe** as *oi* (as in boy), **au** as *ou* or *ow* (as in bough or now), **ei** as a long *a* (as in weight), **eu** as *eu* (as in feud), **ui** as *wee* (as in the French *oui*).

XV

VERBA

Common Words and Expressions

A

a bene placito: at pleasure

a capite ad calcem [from head to heel]: from head to toe (i.e., completely or entirely)

a cuspide corona [from the spear a crown]: honor for military exploits

a datu: from the date

a dextra: on the right

a die: from that day

a fortiori [with greater force]: more conclusively; in logic, an argument made from the lesser to the greater

a latere: from the side

a maximis ad minima: from the greatest to the least

a mensa et toro (or **thoro**) [from table and bed]: (leg.) from bed and board

a mille passibus: a mile away

a minori ad majus: from the lesser to the greater

a posse ad esse: from possibility to realization or reality

a posteriori [from after]: reasoning from specific instances to general conclusions (i.e., inductive or empirical knowledge)

a primo: from the first

a principio: from the beginning

a priori [from before]: reasoning from premise to logical conclusion (i.e., deductive or presumptive knowledge)

a pueris or **a puero:** from boyhood

a quo: from which (opposite of **ad quem**)

a sinistra: on the left

a teneris annis [from tender years]: from childhood or youth

a tergo [in the rear]: behind

a verbis ad verbera: from words to blows

a vinculo matrimonii [from the bonds of marriage]: an absolute divorce

ab: from

ab absurdo: from the absurd

ab aeterno: from the beginning of time

ab asino lanam [wool from an ass]: blood from a stone

ab epistulis [of letters]: secretarial matters

ab extra [from without]: from the outside

ab imo pectore: from the bottom of the heart

ab inconvenienti [from the inconvenience (involved)]: usually designating a law which should not be passed due to certain hardships or inconveniences it would create

ab incunabulis [from the cradle]: from childhood

ab infima ara: from the bottom of the altar

ab initio (ab init.): from the beginning

ab integro: anew

ab intra: from within

ab invito: unwillingly

ab irato [from an angry man]: in a fit of anger (i.e., not to be taken too seriously)

ab origine: from the origin or beginning

ab ovo [from the egg]: from the beginning

ab uno ad omnes: from one to all

ab urbe condita (A.U.C.): from the founding of the city (i.e., Rome)

abacus [a square board]: a hand-held calculating table

abest (pl. **absunt**): he/she is absent

abiit ad plures or **majores** (pl. **abierunt**): he/she has gone to the majority (i.e., is dead)

abnormis sapiens [unconventionally wise]: a natural-born philosopher

abscissio infiniti [cutting off the infinite or negative part]: in logic, the process by which the true conclusion is reached by a systematic comparison and rejection of hypotheses

absente reo (abs. re.): (leg.) the defendant being absent

absit invidia [let there be no ill-will]: no offense intended

absit omen: may the omen augur no evil

absolvo: I absolve

absonus: out of tune

absque [but for]: without

absque hoc [without this]: a legal term used in a special traverse or formal denial

absque ulla nota: without any mark

abusus non tollit usum [abuse does not take away use]: (leg.) abuse is no argument against use

abyssus abyssum invocat: deep calls unto deep

Academia: The Academy (i.e., the grove near Athens where Plato taught his disciples)

accedas ad curiam [you may approach the court]: in English law, a common-law writ to remove a case to a higher court

accentus: part of a church service chanted or sung by the priest and his/her assistant at the altar, distinguished from **concentus** which is sung by the congregation or choir

accepta [receipts]: credits

accessio initium regni: ascension to the throne

accessit (pl. **accesserunt**) [he/she came near]: "honorable mention" in a contest

accessus et recessus: ebb and flow

acerbus et ingens: fierce and mighty

acervatim [in heaps]: summarily

acta sanctorum: holy deeds of the martyred saints

actum agere: to do what has already been done

actum est: it is all over

actus: an act in a play

actus: an action or an actuality

actus Dei: an act of God

actus purus [pure act]: (theo.) a reference to God as a complete and perfect being

actus reus: (leg.) a criminal act

acus: a needle

ad: to or at; (med.) up to

ad absurdum [to what is absurd]: an argument which demonstrates the absurdity of an opponent's proposition

ad amussim [according to a rule]: accurately or exactly

ad annum: a year from now

ad aperturam libri [at the opening of the book]: wherever the book opens (a reference to a certain type of prognostication)

ad arbitrium: at will

ad arma concurrere: to rush to arms

ad astra [to the stars]: to an exalted place or to high renown

ad baculum [to the rod]: an argument or appeal which resorts to force rather than reason

ad captandum: an argument or appeal which is presented for the sake of pleasing the audience

ad captandum vulgus [to catch or attract the crowd]: to please the rabble

ad clerum: to the clergy

ad crumenam [to the purse]: an argument or appeal to one's personal interests

ad eundem gradum (ad eund.): to the same degree or standing

ad exiguum tempus: for a short time

ad extra: in an outward direction

ad extremum [to the extreme]: to the last or to the end

ad extremum tumulum: on the edge of the hill

ad filum aquae: (leg.) to the center of the stream

ad filum viae: to the center of the road

ad finem (ad fin.) [to or at the end]: finally

ad finem fidelis: faithful to the end

ad gloriam: for glory

ad gustum [to taste]: to one's taste

ad hanc vocem (a.h.v.): at this word

ad hoc [to this]: an action taken for a specific purpose, case, or situation

ad hominem [at the man]: an argument which appeals to personal prejudice or emotions rather than reason

ad horam compositam: at the agreed hour

ad hunc locum (a.h.l.): at this place

ad idem: to the same point

ad ignorantiam [to ignorance]: an argument or appeal that is ignorant of the needed facts

ad inferos descendere: to descend into the lower world

ad infinitum (ad inf. or **ad infin.)** [to infinity]: endless, limitless, or forever

ad initium (ad init.): at the beginning

ad instar [after the fashion of]: like

ad interim (ad int.): in the meantime

ad internecionem: to the point of extermination

ad invidiam [to envy]: an argument which appeals to prejudice or envy

ad judicium [to judgment]: an argument which appeals to common sense

ad libitum (ad lib.) [at pleasure]: in music, used as a direction to musicians to improvise a certain number of measures

ad limina apostolorum or **ad limina** [to the threshold of the Apostles]: to the highest authority

ad lineam: in a straight line or perpendicularly

ad litem: (leg.) for the suit or action

ad litteram or **ad literam** [to the letter]: literally

ad locum (ad loc.): to or at the place

ad lunam: by moonlight

ad manum [at hand]: in readiness

ad me: to my house

ad meridiem: southward

ad misericordiam [to pity]: an argument which appeals to pity

ad modum [in or after the manner of]: like

ad multam noctem: until late at night

ad multum diem: until late in the day

ad multus annos: for many years

ad nauseam [to nausea]: to the point of disgust

ad occasum: westward

ad occidentem: westward

ad ostium ecclesiae [at the church door]: at the marriage

ad patres [to the fathers]: dead or passed away

ad paucos dies: for a few days

ad perpendiculum: in a straight line or perpendicularly

ad perpetuitatem: forever

ad populum [to the people]: an argument which appeals to people's prejudices or passions

ad postremum: for the last time

ad quem: at or to which (the opposite of **a quo**)

ad quod damnum: (leg.) to what dammage

ad referendum [for reference]: for further consideration or for the approval of a superior

ad rem [to the matter]: a legal term denoting something relevant to the point at issue

ad sectam (ads.): (leg.) at the suit of

ad summam [on the whole]: in general or in short

ad summum: to the highest point or amount

ad tempus [at the right time]: in due time or according to the circumstances

ad ultimum: to the last

ad unguem [to a fingernail]: to a T (i.e., perfectly)

ad unum omnes [all to a one]: everyone without exception (i.e., unanimously)

ad usum (ad us.): according to custom

ad usum Delphini [for the Dauphin's use]: a work expurgated to avoid offending a prince or other high official

ad utrumque paratus [prepared for either event]: prepared for the worst

ad valorem (ad val.): according to the value

ad verbum [word for word]: literally or to the letter

ad verecundiam [to modesty]: an argument which appeals to modesty

ad vicem: in place of or instead of

ad vitam: for life

ad vitam aeternam [for eternal life]: for all time

ad vitam aut culpam [for life or until misbehavior]: during good behavior

ad vivum [to the life]: lifelike

adde (ad. or **add.):** (med.) let there be added (i.e., add)

adde huc (or **adde eo**) [add to this]: consider this as well

addendum (pl. **addenda**): an attachment to the end of a manuscript indicating the words to be added or corrections to be made

additum (pl. **addita**): something added

ades dum or **adesdum:** come hither

Adeste Fideles: O Come, All Ye Faithful

adfatim: sufficiently

adhuc sub judice lis est: (leg.) the case is still before the court

adiectivum or **adjectivum (adi.** or **adj.):** an adjective

adiratus: (leg.) lost or strayed

adscriptus glebae (pl. **adscripti glebae**) [bound to the soil]: a serf

adsum [I am present]: here!

adsumptio: in logic, the minor premise of a syllogism

adumbratio: a sketch

adversa fortuna: ill fortune

adversaria [written observations]: a diary or journal

adverso colle or **adversus collem:** uphill

adverso flumine: against the stream

adversus (adv.): against

advocatus diaboli: the Devil's advocate (opposite of **promotor fidei** in an ecclesiastical argument in favor of the beatification of a person)

aeger [sick]: a medical excuse

aeger amore: love sick

aegis [a shield]: sponsorship or protection

aegra amans [lover's disease]: love sick

aegri somnia [a sick person's dreams]: hallucination

aegris oculis: with envious eyes

aegrotat (pl. **aegrotant**) [he/she is ill]: a medical excuse

aenigma: a riddle

aequabiliter et diligenter: uniformly and diligently

aequam servare mentem: to keep one's cool

aequanimiter [with equanimity]: with composure

aequi iniqui: friend and foe

aequinoctium autumnale: the autumnal equinox

aequinoctium vernum: the vernal equinox

aequo animo [with an equal spirit]: with equanimity or resignation (i.e., calmly)

aequo marte: a draw (i.e., an indecisive match)

aequum est: it is just

aere perennius [more lasting than bronze]: everlasting

aes alienum [money belonging to another]: debt or debts

aes publicum: a public inscription

aes signatum: coined money

aes triplex [triple brass]: a strong defense

aestas: summer

aestu incitato: at high tide

aetate progrediente: with advancing years

aetatis (**aet.** or **aetat.**): of the age or of one's lifetime

aetatis suae (**A.S.**): of his/her age or lifetime

aeternum vale: farewell forever

afflatus [breath or breeze]: poetic inspiration

afflatus montium: mountain air

Africus: the southwest wind (properly, **ventus Africus**)

age dum: come now

ager publicus: public land

agita (**agit.**): (med.) shake

agmen novissimum or **agmen extremum:** the rear guard

agmen primum: the vanguard

Agnus Dei [Lamb of God]: an appelation of Christ and a section of the Latin Mass

albae gallinae filius [a son of a white hen]: a fortunate son

albo lapillo notare diem [to mark a day with a white stone]: a red letter day

alere flammam: to feed the flame

alias dictus [otherwise called]: an alias

alibi: at another place

alieni appetens [eager for another's property]: covetous

alieni generis: of a different kind

alieni juris: (leg.) subject to the authority of another

alio intuitu: from another point of view

alio pacto: in another way

aliqua: in some way

aliud ex alio: one thing after another

aliunde [from another source]: from elsewhere

alius alias: one now, another later

alius alio: in various directions

alius aliter: in different ways

alma mater [fostering mother]: a university or other institution where a person has been educated

alter ego [one's other self]: a best friend or a bosom buddy

alter idem [another of the same kind]: a second self

alternis annis: every other year

alternis diebus: every other day

alternus: one after the other

alterum tantum [as much again]: twice as much

alteruter: one of two

altum silentium: deep silence or silence from on high

alumna [foster daughter]: a female graduate

alumnus [foster son]: a male graduate

amabo te or **amabo:** please

amantium irae: a lovers' quarrels

amari aliquid [something bitter]: a touch of bitterness

ambigendi locus: room for doubt

ambo [two together]: both

ambrosia: the food or nectar of the gods

amicissimus meus or **amicissimus mihi:** my best friend

amiciter: in a friendly way

amicitia sine fraude: friendship without deceit

amicus curiae [a friend of the court]: a disinterested advisor

amicus humani generis: a friend of the human race

amor habendi: love of possessing

amor nummi: love of money

amor patriae: love of country (i.e., patriotism)

amor proximi: love of one's neighbor

amor sui: self-love

amplissimi viri: men of the highest position

ancilla theologiae [the handmaid of theology]: philosophy

ancora: an anchor

anguis in herba [a snake in the grass]: an unsuspected danger

aniles fabellae: "old wives'" tales

anima bruta [the brute soul]: the vital principle of lower animals

anima divina: the divine soul

anima humana: the human soul

anima mundi [the spirit of the universe]: the creative and energizing force that permeates all nature

anima or **animus** (pl. **animae**): breath, soul, or spirit

animal disputans: an argumentative person

animal rationale: a reasoning person

animo aeger: (med.) heart-sick physically

animo et facto: (leg.) in intention and fact

animo fractus: heartbroken

animo furandi: (leg.) with the intention to steal

animo testandi: (leg.) with the intention of making a will

animus angustus: narrow-minded

animus capiendi: (leg.) the intention of taking

animus furandi: (leg.) the intention of stealing

animus gratus: thankfulness

annales (ann.): records or chronicles

annis tribus: three years ago (properly **abhinc annis tribus**)

anniversarius: yearly

anno aetatis suae (A.A.S.): in the year of his/her age

anno Christi: in the year of Christ

anno Domini (A.D.): in the year of our Lord

anno Hebraico (A.H.): in the Hebrew year (see also **anno mundi**)

anno Hejirae or **Hegirae (A.H.):** in the year of the Hegira (the Prophet Muhammad's flight from Mecca to Medina & the first year of the Muslim era, 622 C.E.)

anno humanae salutis (A.H.S.): in the year of man's redemption

anno interiecto: after the interval of a year

anno mundi (A.M.): in the year of the world since its creation (see also **anno Hebraico)**

anno post Christum natum (A.P.C.N.): in the year after the birth of Christ

anno post Roman conditam (A.P.R.C.): in the year after the building of Rome (ca. 753 B.C.E.)

anno regni (A.R.): in the year of the reign

anno salutis (A.S.): in the year of redemption

anno urbis conditae (A.U.C.): in the year of the founded city (i.e., Rome, ca. 753 B.C.E.)

anno vertente: in the course of the year

annos prope XL natus: almost forty years old

annos tres: three years ago (properly **abhinc annos tres**)

annos vixit (a.v.): he/she lived (so many years)

annua pecunia: an annuity

annus (pl. **anni**): year

annus bisextus: leap-year

annus luctus: year of mourning

annus magnus [great year]: the Platonic year; in astronomy, the year in which the celestial bodies make a complete cycle (about 26,000 years)

annus mirabilis [wonderful year]: a year of wonders (a reference especially to the year 1666 C.E., when the Great Fire ravaged most of London)

ante: before

ante bellum [before the war]: before the American Civil War

ante Christum (A.C.): before Christ

ante Christum natus (A.Ch.N.): before Christ's birth

ante cibum (a.c.): (med.) before meals

ante diem (a.d.): before the day

ante litem motam: (leg.) before litigation has begun

ante lucem: before daybreak

ante meridiem or **ante meridianus (A.M.** or **a.m.):** before noon

ante mortem: before death

ante omnia [before all things]: in the first place

ante partum or **antepartum** [before birth]: before childbirth

ante tempus [too soon]: before its time

ante urbem conditam: before the founding of the city (i.e., Rome)

antecepta informatio: an innate idea

antehac [before this time]: formerly

antenna: a sail yard (i.e., the cross piece of a ship's mast from which a sail hangs)

antiquitatis memoria: ancient history

anxius: uneasy

aper: a wild boar

apis: a bee

apologia pro vita sua: a defense or justification of the conduct of one's life

apotheca: a wine cellar or storage room

apotheosis [deification]: the transformation of a mortal into a deity at death

apparatus belli: munitions or materiel of war

apparatus criticus [critical apparatus]: reference texts used in scholarly work

apparet: it is clear

apricatio: sun-bathing

apricus: sunny

apud [according to]: in the writings of

apud Ciceronem: in the works of Cicero

apud me: at my house

apud patres: in the time of our fathers

aqua (aq.): water

aqua bulliens (aq. bull.): boiling water

aqua caelestis [celestial water]: pure rain water; also, a cordial

aqua destillata (aq. dest.): distilled water

aqua et igni interdictus [forbidden water and fire]: banished

aqua et ignis [water and fire]: the necessary things of life

aqua fontana: spring water

aqua fortis [strong water]: nitric acid

aqua mirabilis [wonderful water]: (pharm.) an aromatic cordial

aqua pura [pure water]: distilled water

aqua regia [royal water]: a mixture of nitric and hydrocloric acids

aqua saliens: a jet of water

aqua tofana [Tofana's water]: a poison made by a certain Tofana, a 17th century Sicilian woman infamous for its use

aqua vitae [water of life]: alcohol (i.e., whiskey or brandy)

aquarius: a water-carrier

aquilo: the north wind

ara: an altar

aranea: a spider

aratrum: a plow

arbiter bibendi [the judge of the drinking]: master of the feast (i.e., a toastmaster)

arbiter elegantiae or **elegantiarum** [a judge of elegance]: a judge in matters of taste

arbitrio suo: (leg.) under his own control

arbor infelix [infelicitous tree]: the gallows

arbor novella: a seedling

Arcades ambo [Arcadians both]: two persons of similar tastes or two simpletons; two of a kind (Virgil)

arcana caelestia [heavenly secrets]: celestial mysteries

arcana imperii: state secrets

arcanum arcanorum [secret of secrets]: a reference to the hidden keys that unlock the secrets of nature underlying alchemy, astrology, and magic

arcanus: secret or esoteric

arcus: a bow

arcus pluvius: a rainbow

ardentia verba [words that burn]: glowing words

ardor: a flame or heat from a flame

area [an open or level space]: a courtyard

arena sine calce [sand without lime]: an incoherent speech (Suetonius)

argentum (ag.): silver

argentum signatum: coined silver

argentum vivum: mercury

argumentum [argument]: a proof

argumentum ab auctoritate: in logic, a proof derived from authority

argumentum ab inconvenienti: in logic, an appeal to hardship or inconvenience

argumentum ad absurdum: in logic, an argument to prove the absurdity of an opponent's argument

argumentum ad baculum: in logic, an appeal to force or the threat of force (also **argumentum baculinum**)

argumentum ad captandum: in logic, an appeal made by arousing popular passions

argumentum ad crumenam [an argument to the purse]: in logic, an appeal to a person's interests

argumentum ad hominem: in logic, an evasive argument relying on attack of opponent's character

argumentum ad ignorantiam: in logic, an argument based on an opponent's ignorance of the facts or on his or her inability to prove the opposite

argumentum ad invidiam: in logic, an appeal to prejudices or base passions

argumentum ad judicium: in logic, an appeal to judgment or common sense

argumentum ad misericordiam: in logic, an appeal to pity

argumentum ad populum [argument to the people]: in logic, an appeal to people's lower nature rather than to their intellect

argumentum ad rem: in logic, a proper argument that bears on the real point of the issue at hand

argumentum ad verecundiam [also **ipse dixit**, or argument from authority]: in logic, an appeal to modesty or to a person's sense of reverence (e.g., a reliance on the prestige of a great or respected person rather than on the independent consideration of the question itself)

argumentum baculinum or **ad baculum:** in logic, an appeal to force or the threat of force

argumentum ex concesso [argument from concession]: an argument based on points already held by one's opponent

aries: a ram

arma accipere [to receive arms]: to be made a knight

arrectus auribus [with ears pricked up]: on the alert

ars amandi [the art of loving]: the art of love

ars artium [art of arts]: philosophical logic

ars artium omnium conservatrix [the art which preserves all arts]: printing

ars dicendi [the art of speaking]: oratory

ars fingendi: the art of sculpture

ars ludicra: the art of drama

ars magica: sorcery

ars moriendi: the art of dying

ars navigandi: seamanship

ars poetica: the art of poetry

ars Punica [the Punic art]: treachery

arteria: a blood vessel

artes ingenuae: the fine arts

artes liberales: the liberal arts

artes perditae: lost arts

arthriticus: pain in the joints of the body (i.e., arthritis)

articulorum dolor: (med.) a form of gout

Artium Baccalaureus (A.B. or **B.A.):** Bachelor of Arts

Artium Magister (A.M. or **M.A.):** Master of Arts

asinus: a jackass

asperges [thou shalt sprinkle]: the sprinkling with holy water at the beginning of the High Mass

assensio mentium [a meeting of the minds]: (leg.) mutual consent

Assensus [assent]: an essential item in Medieval Christian faith (together with **Fiducia** and **Notitia**)

assignatus utitur jure auctoris: (leg.) the assignee is possessed of the rights of the one he or she represents

assumpsit [he undertook]: (leg.) a suit to recover damages for breach of a contract or actionable promise, either expressed or implied

astrum: a star or constellation

atra cura [black care]: (fig.) in mourning

atrium: a hall

auctor ignotus: an unknown author

aucupia verborum: quibbling

audita querela [the complaint having been heard]: (leg.) a common-law writ giving the defendant opportunity to appeal

augustus: majestic

aura (pl. **aurae**): wind, air, or breeze

aura popularis [the popular breeze]: popular favor (Cicero)

aurea mediocritas [the golden mean]: moderation in all things (Horace)

auris: the ear

auritus [long-eared]: attentive

aurora: dawn or the break of day

aurora australis [southern dawn]: the southern lights

aurora borealis [northern dawn]: the northern lights

aurum (**au.**): gold

auspex: an augar who observed the behavior of animals to foretell the future

auster: the south wind

australis: south

ave! [hail!]: Greetings!

Ave Maria: Hail Mary (salutation to the Virgin Mary)

Ave Regina Caelorum: Hail, Queen of Heaven (salutation to the Virgin Mary)

avis: a bird

avunculus [mother's brother]: an uncle (also **patruus**, father's brother)

B

babae!: wonderful!

baccalaris: a young nobleman seeking knighthood

baculum: a staff or walking stick

Bancus Communium Placitorum: (leg.) Court of Common Pleas

Bancus Regis: (leg.) King's Bench

Beata Maria or **Beata Virgo** (**B.M.** or **B.V.**): the Blessed Virgin

Beata Virgo Maria: the Blessed Virgin Mary

beata vita: happiness or bliss

beatae memoriae (B.M.): of blessed memory

beati possidentes [happy are those who possess]: possession is nine-tenths of the law

beatus [blessed]: a candidate for beatification in the Roman Catholic Church

belli denuntiatio: a declaration of war

belli ratio: (mil.) battle tactics

bellicum: (mil.) the signal for march or attack

bellum atrocissimum: a war of atrocities

bellum civile: civil war

bellum domesticum: civil war

bellum internecinum [internecine war]: a war of extermination

bellum intestinum: civil war

bellum lethale: deadly war

bellum omnium in omnes: a war of all against all

bellus: pretty

bene: well or good

bene!: excellent!

bene decessit [he died well]: he died naturally

bene esse: well-being

bene est: it is well

bene exeat [let him/her go forth well]: a certificate of good character

bene facis [I am obliged to you]: much obliged

bene facta: good deeds

bene habet: all right

bene merenti (pl. **merentibus**): to the well-deserving

bene meritus (pl. **meriti**): having well deserved

bene tibi or **bene te:** your health!

bene vale (b.v.): farewell

bene vale vobis [farewell to you]: good luck

benedicite!: bless you!

Benedictus qui venit in nomine Domini [Blessed is he who comes in the name of the Lord]: a section of the Latin Mass

beneficium [kindness or favor]: a benefice

benevolentia: good-will

benigne dicis [much obliged]: thank you or no thank you

benigno numine: by the favor of heaven

bes: two-thirds

bestia: a beast

bibliopola: a bookseller

bibliotheca: a library

biduum: a period of two days

biennium: a period of two years

bifariam: in two parts

bifurcus: having two forks or prongs

bilibra: two pounds weight

billa vera: (leg.) true bill

bimulus: two years old

bimus: lasting two years

bini [twofold]: a pair

bis [twice]: in music, to be repeated

bis bina [twice two]: two pairs

bis in die (**b.i.d.**): (med.) twice a day

bona: (leg.) property

bona aetas: youth

bona fide [in good faith]: sincerely or genuinely

bona fides [good faith]: honest intention

bona fiscalia: (leg.) fiscal or public property

bona gratia: in all kindness

bona mixta malis: a mixture of good and evil

bona mobilia: (leg.) movable goods

bona notabilia: (leg.) noteworthy things

bona pars: a considerable amount

bona peritura: (leg.) perishable goods

bona vacantia: (leg.) unclaimed goods

bona verba: words of good omen

bonae artes: good qualities

bonae memoriae: of happy memory

bonae notae: meritorious

bonis avibus [with good birds]: under favorable auspices

bono animo esse: to be of good cheer

bonum diffusivium sui [diffusing his goodness]: (theo.) a reference to the inherent goodness of the divine creation

bonum omen: a good omen

bonum publicum (**b.p.**): the common good

Boreas: the north wind

bos in lingua [an ox on the tongue]: speechless or silent

brevi praecidam: to put it briefly

breviarium [summary or abridgement]: a medieval devotional book containing the Psalms and other sacred writings

bruma: the winter solstice

brutum fulmen (pl. **bruta fulmina**) [a harmless thunderbolt]: an empty threat

bucina: a curved trumpet

bulla [a seal]: a papal encyclical or declaration

C

cacoëthes: a bad habit, an irrepressible desire or a mania

cacoëthes carpendi: a tendency to find fault

cacoëthes loquendi: a tendency to talk

cacoëthes scribendi: an itch for writing or scribbling

cadaver: a corpse

cadit quaestio [the question falls on the ground]: the discussion has come to an end

caduceus: a prophet's or messenger's staff

caelum: the heavens

calculus [a pebble]: a checker piece, voting pebble, or a counting piece

calidus: hot

caligo [fog or darkness]: mental darkness

callida junctura [skillful joining]: craftsmanship (Horace)

calvaria: the human skull

calvus: bald

calx: the heel

calx [limestone or chalk]: a goal marked with chalk (i.e., a finish line)

calx viva: quicklime

Camera Stellata [Star Chamber]: a tribunal or inquisitorial council; (fig.) a severe and arbitrary court

camera: a vaulted chamber or room

Campus Martius [Field of Mars]: a field used for military exercises

campus: a field or plain

cancer: a crab

candelabrum: a candlestick

candida Pax: white-robed Peace (Ovid)

candidatus [white-robed]: the traditional Roman dress of applicants for public office

candor [bright white]: (fig.) sincere

Canis Major [Greater Dog]: a constellation containing Sirius, the Dog Star

Canis Minor [Lesser Dog]: a constellation to the east of Orion

canis in praesepi [dog in a manger]: someone who keeps others from enjoying the use of what he or she is not using him or herself

Cantabrigiensis (Cantab.): of Cambridge

cantate Domino: sing unto the Lord

cantillatio: chanted portions of a religious service, as in the Mass

cantio or **cantus:** a song

cantor: a singer

cantoris: to be sung by the cantorial side of the antiphonal

cantus firmus [fixed song]: Gregorian melody

cantus planus [plain song]: Gregorian chant

caper: a he-goat

capiat (cap.): (med.) take

capillus: head of hair

capra: a she-goat

capricornus: a horned goat

capsa acuum: a box or container in which to hold pins or needles

captatio benevolentiae: reaching after or currying favor

caput (pl. **capita**): head

caput cenae: the main dish

caput lupinum [wolf's head]: an outlaw or fugitive from the law

caput mortuum [dead head]: worthless residue

caput mundi [capital of the world]: Rome

cardo: the north-south axis of an area divided into four sections by a crossroads

cardo duplex [a double hinge]: a cardinal point; the ends of the earth's axis (i.e., the poles)

caritas: love or charity

Carmen Christi [hymn of Christ]: (theo.) referring to the Pauline hymn to the incarnation of Christ (Philippians 2:5-11)

carmen epicum: epic poetry

carmen triumphale: a triumphal song

casa: a cottage

cassetur billa: (leg.) let the bill be set aside or tabled

casus [a falling or fall]: an occasion, event, or occurrence

casus belli: a cause justifying war

casus conscientiae: a case of conscience

casus foederis [a case of the treaty]: a case within the stipulations of a treaty

casus fortuitus [a fortunate fall]: a chance happening

casus omissus: (leg.) a case omitted or unprovided for

Caurus or **Corus:** the northwest wind

causa: a cause

causa causans [the cause that causes all things]: the Great First Cause; the cause of an action

causa causata [the cause resulting from a previous cause]: an effect

causa cognoscendi: cause of knowledge

causa essendi: cause of being

causa fiendi: cause of becoming

causa finalis: final cause

causa immanens [immanent cause]: change produced from within

causa latentis: hidden cause

causa mali [an evil cause]: a cause of mischief

causa privata: (leg.) a civil case

causa proxima: immediate cause

causa publica: (leg.) a criminal case

causa remota: remote cause

causa secunda: secondary cause

causa sine qua non: an indispensible condition (also **sine qua non**)

causa transiens [cause from beyond]: change imposed from without

causa vera: a true cause

cautim [cautiously]: with security or foresight

caveat [let him beware]: a warning or caution

Cena Domini: the Lord's Supper

cena: dinner

cenatus: after dinner

censor morum: a censor of morals

centum (cent.): a hundred

centum anni [a hundred years]: a century

centuplex: a hundred-fold

cera: wax

cerebrum: the brain

certamina divitiarum [struggles of riches]: strivings after wealth

certiorari [to be certified]: (leg.) a writ calling up the records of a lower court

certitudo salutis: (theo.) assurance of salvation

certo [certainly]: yes

cervix: the back of the neck

cessio bonorum: (leg.) a surrender of goods

cetera or **caetera desunt:** the rest is lacking

ceteris or **caeteris paribus (cet. par.):** other things being equal

ceteris rebus: as regards the rest

charismata: (theo.) spiritual gifts

chimaera: a mythical fire-breathing creature usually depicted with the head of a lion, the body of a goat, and whose tail is that of a serpent

chorea scriptorum: writer's cramp

chorus [to dance in a circle]: in theater, a troop of person's singing and dancing

Christianus: a Christian

Christus: Christ

cibus delicatus: delicacies

cicatrix manet: the scar remains

cingulum Veneris: the girdle of Venus

circa (c. or **ca.):** about, near, or around

circiter (c. or **circ.):** about

circuitus verborum [a circuit of words]: circumlocution

circulus in definiendo [a circle in defining]: a type of circular reasoning (i.e., a vicious cycle)

circulus in probando [a circle in proving]: a type of circular reasoning (i.e., a vicious circle)

circulus vitiosus [a vicious cycle]: circular reasoning

circum (c. or **circ.):** around or about

citato equo: at full gallop

civica corona [civic crown]: an award in recognition for those who had saved the life of a Roman in war

civis bonus [a good citizen]: a patriot

Civitas Dei: the City of God in opposition to the Earthly City (St. Augustine)

Civitas Terrena: the Earthly City in opposition to the City of God (St. Augustine)

clamor bellicus: a war-cry

classicum: a trumpet call

clava: a club

clavis (pl. **claves**) [key]: a glossary

clepsydra: a water clock used to measure the time allotted to orators

cochleare (**coch.**): (med.) a spoonful

cochleare magnum (**coch. mag.**): a tablespoonful

cochleare parvum (**coch. parv.**): a teaspoonful

codex: a book

codex rescriptus: a palimpsest

coelum: the heavens

cognati [connected by blood]: (leg.) relations on the mother's side

cognatus: related by birth

cognitus: known or proven

cognomen: a surname or family name

cognovit or **cognovit actionem** [he has acknowledged the action]: (leg.) the defendant's acknowledgement of the plaintiff's claim

cohors: a battalion

coitus interruptus [interrupted intercourse]: a method of natural birth control

collato pede: hand to hand fighting

collectanea: a miscellany or an anthology

collegium (pl. **collegia**) [a college]: a body or society of persons with common interests or pursuits

collis [high ground]: a hill

collum or **collus:** the neck

colluvies vitiorum [a collection of vices]: a den of iniquity

collyrium: (med.) an eyewash

columna Herculis: the Pillars of Hercules

columna rostrata: a pillar in the Forum decorated with ships' prows

comata silva: in full leaf

comitas inter gentes [comity of nations]: civility among peaceful nations

comitia curiata: the original assembly of the Roman people

commentarii diurni: a diary

commisce: mix together

commodum: at the right or at a suitable time

commune bonum: the common good

communi consensu: by common consent

communibus annis: in common or average years

communicatio essentiae [communication of essence]: (theo.) a doctrine which teaches that Christ the Son receives his divine essence from God the Father

communicatio idiomatum [communication of similarities]: (theo) the transference of divine qualities to humans

communio sanctorum: communion of the saints

communitas: community or fellowship

complexio: in logic, the statement of a syllogism

complexus [an embracing]: an aggregate of parts or a complicated whole

componere lites: to settle disputes

compos mentis [sound of mind]: in one's right mind

compos sui: master of himself

compos voti: having obtained one's wish

concedo [I admit]: I grant (i.e., a concession made in an argument)

concentus [concord or harmony]: part of the church service sung or chanted by the congregation or choir, distinguished from **accentus,** which is sung by the priest and his/her assistant at the altar

concha: a seashell

conchylium: a type of shellfish from which purple dye is extracted

conciliatrix: a procuress

concio ad clerum: discourse to the clergy

concordia: harmony

concordia discors: discordant harmony

concubia nocte: at dead of night

condimentum: seasoning

condiscipulus [fellow student]: a classmate

conditio sine qua non: an indispensible condition (also **sine qua non**)

confer (cf.): compare

confessio: the tomb of a martyred saint

confiteor [I confess]: a prayer of public confession

congius (c.): (med.) a gallon

congressio or **congressus:** a meeting, an association, or a social encounter

conjunctis viribus [with united powers]: a confederation or an alliance

conjunx or **conjux (con.):** a marriage partner

conlegium: a guild

conlibitum est: it pleases or it is agreeable

connubium: intermarriage

consanguinitas: related by blood

conscientia mala: a bad conscience

conscientia recta: a good conscience

consensus: agreement

consensus audacium [agreement of the rash]: a conspiracy

consensus gentium: consent of the nations

consensus omnium: universal consent

consilium: a council or assembly

consortium: participation or a partnership

constat: it is agreed

consuetudo pro lege servatur [custom is held as law]: (leg.) where there are no specific laws, the issue should be decided by custom

consul designatus: a consul-elect

conterminus: bordering upon

continuetur remedia: (med.) let the cure be continued

contra (con.) [opposite]: against or on the opposite side (i.e., on the contrary)

contra bonos mores (cont. bon. mor.): contrary to good manners

contra formam statuti [against the form of the statute]: (leg.) against the letter of the law

contra jus fasque: (leg.) against all law, human and divine

contra jus gentium: (leg.) against the law of nations

contra legem: (leg.) illegally

contra mundum: against the world

contra pacem: (leg.) against the peace

contra rem publicam: to the disadvantage of the state

contradictio in adjecto: a contradiction in terms

contraria contrariis curantur [opposites are cured by opposites]: the principle of allopathy

convenit [it is fitting]: it is agreed

converso ad occidens: facing west

conviva: a party guest

convivium: a feast or banquet

copia fandi: a great flow or abundance of talk

copia verborum [abundance of words]: prolixity

copula [a link or connection]: in logic, a form of the verb "to be" linking the subject and predicate terms of a proposition

cor: heart

coram: [before]: face to face or in the presence of

coram domine rege: before the lord our king

coram judice: (leg.) before a judge

coram nobis [before us]: (leg.) in the court of King's Bench

coram non judice [before a judge without jurisdiction]: (leg.) before one who is not the proper judge

coram paribus [before equals]: before one's peers

coram populo [in public]: in the sight of spectators

cordi est: I like it

cornu: a horn

cornu copiae: the horn of plenty (symbol of abundance)

corona: a crown or garland

corona lucis [crown of light]: a circular chandelier hung from the central interior roof of a church or cathedral

Corpus Christi [body of Christ]: Christian festival in honor of the Holy Eucharist

Corpus Juris Canonici: the body of canon law

Corpus Juris Civilis: the body of civil or Roman law

corpus [body or corpse]: a body or collection of writings

corpus delicti [the body of the crime]: the substance or fundamental facts of a crime

corpus humanum: the human body

corpus juris [body of law]: a collection of laws of a country or jurisdiction

corpus omnis Romani juris: compendium of all Roman law

corpus sine pectore: a body without a soul

corpus vile: a worthless matter

corrigendum (pl. **corrigenda**) [to be corrected]: corrections to be made in a book manuscript before publication

cortina Phoebi: the oracle of Apollo

cos ingeniorum: a whetstone for the wits

cras: tomorrow

cras mane: tomorrow morning

cras mane summendus: (med.) to be taken the next morning

cras mihi: my turn tomorrow

cras nocte: tomorrow night

cras vespere: tomorrow evening

crassa neglegentia or **crassa negligentia:** (leg.) gross negligence

crastinus: on the morrow

creatio ex nihil [creation from nothing]: (theo.) the belief that God created the world from absolute nothingness

crede Deo: trust God

credendum (pl. **credenda**) [a thing to be believed]: an article of faith

creditum: a loan

Credo in unum Deum [I believe in one God]: a section of the Latin Mass

credo [I believe]: a creed

crepusculum: twilight or dusk

crescens luna: a crescent moon

cribrum: a sieve

crimen (pl. **crimina**): (leg.) a crime

crimen falsi: the crime or charge of perjury

crimen laesae majestatis: the crime or charge of high treason

cruciatus tormentorum: the pains of torture

crucis supplicium: crucifixion

crus: a leg or shank

crustum: bread, cake, or pie

Crux: the Southern Cross

crux [cross]: a puzzle or a perplexing problem

crux ansata: the Egyptian ankh

crux commissa: the tau (T) cross

crux criticorum: the crux or puzzle of critics

crux decussata: the chi (X) cross of St. Andrew or St. Patrick

crux medicorum: the crux or puzzle of doctors

crux stellata: a type of cross in which its arms extend into stars

cubitum: the elbow

cui bono? or **cui bono fuisset?** [for whose advantage?]: to what end?

cui fuisset bono?: for whose advantage?

cui malo?: whom will it harm?

cuique suum: to each his own

cuius or **cujus (cuj.):** of which or whose

culmina Alpium: the Alpine summits

culpa: (leg.) fault or negligence

culpa lata: (leg.) gross negligence

culpa levis [a slight fault]: (leg.) excusable negligence

cultus animi [care of the soul]: education

cultus dei: worship of the gods

cultus deorum [care of the gods]: reverence or divine service

cum (c̄): with

cum bona venia: with your good favor

cum eo quod: on that condition

cum grano salis [with a grain of salt]: with reservation

cum imperio esse [to be vested with *imperium*]: to have unlimited power

cum laude [with praise]: with distinction

cum maxime: precisely

cum multis aliis: with many others

cum nimbo [with a cloud]: the halo surrounding the head of saints in sacred art

cum notis variorum: with the notes of various commentators

cum onere: (leg.) with the burden of proof

cum privilegio: with privilege

cum telo: armed

cum uxoribus et liberis: with wife and child

cumulus nimbus [a cloud heap]: rain clouds

cunabula: a craddle

cunae: a bird's nest

cuniculus: a rabbit

cupido: longing or desire

curatius: more carefully

curia advisari vult (cur. adv. vult or **c.a.v.):** (leg.) the court wishes to be advised or to consider the matter

currente calamo [with a running pen]: fluently; offhandedly

curriculum vitae (c.v.) [course of life]: a résumé (also **vitae curriculum**)

cursor [runner]: a messenger or courier

cursus curiae est lex curiae: (leg.) the practice of the court is the law of the court

custodia legis: (leg.) in the custody of the law

custodia libera: (leg.) house-arrest

custos: a custodian or guardian

custos morum: a custodian of morals

custos rotulorum (C.R.) [custodian of rolls]: the principle justice of the peace in an English county

cutis anserina [goose flesh]: goose bumps or goose pimples

cutis capitis: the scalp

cyathus [a ladle used for filling wine glasses]: a fluid measure (i.e., a cupful)

cyathus vinosus: a cupful of wine

cyma recta: a type of arch

cyma reversa: a type of arch

D

da (d.): (med.) give

damnosa haereditas [a damaging inheritance]: an inheritance that entails loss

damnum (pl. **damna**) [damage]: physical harm or material loss

damnum absque injuria [loss without injury]: (leg.) loss due to lawful competition

dante Deo: by the gift of God

dapes inemptae [unbought feasts]: home-made products

data et accepta [things given and received]: expenditures and receipts

datio [giving]: (leg.) the right of alienation

de auditu: from hearsay

de bonis asportatis: (leg.) of goods carried away

de bonis non administratis: (leg.) of the goods not yet administered

de bonis propriis [out of his own goods]: (leg.) out of one's own pocket

de bono et malo [of good and bad]: for better or for worse

de claro die: by the light of day

de die: while still day

de die in diem (de d. in d.): from day to day

de facto [in fact]: in reality or actually the case

de fide [of the faith]: (theo.) required as an article of faith

de fide et officio judicis non recipitur quaestio: (leg.) concerning the good faith and duty of the judge, no quesion can be allowed

de gratia: (leg.) by favor

de industria: intentionally

de integro: afresh or anew

de jure [by right]: (leg.) rightful or rightfully

de lana caprina [about goat's wool]: a non-existent or worthless thing

de lunatico inquirendo: (leg.) a writ to inquire into the sanity of a person

de monte alto: from the high mountain

de more: habitually

de nocte: while still night

de novo: anew or afresh

de pilo pendet [it hangs by a hair]: a precarious situation

de plano [with ease]: easily; (leg.) clearly, patently

de plebe: one of the people

de praesenti: of or for the present

de profundis: out of the depths (Psalm 130:1)

de proprio motu [of its own motion]: spontaneously

de tenero ungui: from childhood

de verbo in verbum or **de verbo** [word for word]: literally

dea: a goddess

debitum (pl. **debita**): (leg.) a debt

debitum naturae [the debt of nature]: death

Decalogus: the Ten Commandments

decani: in music, to be sung by the decanal side of the antiphonal

decanta: pour off

decanus [leader of ten]: a dean

decem anni: a decade

deceptio visus: an optical illusion

decessit sine prole (**d.s.p.**): died without issue

decet [it is fitting]: it is proper, either morally or physically

decor: grace or beauty

decretum (**d.**): a decree or an ordinance

decuma (or **decima**) [a tenth part]: a tithe

decumanus: the east-west axis of an area divided into four sections by a crossroads

dedita opera: intentionally

dediticii [those having surrendered]: subjects of Rome without rights

defectio lunae: a lunar eclipse

defectio solis: a solar eclipse

defectus sanguinis: (leg.) failure of issue

definiendum [that which is defined]: in definitions, the term that is to be defined

definiens [that which does the defining]: the definition of a term

definitum: a defined thing

Dei judicium [judgment of God]: trial by ordeal

Dei propitii: the favor of heaven

delenda: things to be deleted

delictum (pl. **delicta**) [fault or crime]: (leg.) an offense or misdemeanor

delineavit (**del.**): he or she drew it

delirium tremens (**D.T.**) [trembling delirium]: mental delusions caused by alcohol poisoning

dementia: insanity

dementia a potu [insanity from drinking]: delirium tremens

dementia praecox: (med.) a form of early insanity

deminutio capitis: loss of civil rights

demissi capilli: hair growing long

demonstratio: a type of oratory concerned with praise and censure

demortuus: the late (i.e., deceased)

denarius: a Roman siver coin

dens (pl. **dentis**): a tooth

descendere ex equo: to dismount a horse

desertus: a solitary place

desideratum: something desired (also **desiderium:** a yearning or desire for something)

desilio ad pedes: to dismount

desuetudo: disuse

desunt caetera or **desunt cetera:** the rest is wanting (e.g., the missing part of a quotation)

desunt multa: many things are wanting

detur [let it be given]: a book prize given to undergraduates at Harvard

Deus absconditus [the hidden God]: (theo.) the doctrine that God's nature is not fully revealed to humanity, even after the advent of Christ (Martin Luther)

Deus pro nobis [God for us]: (theo.) those aspects and manifestations of God open to the finite human mind; God's direct relation to humans through Christ

deus: a god

deus ex machina [a god from a machine]: providential intervention, esp. in a play or a novel

deus ignotus: an unknown or ignorant god

deus incognitus: the unknown, unknowable God

deus mobilis: a changing or changeable god

deus philosophorum: the god of the philosophers (Lactantius)

deverticula flexionesque: twists and turns

dextimus: on the right hand or side

dextra: the right hand

dextras dare [to give right hands]: to shake hands as a pledge of good faith

dextro tempore [at the right time]: at the opportune moment

di or **dii majores** [the greater gods]: men of outstanding merit

di or **dii minores** [the lesser gods]: men of lesser merit

di or **dii penates:** household gods

diabolus: a devil

dic bona fide: tell me in good faith (Plautus)

dic quid sentias: give me your opinion

dicis causa or **dicis gratia** [for form's sake]: for the sake of appearances

dicitur [it is said]: they say

dictum (pl. **dicta**) [a word or speech]: a truism or witty saying

dictum de dicto [report upon hearsay]: second-hand story

dictum factum: said and done

diebus alternis: every other day

diebus tertiis: every third day

diem ex die: from day to day

Dies Irae [day of wrath]: Day of Judgment (a hymn sung during the requiem mass)

dies: daytime or day

dies datus [a day given]: (leg.) a day appointed for hearing a lawsuit

dies dominicus: the Lord's day (i.e., Sunday)

dies faustus or **fasti:** a lucky day (i.e., the days'on which the praetor could administer justice)

dies festus: a festival or holiday

dies infaustus: an unlucky day (inauspicious days for civic affairs or for court judgments)

dies juridicus: (leg.) a day on which the court sits

dies natalis: a birthday

dies nefasti or **nefasti** [forbidden days]: days on which no public business is transacted

dies non juridicus or **dies non:** (leg.) a day on which the court does not sit

dies profesti [common days]: week days (i.e., non-holy days)

difficiles nugae: hard-earned trifles

digitale: a thimble

digito monstrari [be pointed out with the finger]: to be famous

digitulus [little finger]: the touch of a finger

digitus [finger]: a finger's breadth (i.e., one inch)

digitus anularius: the ring finger

digitus auricularis: the little finger

digitus index: the index finger

digitus medius: the middle finger

digitus pollex: the thumb or big toe

dignus vindice nodus [a knot worthy of a liberator]: a difficulty needing divine intervention

diluculo: in the morning twilight

diluculum: dawn or daybreak

dilue (dil.): (med.) dilute or dissolve

diluvium: a flood or deluge

dimidia pars: half

dimidio minus [less by half]: half as much

dimissio: dismissal

dirae: bad omens

disciplina arcana [secret teaching]: rituals and doctrines known only to those fully initiated into a religion

discursus: running to and fro

disjecta membra: scattered parts or remains (i.e., fragments)

disparatum: in rhetoric, the contradictory proposition

dispendia morae: loss of time

dispudet: it is a great shame

dissolutio criminum: a refutation

dissolutio naturae: death

dissolutio navigii: shipwreck

diverbium: in theater, dialogue on the stage

divina particula aurae [divine particle of light]: the divine spirit in the human person

divinatio: (leg.) the selection of a prosecutor by the court

divinitas [divinity]: the power of prophecy or divination

Divinitatis Baccalaureus (D.B.): Bachelor of Divinity

Divinitatis Doctor (D.D.): Doctor of Divinity (an honorary degree)

divinitatis sensus: (theo.) an awareness of the divine presence in the world

divinus: superhuman or divine

dixi: I have spoken

do ut des [I give that you may give]: (leg.) a form of commutative contract

do ut facias [I give that you may do]: (leg.) a form of commutative contract

doctor utriusque legis: doctor of both Canon and Civil laws

doctrina: teaching or instruction

doctus cum libro [learned with a book]: a person who lacks practical knowledge

dodrans: three fourths in length (i.e., nine inches of a standard foot)

dogma: a philosophical doctrine

dolor: pain or sorrow

dolor artuum: (med.) gout

dolus: (leg.) fraud or deceit

dolus bonus: (leg.) permissible deceit

dolus malus: (leg.) unlawful deceit

domi [in the house]: at home

domi meae: at my house

domicilium or **domus:** a house

dominus et domina: lord and lady

domo: from home

domo carens: homeless

domo profugus: homeless

domum: homewards

Domus Procerum (D.P. or **Dom. Proc.):** the House of Lords

Dona Nobis Pacem: Grant Us Peace (concluding section of the Latin Mass)

dono dedit (d.d.): given as a gift

donum superadditum [additional endowment]: (theo.) refers to those divine gifts humans lost at the Fall, such as knowledge, eternal happiness, and love

dorsum: the back

dramatis personae (dram. pers.): the cast of characters in a play

duces tecum [thou shalt bring with thee]: a subpoena

ductus oris: the lineaments of the face

dudum: some time ago

dulce 'Domum': sweet 'Home' or "Homeward" (English song sung at the end of the school term)

dulcis unda: fresh water

dum [while]: on the condition that

dum sola [while alone]: (leg.) while unmarried

dummodo [so long as]: provided that

duo: two

duo sextarii: a quart

duodecim: a dozen

duplex: doublé

duplus [twice as much]: (leg.) a double penalty

durante: during

durante absentia: (leg.) during absence

durante beneplacito [during our good pleasure]: (leg.) appointments made and unmade at the pleasure of the magistrate

durante minore aetate: (leg.) during minority

durante vita: (leg.) during life

dux: a leader or a guide

dux gregis [leader of the flock]: the leader of the pack

E

e contra: on the other hand

e contrario: on the contrary

e longinquo: from a distance

e re nata [under the present circumstances]: as matters stand

e re publica: in the interests of the state

e republica [in the public interest]: for the benefit of the state

e verbo [in word]: literally

ebriolus: mildly intoxicated (i.e., tipsy)

ebrius: drunk

Ecce Homo [behold the man!]: a representation of Christ crowned with thorns

ecce: behold!

ecce signum [behold the sign!]: here is the proof

eccere!: there you are!

ecclesia: a church

edere animam [to breathe (one's last) breath]: to die

edictum: a decree

editicius judices: jurors chosen by a plaintiff

editio cum notis variorum: an edition of a text with notes and commentary

editio princeps (pl. **editiones principes**): the first printed edition of a book

editio tribuum: (leg.) a proposal by a plaintiff for the choice of a jury

Editio Vulgata [common edition]: the Latin Vulgate version of the Bible

efferatus: stuffed full

efficiens causa: in philosophy, the efficient cause

ego: I

ego ipse: I myself

ejus modi [of this kind]: in that manner

ejusdem farinae: of the same flour

ejusdem generis: of the same kind

elapso tempore: the time having elapsed

elixir vitae: elixir of life

elogium: an epitaph on a tombstone or a codicil to a will

emeritus (fem., **emerita**) [veteran]: a title of honor denoting long and distinguished service

eminus: at or from a distance

empiricis: a physician who relies on practical rather than scientific knowledge (i.e., a quack)

emplastrum (pl. **emplastra**, pharm.): a plaster

emporium: a market or place of trade

emptor: a buyer

emunctae naris [of wiped nose]: a person of keen or mature judgment (Horace)

enim: namely

enimvero [to be sure]: certainly

enodis [without knots]: clear or plain

Ens Entium [Being of Beings]: the Supreme Being

ens (pl. **entia**): being or existence; an entity

ens rationis [a creature of reason]: a product of mental action

entia naturae: things of nature

entia rationis: things of reason

enuntiatum: a proposition

enuntio: in logic, to state a proposition

eo animo: with that intention

eo instante: at that moment

eo ipso [by that itself]: by that fact

eo loci: at that very place

eo nomine [by that name]: on this account

episcopus: a bishop

epistula: a letter

equi biiugi: two horses yoked abreast

equo admisso: at full gallop

equo incitato: at full gallop

equo vecto: mounted on horseback

equus: horse

equus bellator: a war-horse

ergo: therefore

erratum (pl. **errata**): an error or mistake

esse: being or existence (as opposed to **posse**)

esse in oculis: to be visible

esse in pretio: to be prized

est operae pretium: it is worth while

et: and or also

et alibi (et al.): and elsewhere

et alii (fem., **aliae; et al.**): and others

et cetera (etc.): and so forth

et conjunx (et conj.) [and husband or and wife]: and spouse

et hoc genus omne: and everything of this kind

et id genus omne: and everything of the kind

et nunc et semper: now and always

et sequens (et seq.): and the following

et sequentes (et seq.): and what follows

et sequentia: and what follows

et sic de ceteris: and so of the rest

et sic de similibus: and so of the like

et similia: and the like

et uxor (et ux.): and wife

etiam: yes

etiam atque etiam: again and again

eu! or **euge!** [well done!]: bravo!

Eurus: the southeast or east winds

evangelium: the Gospel

evocati: veterans called back to duty

ex abrupto [abruptly]: without preparation

ex abundante cautela: from excessive caution

ex abundantia: out of the abundance

ex acervo: out of a heap

ex adverso [from the opposite side]: in opposition

ex adyto cordis: from the bottom of the heart

ex aequo: on equal terms

ex aequo et bono: [according to what is right and good]: justly and equitably

ex animo [from the heart]: sincerely

ex animo effluere: to escape from the mind

ex auctoritate mihi commissa: by virtue of the authority vested in me

ex bona fide [in good faith]: on one's honor; sincerely

ex capite [out of the head]: from memory

ex cathedra [from the chair]: officially; with authority

ex commodo: conveniently

ex concesso [out of concession]: from what has been granted

ex consuetudine mea: according to my custom

ex contrario [on the other side]: on the contrary

ex curia: (leg.) out of court

ex delicto [from offense]: (leg.) by reason of an actionable wrong or a criminal deed

ex dono [by the gift]: as a present

ex dono Dei: by the gift of God

ex equo desilire: to dismount from a horse

ex facie [from the face]: on its face; (leg.) evidently

ex gratia [of or by favor]: (leg.) in absence of legal right

ex hypothesi: by hypothesis

ex improviso: unexpectedly

ex industria: on purpose

ex inopinato: unexpectedly

ex instituto: according to traditional usage

ex lege [arising from the law]: as a matter of law

ex libris or **e libris** [from the books of]: an inscription denoting ownership of a book (i.e., a bookplate)

ex longinquo: from a distance

ex memoria [from memory]: by heart

ex mera gratia: through mere favor

ex merito [according to one's desserts]: from merit

ex mero motu [of a mere impulse]: of one's own accord

ex morbo convalescere: to recover from a disease

ex more [according to custom]: habitually

ex necessitate rei [from the necessity of the case]: necessarily

ex officio (e.o.): by virtue of one's office

ex opere operantis [out of the work]: (theo.) refers to the efficacy of the sacrament coming from the goodness of the one dispensing it

ex opere operato [out of the operation of the work]: (theo.) refers to the efficacy of the sacrament despite the moral condition of the one dispensing it

ex parte [from one party]: in the interests of one side only; in part

ex pede Herculem [from the foot we recognize Hercules]: from a part we may divine the whole

ex post facto [after the deed is done]: after the fact

ex professo [by declaration]: avowedly or openly

ex proposito [by design]: purposely

ex propriis: from one's own resources

ex proprio judicio: from its own judgment

ex proprio motu: of his (or its) own accord

ex pueris excedere [to leave boyhood behind]: to become a man

ex quo [from which time]: since

ex quo tempore: since that time

ex quocunque capite: for whatever reason

ex re et ex tempore: according to time and circumstance

ex sanguis [without blood]: deathly pale

ex sententia: as one would wish

ex somnis: sleepless

ex tacito: tacitly

ex tempore: on the spur of the moment

ex toto: on the whole

ex usu [of use]: useful or advantageous

ex utraque parte: on either side

ex vi termini: by force of the term, limit, or restriction

ex voto: according to one's vow

ex vulnere mori: to die of wounds

exactio capitum: a poll tax

exanimis or **exanimus:** lifeless

exceptis excipiendis: (leg.) due exceptions or objections being made

excerpta [excerpts]: selections

excudit (exc.): he/she fashioned it

excursus: a digression

exempli causa: for instance

exempli gratia (e.g.) [for the sake of example]: for example

exemplum (pl. **exempla**): a sample or copy

exeunt (sing. **exit**) [they go out]: they leave the stage

exeunt omnes [all go out]: all leave the stage

exinde or **exin:** in logic, consequently or accordingly

exit (pl. **exeunt**): he/she leaves the stage

exlex: outside the law

expedit mihi: it is in my interest or to my advantage

experimentum crucis: a crucial test or experiment

explicit [here ends]: the end (written at the end of a book manuscript)

exploratum habeo: I am sure

expressio unius est exclusio alterius: (leg.) the express mention of the one is the exclusion of the other

expressio verbis: in express terms

exstat liber: the book is still extant

extra jocum [joking apart]: all joking aside

extra modum: beyond measure

extra muros: beyond the walls

extra ordinem: in an unusual manner; extraordinarily

extremum bonorum: the highest good

extremum malorum: the highest evil

extremus: the outermost

F

fabella: a fable or a little story

faber ferrarius: a blacksmith

faber tignarius: a carpenter

fabula: a comedy or a farce

fabulae!: nonsense!

fac sciam: let me know

fac ut sciam: tell me

facere sacramentum: to swear an oath

facies Dei revelata: (theo.) the revealed face of God

facile princeps [easily chief]: easily the first

facio ut des [I do that you may give]: (leg.) a type of commutative contract

facio ut facias [I do that you may do]: (leg.) a type of commutative contract

factum: an act or a deed

factum est: it is done

faeneus homines: men of straw

faex populi (pl. **faeses populi**) [dregs of the people]: the common rabble

fallacia consequentis [fallacy of the consequent]: in logic, a **non sequitur**

falsa lectio (pl. **falsae lectiones**): a false or erroneous reading

falsi crimen: (leg.) the crime of falsification

fama clamosa [noisy rumor]: a current scandal

fama est [it is rumored]: there is a rumor

familia: household

fanum [a temple and its grounds]: a holy place

farina: meal or flour

farrago libelli [the medley of that little book of mine]: a hodgepodge

fartum: stuffing

fas est [it is allowed]: it is lawful

fasces [bundle of sticks with protruding axe]: symbol of high office, such as a Roman Magistrate or Consul (later a symbol of fascist Italy under Benito Mussolini)

fasti [calendar of events]: annals

fasti et nefasti dies: lucky and unlucky days

faustis ominibus: with favorable omens

Favonius: the west winds

fax [a torch]: an instigator; a stimulus

febris: a fever

februum: religious purification

fecerunt (ff.) [they made it]: appended to the artists' names on a painting

fecit (fec.) [he/she made it]: appended to an artist's name on a painting

feles or **felis:** a cat

feliciter [happily]: fortunately

felix culpa! [O fault most fortunate!]: St. Augustine's allusion to the Fall of humanity that necessitated the coming of the Redeemer

felo-de-se (pl. **felones-de-se**): (leg.) suicide; also, an illegal act that results in the death of the felon

femina: a woman

femininum (f.): (gram.) feminine (also feminus)

femur: the thigh

fenestra [a window]: (leg.) a loophole

ferae naturae [of a wild nature]: undomesticated

ferrum (fe.): iron

ferus [a wild animal]: wild or uncivilized

fessa aetas: old age

fessus de via: travel weary

fessus viator: a weary traveler

fiat (ft.): let it be so!; (med.) let it be made

fiat haustus (ft. haust.): (med.) let a draft be made

fiat mistura (ft. mist.): (med.) let a mixture be made

fiat pulvis (ft. pulv.): (med.) let a powder be made

fictilia: pottery

fictilis (fict.) [earthen]: made of potter's clay

ficus: a fig tree; a fig

fide mea: on my word of honor

fidei defensor (F.D. or fid. def.): Defender of the Faith (a title of the English monarch)

fideliter: faithfully

fides publica: a promise of protection or of safe-conduct

Fiducia [trust]: an essential item in Medieval Christian faith (together with **Assensus** and **Notitia**)

fiducia sui: self-confidence

fieri facias (fi. fa.) [cause it to be done]: a writ commanding the sheriff to execute a judgment

filatim: thread by thread

filia: daughter

filioque [and from the son]: the clause later added to the Nicene creed by the Western Catholic Church that precipitated further schism between Roman and Byzantine Christianity

filius: son

filius nullius [a son of nobody]: an illegitimate son

filius populi [a son of the people]: a bastard

filius terrae [a son of the earth]: a man of low birth or unknown origin

filiusfamilias: a son still under the power of his father

filum (pl. **fila**) [a thread]: a filament; a filar structure

finem respice [consider the end]: have regard for the outcome

finis: the end

finitum non capax infiniti [the finite cannot contain the infinite]: (theo.) a doctrine reaffirming the humanity of Christ

firmamentum: in rhetoric, the main point of an argument

fistula: a water pipe

flabellum or **flabrum:** a fan

flagrante bello [while the war is blazing]: during hostilities

flagrante delicto [while the crime is blazing]: in the very act of the crime (i.e., red-handed)

flatus vocis [a mere word]: not real (St. Anselm)

flebile ludibrium [a lamentable mockery]: a tragic farce

floreat: may it flourish

flores (fl.): flowers

floruit (fl. or **flor.):** flourished

flos: a flower or blossom

flos aetatis: the heyday

fluidum extractum (fldxt.): (med.) fluid extract

fluidus [liquid]: fluid

flumine adverso [against the stream]: upstream

flumine secundo [with the stream]: downstream

folio recto (f.r.): on the front of the page (i.e., the right-hand page)

folio verso (f.v.): on the back of the page (i.e., the left-hand page)

folium or **frons:** a leaf

fons: a fountain or fresh water spring

fons malorum: the source of evils

foramen magnum [great opening]: (anat.) the passage from the cranial cavity to the spinal canal

forceps: a pair of tongs

forfex: a pair of scissors

formica: an ant

fortitudini: for bravery

fortuna adversa: misfortune

fortuna prospera: good fortune

fortuna secunda: good fortune

forum: an open market or a public square

forum bovarium or **boarium:** the cattle market

forum holitorium: the vegetable market

forum piscarium or **piscatorium:** the fish market

fossa: a ditch

fossio: an excavation

frater (pl. **fratres**): a brother

frater germanus: one's own brother (as opposed to a step brother)

fratres: brothers and sisters

fraus est celare fraudem: (leg.) it is fraud to conceal fraud

fraus pia: a pious fraud
freno remisso: (to ride) with loose reins
frustillatim: bit by bit
frustra: in error; in vain
fuimus: we have been
fulmine ictus: struck by lightning
functus officio [having performed the office]: having resigned from office
funditus [from the bottom]: completely or entirely
fundus: the ground
fundus animae: the basis or basic essence of the soul
fungus: a mushroom
furca [two-pronged fork]: a pitch-fork
furnus: an oven
furor: madness
furor loquendi: a passion for speaking
furor poeticus: poetic inspiration
furor scribendi: a passion for writing
fusus crines: flowing free

G

Gallice [in Gaulish]: in French
gaudium certaminis: delight of battle
geminus (pl. **gemini**): twin
gemma: a gem or jewel
generalia: general principles
genesis [beginning]: the constellation that presides over one's birth
genitalis dies: birthday
genius loci (pl. **genii loci**) [the spirit of the place]: a guardian deity
gens togata [the togaed nation]: Roman citizens (Virgil); civilians generally
genus dicendi: a turn of speech or phrase
glebae ascriptus: attached to the soil
Gloria: glory
Gloria in Excelsis Deo: Glory be to God Most High (the "greater doxology")
Gloria Patri: Glory be to the Father (the "lesser doxology")
gloriae cupidus: one desirous of glory
gluten: glue
gluteus maximus: (anat.) the major muscle of the buttocks
gradarius: going step by step
gradatim [step by step]: gradually or by degrees
Gradus ad Parnassum or **Gradus** [a step to Parnassus]: an aid in writing Latin verse
grandis natu: aged

granum (gr.): (med.) a grain

gratia praeveniens [prevenient grace]: a Christian doctrine holding that God not only provides Grace but also the desire within the individual believer to receive it (St. Augustine)

gratias agere: to give thanks

gratias tibi ago: thank you

gratis dictum: a mere assertion

gratuitus: without cost (also **gratis**)

gratus animus: gratitude

gravatim: reluctantly

gravitas: seriousness or weightiness

graviter ictus: severely wounded

gregatim [in flocks or in herds]: in droves

grege facto: (mil.) in close order

grex venalium: a venal throng

gubernaculum: a ship's rudder

gubernator [a pilot]: a governor or director

gurges: a whirlpool or eddy

guttae (gtt.): (med.) drops

guttatim: drop by drop

gyrus: a ring or a circle

H

habeas corpus ad subjiciendum or **habeas corpus (hab. corp.)** [that you have the body]: (leg) a writ requiring that officials bring a detained individual before a court to decide the legality of that individual's detention or imprisonment

habemus papam! [we have a father!]: the cheer of the people upon the election of a new Catholic pope

habet! [he has it]: he is hit (the cheer of the crowd when a gladiator is wounded, also **hoc habet!**)

hac lege [with this law]: with this proviso

hactenus: up to this point

haesitantia linguae: a speech impediment

hallex: the thumb or the big toe

haruspex: an augur who examined entrails of sacrificed animals or other natural phenomena, such as lightning, to foretell the future

haud dubie [not a doubt]: certainly

haud longis intervallis [at intervals by no means long]: at frequent intervals

haud or **haut:** by no means

haud passibus aequis [not with equal steps]: with unequal steps

haustus (haust.): (med.) a draught

Hecatean: magical

heliotropium: a sunflower

helluo librorum [a devourer of books]: a bookworm

hemina: half a pint

herba: grass

heres (pl. **heredes; her.**): (leg.) heir

heres ex asse: (leg.) a sole heir

heres ex besse: (leg.) heir to two-thirds of the property

heres ex dodrante: (leg.) heir to three-quarters of the estate

heri: yesterday

Hesperius: western

Hesperus: the Evening Star

hesterni quirites [citizens of yesterday]: slaves recently set free

hesternus: yesterday

heus: hello!

hiatus valde deflendus [a gap much to be regretted]: a person whose achievements fall short of earlier promise (also used to denote a blank space in a work)

hibernus: for the winter

hic et nunc: here and now

hic et ubique: here and everywhere

hic iacet or **hic jacet (H.I.):** here lies

hic iacet sepultus (H.I.S.): here lies buried

hic sepultus (H.S.): here [lies] buried

hic situs est . . . : here lies . . .

hinc atque illinc: on this side and on that

hippodromos: a horse track or race course

his non obstantibus: notwithstanding these things

hoc age [this do]: mind what you are about (i.e., be attentive)

hoc anno (h.a.): in this year

hoc loco (h.l.): in this place

hoc mense (h.m.): in this month

hoc mihi placet: this pleases me

hoc monumentum posuit (H.M.P.): he/she erected this monument

hoc nocte [this night]: tonight

hoc quaere (h.q.): look for this

hoc sensu (h.s.): in this sense

hoc tempore (h.t.): at this time

hoc titulo (h.t.): under this title

hodie [this day]: today; at present

homicidium: murder

hominis iussu: with the sanction of a person

Homo Religiosus: religious man (Eliade)

Homo Sapiens [wise man]: the human species of the genus **Homo**

homo (pl. **homines**): human being or man

homo ansatus: a person standing with arms akimbo

homo dissolutus: a libertine

homo doctus: a man of letters

homo ebriosus: a drunkard

homo elegans: a well-dressed person (i.e., a dandy)

homo erectus [upright man]: an early species of humans which stood upright

homo gloriosus: a braggert

homo ingeniosus: a person of talent or genius

homo liberalis: a generous or courteous person

homo ludens [playful man]: a definition of humans and human culture in terms of play (Huizinga)

homo montanus: a highlander

homo multarum literarum [a man of many letters]: a man of great learning

homo nefarius: an evil person

homo nullius coloris: a man of no party

homo plebeius: a man of the people

homo reus: (leg.) an accused or guilty person

homo Roma natus: a native of Rome

homo scelestus: a scoundrel

homo seditiosus: a rebel or insurrectionist

homo sine censu [a man without property]: the unlanded classes; the homeless

homo solitarius: a recluse

homo studiosus: a partisan

homo stultus: a fool

homo trium literarum [a man of three letters]: a thief (i.e., **fur**, a thief; Plautus)

homo viator: man the wanderer (Marcel)

homo voluptarius: a self-indulgent person

honoris causa [for the sake of honor]: with due respect; honorary

honoris gratia: honorary

hora (H. or **hor.):** (med.) hour

hora decubitus (hor. decub.): (med.) at bedtime

hora quota est?: what time is it?

horae canonicae [canonical hours]: hours for prayer

horae subsicivae: leisure hours

horno: this year

horologium: a timepiece

horribile dictu: horrible to tell

horribile visu: horrible to see

horsum: in this direction

hortus siccus [a dry garden]: an herbarium

hospes: a guest

hospes hostis: a stranger or enemy

hostia [an animal given in sacrifice]: a victim

hostis patriae: a rebel
huc et illuc: hither and thither
hui [hello!]: wow!
hujus anni: of this year
hujus mensis: of this month
Humaniora: the Humanities
humanitas: humanity
humi: on the ground
humili loco natus: of humble origin
Hydra: a many-headed water snake
hyperbole: an exaggeration
hypogeum: an underground vault

I

Iapyx or **Japyx:** the west–northwest wind
ibidem (ib. or **ibid.):** in the same place (e.g., in a book)
id aetatis: of that age
id demum: that and that alone
id est (i.e.) [that is]: that is to say
id genus omne: all that sort
id temporis: at that time
idem (id.) [the same]: the same as above
idem quod (i.q.): the same as
idem sonans [sounding alike]: having the same sound or meaning
identidem: repeatedly
iecur: the liver (thought to be the seat of the passions)
ieiunium: days of abstinence
ientaculum: breakfast
ignis: fire
ignobile vulgus [the lowborn multitude]: the great unwashed
ignorantia juris non excusat: (leg.) ignorance of the law does not excuse
ignoratio elenchi [ignorant reasoning]: in logic, the fallacy of refutation by
    indirection (i.e., disputing a point not raised by one's opponent)
ignotus (ign.): unknown
Ilias malorum [an Iliad of woes]: a series of calamities
ilicet [forthwith]: immediately
ilico: on the spot
illotis manibus [with unwashed hands]: unprepared
imagines majorum: portraits of ancestors
imago Dei [the image of God]: the divine aspect of the human person (Genesis 1:27)
imago mundi: a symbolic representation of the world

imitatio dei: religious rituals or other symbolic acts that replicate some divine action or sacred event (e.g., the Jewish Passover, the Christian Eucharist, the Hajj)

immedicabile vulnus: an incurable wound (Ovid)

immo: on the contrary

immodicus: excessive

immunis: exempt

immutata oratio: an allegory

imo pectore: from the bottom of the heart

impari Marte: with unequal military strength

impendio: very much

imperium singulare: absolute power

impermissus: forbidden

impietas: unbelief

implicite: by implication

impos animi [having no power over the mind]: an imbecile

impotens sui [having no power over one's self]: unrestrained; passionate

impotentia: poverty

impraesentiarum: for the present

imprimis [in the first place]: first in order

impulsu tuo: at your instigation

imum mare: the bottom of the sea

in absentia (i.a.): in absence

in absoluto: absolutely

in abstracto: in the abstract

in actu [in act or in reality]: in the very act

in adversum montem: up the mountain

in aequo: on equal terms

in aeternum [forever]: from everlasting to everlasting

in alio loco: in another place

in ambiguo [in doubt]: in a doubtful manner

in armis [in arms]: under arms

in articulo mortis: at the point or moment of death

in banco: (leg.) in full court

in banco regis: in the King's Bench

in bello: in time of war

in bonis: (leg.) in or among the goods or property

in camera [in chamber]: (leg.) at chambers (i.e., in private, not in open court); a meeting that is held in secret

in capite [in chief]: (leg.) rights bestowed by a feudal lord

in carcerem: in prison

in cassum: in vain

in commendam [in trust for a time]: (eccles.) a benefice held by a person in absence of an incumbent

in concordia vocum: in unison

in contrarium: in an opposite direction

in contumaciam: (leg.) in contempt of court

in corpore [in body]: in substance

in cumulo: in a heap

in curia: in open court

in custodia legis: (leg.) in the custody of the law

in custodiam: in prison

in deposito [on deposit]: as a pledge

in die: on the day

in diem vivere [to live for today]: to live from hand to mouth

in dies (in d.): (med.) daily

in dies singulos: from day to day

in directum: in a straight line

in discrimine esse: to be at stake

in discrimine rerum [at the point of crisis]: at the turning point

in dorso: in or on the back

in dubio [in doubt]: undetermined

in dubium vocare: to call into question

in eo est [the position is such]: it depends on this

in equilibrio: in equilibrium

in esse [in being]: in actual existence (as opposed to **in posse**)

in excelsis: in the highest

in extenso: at full length (i.e., unabridged)

in extremis: at the point of death

in extremo libro: at the end of the book

in facie curiae: (leg.) in the presence of or before the court

in fieri [pending]: (leg.) in course of completion

in flagrante delicto [while the crime is blazing]: (leg.) in the very act (i.e., caught red-handed)

in folio [in leaves]: in a folio volume (i.e., in the form of a sheet folded once)

in forma pauperis [as a poor man]: (leg.) not liable to costs

in foro conscientiae: in the court or tribunal of conscience

in foro domestico: in a domestic court (as opposed to a foreign court)

in fumo: in smoke

in futuro: in the future

in futurum: for the future

in genere: in kind

in gremio legis [in the bosom of the law]: under the protection of the law

in hac parte: on this part

in horam vivere: to live for the moment

in horas: hourly

44

in illo tempore [in those days]: in the Golden Age (i.e., in the time when gods and goddesses walked the earth)

in incertum: for an indefinite period

in infinitum [to infinity]: forever

in intellectu: in the mind

in invidiam [in ill-will]: to excite prejudice

in invitum [against the unwilling]: compulsory

in ipso articulo temporis: in the nick of time

in ipso periculi discrimine: at the critical moment

in itinere [on the journey]: by the wayside

in jure: (leg.) according to the law

in limine (in lim.) [on the threshold]: in the beginning

in limine belli: at the outbreak of war

in litus or **in litore:** ashore

in loco [in the place]: in the proper or natural place

in loco citato (loc. cit.): in the place cited

in loco parentis: in the place of a parent

in longitudinem: length-wise

in majus: to a higher degree

in malam partem: in a bad sense

in manibus [hand to hand]: on hand

in medias res [into the midst of things]: into the heart of the matter (in literature, a story that begins in the midst of the plot)

in mediis rebus: in the midst of things

in medio: in the middle

in meditatione fugae: (leg.) in contemplation of flight

in melius mutari: to take a turn for the better

in memoriam [in memory]: in memory of

in meridiem: in the south

in mora [in delay]: (leg.) in default

in naturalibus [in a state of nature]: in the nude

in nomine: in the name of

in notis: in the notes

in nubibus [in the clouds]: befogged or confused

in nuce: in a nutshell

in obliquum [in an oblique direction]: sideways

in oculis civium [in the eyes of citizens]: in public view

in omne tempus: forever

in omnes partes: in all directions

in omnia paratus: prepared for all things

in omnibus [in all things]: in all respects

in ovo [in the egg]: undeveloped

in pace: in peace

in pari causa: in an equal cause

in pari delicto: (leg.) two equally at fault

in pari materia: in an analogous case

in partibus infidelium (i.p.i.) or **in partibus (i.p.)** [in the lands of the unbelievers]: a titular bishop whose title is that of an extinct Roman Catholic see

in pectore [in the breast]: in secret; in reserve

in periculo mortis: in danger of death

in perpetuam rei memoriam: in perpetual remembrance

in perpetuum: forever

in persona: in person

in persona Christi: in the person of Christ

in personam [against the person]: (leg.) against a particular person as distinguished from a particular thing (**in rem**)

in plano: on a plane or level surface

in pleno: in full

in pontificalibus [in pontificals]: in episcopal robes

in posse [in possibility]: potentially (as opposed to **in esse**)

in posterum [for the next day]: for the future

in potentia [in possibility]: potentially

in praesens: for the moment

in praesens tempus: for the present time

in praesenti: at the present time

in praesentia: for the present

in primis: especially

in principio (in pr.): in the beginning

in privato: in private

in procinctu [with loins girded]: in readiness for battle

in promptu [in readiness]: at a moment's notice

in propatulo [in public]: publicly

in propria causa: (leg.) in his or her own suit

in propria persona: (leg.) in one's own person

in prospectu: in prospect

in publico [in the streets]: in public

in puris naturalibus: stark naked

in re [in the matter of]: concerning

in rebus multis [in many things]: tending to many things; busy in a matter

in rem [in or against a thing]: to one's advantage; (leg.) against a particular thing as distinguished from a particular person (**in personam**)

in rerum natura: in the nature of things

in saecula saeculorum [for ages of ages]: forever and ever

in se: in itself

in singulos menses: in each month

in situ [in its place]: in proper position

in solidum or **in solido** [for the whole]: (leg.) jointly

in somnis: in a dream

in somno: asleep; in a dream

in statu pupillari: in a state of pupilage

in statu quo: in the state in which it was before

in statu quo ante bellum: in the state in which it was before the war

in tempore: at the right moment in time

in tempore ipso: at the very instant

in tempore opportuno: at the opportune time

in tempus [for a time]: temporarily

in tenebris [in darkness]: in a state of doubt

in terminis [in express terms]: definitely

in terram demergi: to sink into the earth

in terrorem: as a warning

in testimonium: in witness

in totidem verbis: in so many words

in toto [on the whole]: altogether

in toto caelo: as far as possible

in transitu (**in trans.**) [in transit]: on the way

in transversum: across

in tuto esse [to be in a position of safety]: in a safe place

in unguem [to a fingernail]: to a T (i.e., perfectly)

in universum [on the whole]: universal or universally

in unum: in or into one place

in usu: in use

in utero: in the womb

in utramque partem: pro and con

in utraque re: in both cases

in utroque fidelis: faithful in both

in utroque jure: (leg.) under both laws (i.e., civil and canon)

in utrumque paratus: prepared for either event

in vacuo: in a vacuum

in vadio: in pledge

in ventre: (leg.) in the womb

in vicem or **in vices** [in turn]: alternately; reciprocally

in vita esse: to be alive

in vitro [in glass]: in a test tube or petri dish

in vivo: (med.) in the living organism

inanis equus: riderless

Incarnatus [incarnate]: a part of the Nicene Creed referring to the incarnation of Christ

incipit: (lit.) here begins (i.e., the beginning of a literary text)

incoctus [uncooked]: raw

incognita causa: (leg.) without examination

incommodo tuo: to your disadvantage

incubus [nightmare]: a male spirit or demon believed to prey sexually on young women while asleep in their beds

Index Expurgatorius: a list of books from which offending passages must be purged before they may be read by Catholics

Index Librorum Prohibitorum: a list of prohibited books drawn up at the Roman Catholic Council of Trent, first published in 1557 and regularly updated

index [a sign]: the forefinger

index rerum [an index of matters]: a reference notebook

index verborum: an index of words

indicium (pl. **indicia**) [an indicating mark or sign]: a symptom

indicta causa: (leg.) without a hearing

indictum sit: be it unsaid

indidem: from the same place or matter

indolatus corpora: without funeral honors

indolentia: free from pain

inedita: unpublished compositions

inemptus: unbought

infamia: ill-fame

infaustus: unlucky

infelicitas: misfortune

infernus [below]: of the lower world

infidelis: unfaithful

infima species (pl. **infimae species**): the lowest species of a genus or class

infimo loco natus: from the lowest classes

infimus mons: at the foot of the mountain

infirmus [weak or feeble]: sickly

inflatilia: (music) wind instruments

inflatus [pompously]: on a greater scale

infra (inf.) [below]: further on (e.g., in a book)

infra dignitatem (infra dig.) [beneath one's dignity]: unbecoming

infrons: leafless

ingens aequor: the vast ocean

ingratus: thankless

ingratus animus: ingratitude

inhumatus: unburied

inibi: near at hand

inimicus: a public enemy

iniquus [uneven]: one-sided

initio (init.): in or at the beginning or start (usu. referring to a passage in a book)

initio anni: at the beginning of the year

inlex: lawless

inlicitus: illegal

innuba or **innupta:** unmarried

inolens: without smell

inquirendo [by inquiring]: (leg.) authority to inquire into something for the Crown

insalutato hospite [without saluting one's host]: without saying goodbye

insanabilis: incurable

insculpsit: he or she engraved it

insepultus: unburied

insomnis: sleepless

instar omnium: worth all of them

insula: an island

insuper: above; besides

integer vitae [blameless of life]: an upright person

intempesta nox: the dead of the night

inter: between or among

inter alia: among other things

inter alios: among other persons

inter cenam: during dinner

inter epulas [during the feast]: while feasting

inter nos [between ourselves]: mutually

inter pares: among equals

inter pocula [between cups]: over a glass

inter regalia: among or part of the regalia

inter se [between or among themselves]: reciprocally

inter vivos: among the living

intercus: under the skin

intercus aqua: (med.) dropsy

interdictum: a prohibition

interdius [in the daytime]: by day

interdum: now and then

interim: meanwhile

interlunium: the period of the new moon

intermundia: the space between the worlds

internus: inward; internal

interregnum: a period between two reigns

interrex: a regent or temporary chief magistrate

interrogatio: in logic, an argument (i.e., syllogism)

intertextus: interwoven

intra: inside; within

intra jactum: (mil.) within range

intra muros: within the walls [of a city]

intra parietes: within the walls [of a house]

intra vires: within the powers (of)

intrepidus: calm
intro: inwards; within
intuitu: in respect of
intumulatus: unburied
intus: from the inside; inwardly
inurbanus: rude
inutilis: useless
invenit (inv.): he or she designed it
inverso ordine: in inverse order
inversus: overturned; upside down
invictus: unbeaten
invidia: envy or jealousy
invitatu: by invitation
invitatus a me: at my invitation
invitatus a te: at your invitation
ipse dixit [he himself has spoken it]: a dictum
ipsissima verba: the very words
ipsissimis verbis: in the very words
ipso facto [by the fact itself]: by that very fact
ipso jure: by the law itself
ira deorum: the wrath of god; divine retribution
irrevocabile verbum: an irrevocably spoken word
ita: yes
ita res est or **ita est:** it is so
ita?: really?
Italice [in Italian]: in the Italian manner
item or **itidem:** likewise
iter impeditum: an impassable road
iter pedestre: going by foot
iter terrestre: going by land
iter unius diei: a day's journey
iterum [again]: anew; for the second time
itinera diurna nocturnaque: traveling day and night
Iudaeus: Jew
iussu: by order or by command

J

(**N.B.**, the letter **j, J** was not known in Classical Latin but was created by Renaissance Italian humanists in order to distinguish consonated from non-consonated forms of **i, I**)

jam satis: already enough
januis clausis [with closed doors]: in secret

januae mentis [gates of the mind]: inlets of knowledge

joci causa: for the sake of the joke

judex: a judge

judex incorruptus: an impartial judge

judicia nulla [lawlessness]: anarchy

judicis: panel of jurors

judicium: a trial or legal decision

judicium Dei: the judgment of God

judicium perversum: a miscarriage of justice

jugulum (also **iugulum** or **iugulus**): the throat

jumentum: a beast of burden

junior: younger

Juppiter Tonans: Jupiter the Thunderer

jurare in verba magistri [to swear the words of the master]: a confession

jure: by right or by law

jure coronae: by right of crown

jure divino: by divine right or divine law

jure humano [by human law]: by the will of the people

jure mariti [by a husband's right]: by marital law

jure non dono: by right, not by gift

jure propinquitatis: by right of relationship

jure sanguinis: by right of blood

Juris or **Jurum Doctor [J.D.]:** doctor of law (a professional degree)

Juris Utriusque Doctor [J.U.D.]: doctor of both Canon and Civil laws

juris peritus: an expert in the law

jurisdictionis fundandae causa (or **gratia**): for the sake of establishing jurisdiction

jus (pl. **jures**): law; legal right

jus canonicum: canon law

jus civile: civil law

jus commune: common law

jus divinum: divine law

jus et norma loquendi [the law and rule of speech]: ordinary usage

jus gentium [law of nations]: international law

jus gladii [law of the sword]: supreme jurisdiction

jus in re: a real right

jus mariti: the right of a husband

jus naturae (or **naturale**): natural law

jus nullum: absence of justice

jus pignoris: the right of pledge

jus possessionis [right of possession]: hypothecation

jus postliminii [law of postliminium]: restoration or repatriation of goods or persons captured during war upon coming once again under the jurisdiction of the original nation from which the goods or persons were taken

jus primae noctis: the right of the first night

jus proprietatis: right of property

jus regium: right of royalty

jus relicti: the right of the widow

jus sanguinis: the law of consanguinity (i.e., the citizenship of the parents determines the citizenship of the child)

jus soli: the law of the soil (i.e, the place of birth determines the citizenship of the child)

jusjurandum (pl. **jusjuranda**): an oath

jussu: by order or by command

justitiae tenax: tenacious of justice

justo tempore: at the right time

juxta [close by]: equally

juxta solem cadentem: in the west

K

Kyrie eleison [Lord, have mercy]: a section of the Latin Mass

L

labia or **labium:** the lip

labores solis: an eclipse of the sun

labrum: a bath tub or wash basin

lac: milk

lac concretum: curdled milk

lac recens: fresh milk

lacerta: a lizard

lacertus: the upper arm with its muscles

lacrima Christi: the tear of Christ

lacteus orbis: the Milky Way (also **orbis lacteus**)

lacuna: a gap or deficiency

laesa majestas [lese majesty]: high treason

laeva [left]: left-handed

lana caprina [goat's wool]: a nonexistent thing; a trifle

lapidarius: a stonemason

lapis (pl. **lapides**): a stone

lapis philosophorum: the philosopher's stone (an imaginary substance which alchemists believed would change base metals into gold)

lapsus [a slip]: a lapse or blunder

lapsus calami: a slip of the pen

lapsus linguae: a slip of the tongue

lapsus memoriae: a lapse of memory

lar (pl. **lares**): a tutelary deity or beneficent ancestral spirit

lar familiaris [household deity]: the spirit of the founder of the family

lares et penates [household deities]: the home

Latine [in Latin]: in the Latin manner or style

Latine dictum: spoken in Latin

Latissimus dorsi: (anat.) the back muscle

lato sensu: in a broad sense (the opposite of **stricto sensu**)

laudatio funebris: a eulogy

laudis cupidus: one desirous of praise

lectio senatus: the roll call of senators

lector benevole: gentle reader

lectori benevolo (L.B.): to the gentle reader

legalis homo [legal man]: a person of full legal rights

legatus a latere: a papal legate

legenda: things to be read

leges nullae [lawlessness]: anarchy

legis pacis: conditions of peace

Legum Baccalaureus (LL.B.): Bachelor of Laws

Legum Doctor (LL.D.): Doctor of Laws

leo: a lion

leonina societas: a leonine partnership (a legally invalid partnership in which the partner shares in the losses but not in the profits)

lepus: a hare

lex (pl. **leges**): law or statue

lex irrita est: a law is invalid

lex loci: the law of the place

lex mercatoria or **mercatorum:** mercantile law

lex non scripta [unwritten law]: common law

lex rata est: a law is valid

lex salica [law of the Salian Franks]: the ancient law denying the French monarchy to women

lex scripta [written law]: statute law

lex talionis: the law of retaliation (e.g., an eye for an eye)

lex terrae: the law of the land

libellus: a letter or petition

liber (pl. **libri; L.** or **lib.**): book

libertas: liberty or freedom

liberum arbitrium [free will]: free choice

libido (pl. **libidines**) [desire]: the sex instinct or sex drive

libra (lb.) [a pair of scales]: a Roman pound (i.e., 12 oz.)

licentia: excessive liberty or license

licentia vatum: poetic license

licet [it is permitted]: it is legal

lignator: a woodcutter

limbus [limbo]: the border regions of hell

limbus fatuorum: fool's paradise

limbus infantium [infants' paradise]: limbo for unbaptized children

limbus patrum [paradise of the Fathers]: the place for the souls of the righteous before the advent of the Christian Gospel

limbus puerorum: children's paradise

limen: a threshold

lingua [the tongue]: a language or tongue

lis pendens: (leg.) a pending lawsuit

lis sub judice: (leg.) a lawsuit before a judge yet to be decided

lite pendente: (leg.) during the trial

literati or **litterati** [persons of letters]: the learned class

literatim or **litteratim** [letter for letter]: literally

literatus or **litteratus** [well-read]: learned or educated

littera scripta manet: the written letter remains

Litterae Humaniores (Lit. Hum.): the Humanities (e.g., the ancient Classics)

litterae scriptae [written letters]: manuscripts

Litterarum Doctor (Litt.D.): Doctor of Letters

Litterarum Humaniorum Doctor (L.H.D.): Doctor of Humanities

loca deserta: the desert lands

loca inculta: uncultivated country

loca longinqua: distant places

loca plana [level country]: the plains

locatio [a letting]: (leg.) leasing

loci communes (sing. **locus communis**): public places

loco: in the place

loco citato (loc. cit. or l.c.): in the place cited

loco laudato (loc. laud.): in the place cited with approval

loco supra citato (l.s.c.): in the place cited before

locum tenens (pl. **locum tenentes**): a substitute or deputy, esp. for a physician or a cleric

locus (pl. **loci**) [a place]: a written passage

locus citatus: the quoted passage

locus classicus (pl. **loci classici**) [classical passage]: an oft-cited passage

locus communis (pl. **loci communes**) [a common place]: a public place; a place of the dead

locus criminis: the scene of the crime

locus delicti: the scene of the crime

locus in quo [place in which]: the place where a passage occurs

locus poenitentiae: a place or opportunity for repentance

locus pugnae: a battlefield

locus sigilli (L.S.): the place of the seal

locus standi [a place of standing]: recognized position; (leg.) right to appear before a court (i.e., a right to be heard by a judge)

logos: word

longitudo: length

longo intervallo: by a long interval

longus pedes sex: six feet long

loquitur (loq.): he/she speaks

lotio (lot.): (med.) a lotion

lubricus: slippery

lucescit [it grows light]: day is breaking

lucet [it is light]: it is day

lucidus ordo: a clear arrangement

lucifer [light-bringing]: the morning star

lucri causa: for the sake of gain

luctator: a wrestler

lucubratus [work done by a night lamp]: late night study

lucus a non lucendo [grove from not being light]: explanation by contraries (a play on words between *lucus* [grove] and *lucre* [to shine] which appear etymologically related but are not—hence the logical fallacy of drawing incorrect conclusions from seemingly related facts)

ludus gladiatorius: a school for gladiators

ludus litterarius: an elementary school

lues: a plague

lues venerea: (med.) syphilis

lumen fidei: light of faith

lumen gratiae: light of grace

lumen naturale [light of nature]: natural intelligence

lumen naturale rationis [natural light of reason]: (theo.) knowledge of divine things without the direct assistance of God

luna: the moon

luna crescens: a crescent moon

luna decrescens: a gibbous moon

lunae lumen: moonlight

lusus naturae: a freak of nature

lux: light

lux mundi: the light of the world

M

mactatio [a sacrifice]: (theo.) refering to the sacrificial death of Christ

macte animo! [be increased in courage]: take courage!

macte virtute! [be increased in virtue]: go on and prosper!

macte!: well done! or good luck!

maculis distinctus: spotted

maculis interfusa: stained here and there

Magister Artium (M.A.): Master of Arts

magister: master or teacher

magister ceremoniarum: master of ceremonies

magister dixit: the master has spoken it (an invocation of the authority of Aristotle in Medieval scholasticism)

magister internus: inward teacher

magister ludi [master of the games]: an elementary school teacher

Magisterium: The Roman Catholic tradition, its authority, teachings, and holy offices

Magna Carta: the Great Charter of civil rights and freedoms signed by King John and the English nobility in 1215 C.E.

Magna Mater [the Great Mother]: a deity related to the ancient cult of Mithras

magna cum laude: with great praise

magna ex parte: to a great extent

magna voce: aloud

magni momenti: a great moment (i.e., a turning point)

magnificat [it magnifies]: a hymn of praise

magno cum detrimento: with great loss (of life)

magno cum fletu: with many tears

magno opere [very much]: greatly

magno pretio or **magni pretii:** at a high price (i.e., costly)

magnum bonum: a great good

magnum iter: (mil.) a forced march

magnum opus or **opus magnum** (pl. **magna opera**) [a great work]: an author's greatest work; a masterpiece

magus (pl. **magi**): a wizard or magician

Majestas Dei: (theo.) the majesty of God

major natu: older child

major pars: the majority

majusculae [uncials]: large capital letters characteristic of early Latin MSS

mala fide [in bad faith]: false or falsely; treacherously (opposite of **bona fide**)

mala in se: inherently evil

mala praxis: malpractice

male gratus: unthankful

maledictum: cursing

malevolentia: ill-will; malice

mali exempli [of bad example]: of bad precedent

malis avibus [with unfavorable birds]: under bad auspices

malleus: a hammer or mallet

malo animo: with intent to do evil

malo modo: in an evil manner

malum (pl. **mala**): an evil

malum in se [a thing evil in itself]: (leg.) a thing unlawful in itself, regardless of statute

malum prohibitum (pl. **mala prohibita**) [a prohibited evil]: (leg.) an act that is unlawful because it is forbidden by law (i.e., a legal crime though not necessarily a moral crime)

malus pudor: false modesty

mamma: the breast

mandamus [we command]: in English law, a high court writ issued to a lower court ordering performance of a legal duty or enforcement of a legal directive

mandatum: a message or commission

manes: spirits of the dead

manet [he/she remains]: he/she remains on stage

manet cicatrix: the scar remains

mania a potu [mania from drinking]: delirium tremens

manica [manicles]: handcuffs

manipulus: a handful

manu forti [with a strong hand]: by force

manu propria: with one's own hand

manumissio: emancipation from slavery

manuscriptum (**MS**; pl. **manuscripta, MSS**): a manuscript

mare clausum [closed sea]: a sea within the jurisdiction of a particular country

mare liberum [open sea]: a sea open to all

Mare Nostrum [our sea]: the Mediterranean Sea

margarita: a pearl

marginalia: marginal notes

marita: a wife

maritus: a husband

Marsicum bellum: the Social War between Marius and Sulla (90–88 B.C.E.)

mas or **masculus:** male or manly

masculinum (**m.**): masculine

mater: mother

Mater dolorosa [the sorrowing Mother]: the Holy Mother sorrowing at the Cross

materfamilias [a married woman]: the mother of the family or of the household

materia medica: (med.) notions and remedies used by physicians to heal patients

maximam partem: for the most part

maximus natu: the eldest child

me absente: in my absence

me auctore: by my advice

me duce: under my leadership or direction

me indicente: without my saying a word

me invito: against my will

me judice [I being judge]: in my opinion

me libente: with my pleasure or good-will

me paenitet [I regret it]: I'm sorry

me vivo: in my lifetime

mea culpa [my fault]: by my fault

mea de causa: on my account

mea gratia: for my sake

media acies: the center of the field of battle

media nox: midnight

media urbs: the city center

media via: the middle of the road; the middle way

Medicinae Doctor (**M.D.**): Doctor of Medicine

medicus: a physician

mediocris: middling; ordinary

meditatio fugae: (leg.) contemplation of flight

mediterraneus: inland

mel: honey

melioribus annis [in the better years]: in happier times

membratim [limb by limb]: one by one; piecemeal

membrum virile [the male member]: the penis

memento mori [remember you must die]: an object serving as a reminder of death

memorabilia: things worthy of remembrance

memoria in aeterna: in everlasting remembrance

memoria technica [artificial memory]: a system of memory (i.e., mnemonics)

memoriter [from memory]: by heart

mendicus: a beggar

mens divinior [a mind of diviner cast]: an inspired soul (Horace)

mens legis: the spirit of the law

mens rea: a guily intent

mensa: a table or altar

mensa et toro (or **thoro**): (leg.) from bed and board

mensa secunda: dessert

mensis: month

menstruus: monthly or month-long

mente captus: beside oneself

mentum: the chin

meo judicio: in my judgment

meo nomine: on my account

meo periculo [by my peril]: at my own risk

meo voto: by my wish

mercator: a merchant

mercatus: merchant business or trade

merda: excrement

meretrix: a harlot

meridies (M. or **m.)** [midday]: noon

messis ingrata: a poor harvest

messis opima: a good harvest

meum et tuum: (leg.) mine and thine (expressing rights of property)

meus [mine]: my friend (e.g., **Claudius meus:** my friend Claudius)

miles gloriosus: a boastful soldier

militia: warfare

mille passuum [a thousand paces]: a Roman mile

minimum: a very little

minimus: the smallest or the least

minor natu: younger

minus bene [less well]: unsatisfactorily

minusculae [small letters]: lower-case Roman letters in later Latin MSS

minutatim [bit by bit]: gradually

minutia (pl. **minutiae**) [smallness]: a trifle

mirabile dictu: wonderful to say

mirabile visu: wonderful to behold

mirabilia [wonders]: miracles

mirum in modum [in a wonderful manner]: surprisingly

misce: (med.) mix

miserabile dictu: sad to relate

miserable vulgus: a wretched mob

miserere mei: have mercy on me

misericordia [heart of mercy]: pity or compassion

Missa (pl. **Missae**): the Mass

Missa ad canones: (mus.) a Mass in canonic style

Missa ad fugal: (mus.) a Mass in fugal style

Missa bassa: Low Mass

Missa brevis: (mus.) a brief Mass

Missa cantata: Mass sung, but without deacon and sub-deacon

Missa catechumenorum: Mass of the catechumens

Missa fidelium: Mass of the faithful

Missa in Tempore Belli: Mass in Time of War (Haydn)

Missa sine nomine: (mus.) Mass without a name

Missa solemnis: High Mass

mitis sapientia: gentle wisdom

mitra [headdress]: a ceremonial hat worn by popes, bishops, and abbots

mittimus [we send]: a warrant of commitment to prison; a writ to remove records
from one court to another; a dismissal or a discharge

mobile perpetuum: perpetual motion

mobile vulgus (mob.): the fickle masses (i.e., the mob)

modestia: sense of discipline

modo et forma: in manner and form

modo praescripto (mod. praesc.): (med.) as directed or prescribed

modus (pl. **modi**): a mode, method, or manner

modus operandi: a mode of operating

modus ponendo tollens: in logic, a mode of reasoning that denies by affirming (e.g., either p or q (but not both); p, therefore not q; or vice versa)

modus ponens: in logic, a mode of reasoning that affirms by affirming (e.g., if p then q; p, therefore q)

modus tollendo ponens: in logic, a mode of reasoning that affirms by denying (e.g., either p or q; not p, therefore q)

modus tollendo tollens or **modus tollens:** in logic, a mode of reasoning that denies by denying (e.g., if p then q; not q, therefore not p)

modus vivendi [manner of living]: (leg.) a temporary working agreement or compromise between two disputants pending a settlement of differences

moles belli: siege machines

mollia tempora: favorable occasions

momentum: movement or motion

mons: a mountain

morbo corripi: racked with disease

morbus comitialis: (med.) epilepsy

morbus ingravescit: (med.) the disease grows worse

mordicus [by biting]: with the teeth

more [after the manner of]: in the fashion of

more Anglico: in the English fashion

more dicto: in the manner directed

more Hibernico: in the Irish fashion

more meo [in my usual manner]: in my own way

more Socratico [after the manner of Socrates]: dialectically

more solito: in the usual manner

more suo [in his usual manner]: in his own way

mores (pl. **mos**) [customs, habits]: customary usages; (leg.) unwritten laws

mors immatura or **mors praematura:** an untimely death

mortis causa: by reason of impending death

mortuus: dead; defunct

morum praecepta: moral teaching

mos majorum: ancestral custom

mos pravus: a bad custom

mos pro lege [custom for law]: usage has the force of law

motu proprio [by one's own motion]: of one's own accord

mox: soon

mox nox: soon night

mulier: a woman

multa de nocte or **multa nocte:** late at night

multa paucis [much in little]: many things in few words

multi [the many]: the common crowd

multimodis [in many ways]: variously

multis cum lacrimis: with many tears

multis partibus: many times

multis rebus: in many respects

multo mane: early in the morning

multo post: much later

multorum deorum cultus: polytheism

multum in parvo: much in little

multus sermo: a long conversation

mundanus: a citizen of the world

mundi universitas: the universe

mundus: the world

mundus imaginalis: the world of images

mundus intelligibilis: the intelligible world

mundus sensibilis: the sensible world

muralis corona: the crown of honor given to the first person over the wall of a besieged city

murus: a wall

mus: a mouse

musca: a fly

muscae volitantes [flying flies]: (med.) specks before the eyes

mutanda: things to be altered

mutatis mutandis (m.m.): the necessary changes being made

mutato nomine: the name having been changed

mutuus consensus: mutual consent

mysteria: cultic mysteries or secret rites

mysterium fascinosum [a fascinating mystery]: (theo.) the feeling of awe-inspiring fascination in the presence of the Almighty God (Otto)

mysterium stupendum [an astounding mystery]: (theo.) to be dumbfounded or thunderstruck by the awareness of the presence of the Almighty God (Otto)

mysterium tremendum [a tremendous mystery]: (theo) the feeling of awful dread in the presence of the Almighty God (Otto)

N

nares or **naris:** the nose

natale solum: native soil

natu: by birth

natura naturans [nature naturing]: (theo.) refers to God as the creative principle of created things (i.e., the infinite creating the finite)

natura naturata [nature natured]: (theo.) refers to created things which find their principle being in God (i.e., the finite dependent on the infinite)

naturae bona: natural advantages

naturae bonitas: innate goodness

naturalia: the sex organs

natus (n.): born

natus ad gloriam: born to glory

natus nemo [not a born soul]: not a human being; (fig.) a nobody (Plautus)

nauta: a sailor

navis: a ship

navis constrata: a decked ship

navis longa: a man-of-war

navis magister: a ship's captain

navis oneraria: a transport ship

navis praetoria: a flag ship

Ne Temere [not rashly]: a decree by the Roman Catholic Church invalidating all marriages not consecrated before a priest and the proper witnesses

ne admittas: do not admit

ne exeat regno or **ne exeat** [let him not go out of the realm]: a writ of restraint

ne multa: in brief

ne nimium [not too much]: do nothing in excess

ne obliviscaris [lest ye forget]: do not forget

ne plus ultra [not more beyond]: the highest point attainable or attained

nebula: a fog; a vapor

nebulo: a fog-headed person (i.e., good-for-nothing)

nec caput nec pedes [neither head nor foot]: in confusion

nec cede malis: yield not to misfortunes

nec cupias nec metuas: neither desire nor fear

nec more nec requies [neither delay nor rest]: without intermission (Virgil)

nedum: not to say

nefasti dies: unlucky days (in ancient Rome, assemblies did not convene and legal pronouncements were not made on these days)

negotia publica: public affairs

nemine contradicente: no one contradicting

nemine dissentiente: no one dissenting

nemo alius: no one else

nemo doctus: no man of learning

nemo est heres viventis: (leg.) no one is heir of a living man

nemo non: everyone

nepos: nephew or grandson

neptis: a granddaughter

nervus probandi [the sinew of proof]: the chief argument

nervus rerum [the sinew of things]: the strength of things

nescio quid: I know not what

neuter [neither]: of neither sex; in neither direction

neutrum (n.): neuter

nexus [a tying together]: connectedness

niger cycnus [black swan]: a prodigy (v.i., **rara avis**)

nigro notanda lapillo [to be marked with a black pebble]: a bad day

nihil: nothing

nihil ad rem [nothing to the point]: beside the point (i.e., irrelevant)

nihil attinet: it is pointless

nihil debet [he/she owes nothing]: (leg.) a plea denying a debt

nihil dicit or **nil dicit** [he says nothing]: (leg.) a common-law judgment when the defendant declines to enter a plea or to answer a charge

nihil non: everything

nihil obstat: there is no objection

nihil obstat quominus imprimatur [nothing hinders the work from being published]: the phrase that indicates acceptability to the Censor of the Roman Catholic Church, printed on the title page of a published work

nihil omnino: not in the least

nil ultra [nothing beyond]: the farthest point or utmost limit

nimbus: a cloud; a rain cloud

nimis: more than enough; too much

ningit: it is snowing

nisi [if not]: unless

nisi prius [unless before]: (leg.) a trial held for civil cases before a judge and a jury

nisus: effort; striving

nisus formativus [creative effort]: the vital principle

nitrum: soda

nix: snow

nobilis [of noble birth]: known or celebrated

nobilis genere natus: of noble birth

nocte (n.): at night

nocte intempesta: at dead of night

noctiluca [light of the night]: the moon

noctu or **nocturnus:** by night

nolens volens [whether willing or not]: perforce (i.e., willy-nilly)

nolle prosequi (nol. pros.) [to be unwilling to prosecute]: an entry into court records indicating a stay or discontinuance of proceedings, either wholly or in part

nolo contendere [I do not wish to contest]: (leg.) a plea of "no contest" to criminal charges by the defendant without admitting guilt

nolo episcopari [I do not wish to be made a bishop]: official refusal of a royal offer of a bishopric

nomen (pl. **nomina**): name

nomen atque omen: a name and also an omen (Plautus)

nomen genericum: a generic name

nomen nudum (pl. **nomina nuda**) [naked name]: in biology, a mere name without a proper description

nomen Romanum: the Roman Power

nomen specificum: a specific name

nomenclator: a servant or slave who reminded his master of names

nomine meo [in my name]: on my behalf

non: no

non adfici: to remain unaffected

non assumpsit [he/she did not undertake]: (leg.) a general denial in an action of *assumpsit*

non bis in idem [not twice for the same thing]: the legal principle of double jeopardy

non causa pro causa [not a cause for a cause]: in logic, the fallacy of false cause

non compos mentis: (leg.) not of sound mind

non constat [it does not appear]: (leg.) the evidence is not before the court

non dolet: it does not hurt

non ens [nonexistent]: a nonentity

non erat his locus: that was not the appropriate place for them

non esse [nonbeing]: nonexistence

non est: he/she/it is not

non est inventus [he/she has not been found]: (leg.) a statement by a sheriff on return of a writ of arrest when the defendant is not to be found

non est meus actus: (leg.) it is not my act

non est tanti: it is not worthwhile

non ita: not particularly

non laccessitus: unprovoked

non legitimus: unconstitutional

non libet: it is not pleasing

non licet (n.l.): it is not permitted

non liquet (n.l.) [it is not clear]: (leg.) the case is not proven

non nihil: something

non obstante (non obs.): notwithstanding

non obstante veredicto [notwithstanding the verdict]: (leg.) a verdict for the plaintiff setting aside a verdict for the defendant

non placet [it does not please]: a negative vote

non possumus [we cannot]: a statement expressing inability to act in a matter

non prosequitur (non pros.) [he/she does not prosecute]: a judgment where the plaintiff does not appear

non sequitur (non seq.): it does not follow

non sine causa [not without cause]: with good reason

nondum: not yet

nondum editus: unpublished

nondum natus: unborn

norma: a rule; a standard

nostri: our people

nostro periculo: at our own risk

nota bene (N.B. or **n.b.)** [note well]: take notice

nota per experientiam: in logic, a proposition that is evident by experience as derived by the principle of induction

notandum (pl. **notanda**): a memorandum

notatu dignum: worthy of note

Notitia [understanding]: an essential item in Medieval Christian faith (together with **Assensus** and **Fiducia**)

notitia illata: acquired knowledge

notitia innata: innate knowledge

notitia intuitiva: intuitive knowledge

nova luna: a new moon

novae res: a political revolution

novae tabulae [new ledgers]: a cancellation of debts

novalis: fallow ground; also a cultivated field

novena (pl. **novenae**): a nine-day period of religious observance or devotion

novissima verba: a person's last words

novus homo [a new man]: an upstart; a parvenu

novus rex, nova lex: new king, new law

nox (pl. **noctis**): night

nox luna inlustris: a moonlit night

nucleus: a pit or stone

nuda veritas: the naked truth (Horace)

nudatum corpus: the naked body

nudis verbis: in plain words

nudius tertius: the day before yesterday

nudum pactum [a nude pact]: (leg.) an informal contract or agreement without consideration or cause and therefore invalid unless under seal

nugae [trifles]: trivial works

nugae canorae [melodious trifles]: nonsense

nulla bona [no goods]: (leg.) no effects

nulli secundus: second to none

nullius filius [nobody's son]: an illegitimate son

nullo modo: by no means

nullo negotio: without any trouble

nullo pacto: by no means

numen: a spirit or deity

numen divinum: the will of heaven

numen loci [spirit places]: sacred places

numen praesens: (theo.) the feeling of some spiritual presence

numerus clausus [closed number]: a quota

nummi adulterini: bad money

nummi boni: a genuine coin

nunc: now

nunc aut nunquam: now or never

nunc pro tunc [now for then]: in law, designating a delayed action which takes effect as if it were done at the proper time

nupta: married

nuptiae [nuptials]: marriage

nutus et pondus: gravity

nux: a nut

O

ob rem: with advantage

obesus: fat or swollen

obiit (ob.): he/she died

obiit sine prole (ob.s.p.): he/she died without issue

obiter (ob.) [by the way]: incidentally; in passing

obiter dictum (pl. **obiter dicta**) [an incidental remark]: an unofficial expression of opinion

obiter scriptum (pl. **obiter scripta**): an incidental composition

oblique: sideways

obscuro loco natus: of unknown origin

observandum (pl. **observanda**): a thing to be observed

obsignator: (leg.) a witness to a will

obsoletus [worn out]: out of date

obviam: in or on the way

occidens [setting]: the setting sun (i.e., the West)

occultus: hidden; concealed

occupatus: busy; engaged

Oceanus: in ancient time, the ocean believed to encompass the earth

octarius (o.): (med.) a pint

octipes: having eight legs

oculatus [having eyes]: conspicuous; catching the eye

oculis et auribus captus: blind and deaf

oculis opertis: a blindfold

oculus: the eye

oculus dexter (o.d.): the right eye

oculus sinister (o.s.): the left eye

odium: hatred; bitter dislike

odium aestheticum [the hatred of artistic rivals]: the bitterness of aesthetical controversy

odium medicum [the hatred of rival physicians]: the bitterness of medical controversy

odium musicum [the hatred of rival musicians]: the bitterness of musical controversy

odium theologicum [the hatred of rival theologians]: the bitterness of theological controversy

odor lucri [the smell of profit]: the expectation of gain

officina [workshop]: a laboratory

officina gentium: the laboratory of the nations

officium: sense of duty; a dutiful act

oleo tranquillior: smoother than oil

oleum (ol.): oil (also olive oil)

oleum perdisti [you have lost oil]: you have wasted your time

olim [at that time]: formerly; for a long time now

olivum: olive oil

omen faustum: a favorable omen

omen infaustum: an evil omen

omen sinistrum: an evil omen

omne scibile: everything knowable

omnes ad unum [all to a person]: unanimous

omni ex parte: from every point of view

omni hora (o.h.): every hour

omni nocte (o.n.): every night

omni quadranta hora (o.q.h.) [every quarter hour]: every fifteen minutes

omni mane vel nocte: every morning or night

omnibus idem: the same to everyone

omnibus rebus: in every respect

omnigenus: of all kinds

omnimodis: in every manner or way

omnino [altogether]: in general; in all

omniparens: all-producing

omnipotens: all-powerful

omnipotentia Dei: almighty God

omnituens: all-seeing

onus probandi: (leg.) the burden of proof

ope et consilio [with aid and counsel]: (leg.) an accessory to the crime

opera mea: thanks to me

operae pretium: worth while

opere citato (op. cit. or o.c.): in the work cited

opere in medio: in the midst of the work

operis exactor: a task-master

opinio dei: belief in god

opinio vana: an illusion

oportet [it is proper]: one should; one ought

opposuit natura [nature has opposed]: it is contrary to nature

opprobrium medicorum [the reproach of physicians]: (med.) an incurable disease

optato: according to one's wish

optimas [one of the best]: aristocratic

optimates [the aristocrisy of ancient Rome]: the noble class

optime [most excellent]: very good

optimo jure: with full right

opus (pl. **opera**; **op.**) [a work]: a musical composition

opus est [there is work]: there is need

opus magnum or **magnum opus** [a great work]: a masterpiece

opus operatum (pl. **opera operata**) [a work wrought]: in Christian theology, the inherent efficacy of the sacrament

oraculum: an oracle

orate fratres: pray, brothers

orate pro anima: pray for the soul of. . . .

oratio composita: an elaborate speech

oratio gravis: a weighty address

oratio meditata: a prepared speech

oratio obliqua [a second-hand report]: hearsay

oratio subita: an extemporaneous speech

orationem concludere: to end a speech

Orbis Factor: Maker of the World

Orbis Pictus: the World in Pictures (Comenius)

orbis finiens: the horizon

orbis lacteus: the Milky Way (also **lacteus orbis**)

orbis medius: the temperate zone

orbis scientiarum: the circle of the sciences

orbis signifer: the Zodiac

orbis terrae or **orbis terrarum:** the world (i.e., all those countries comprising the Roman Empire)

ordinandi lex: procedural law

ordinatum est [it is ordered]: so ordered

ordine [in turn]: in due order

ordines majores [major orders]: the higher offices of the Catholic Church

ordines minores [minor orders]: the lower offices of the Catholic Church

ordo albus [white order]: the Augustinian Order

ordo griseus [grey order]: the Cistercian Order

ordo niger [black order]: the Benedictine Order

ordo salutis [orders of salvation]: (theo.) the Holy Orders of the Catholic Church

ore rotundo [with a round mouth]: a nicely given speech (Horace)

ore tenus [merely from the mouth]: by word of mouth

oriens [rising]: the rising sun (i.e., the East)

origo mali: (theo.) the origin of evil

os (pl. **ora**) [mouth]: an opening

os (pl. **ossa**): a bone

oscillatio: swinging to and fro

osculum pacis: kiss of peace

ossa: a skeleton

ossium compages: the skeletal system

ostiatim: from door to door

ostrinus: purple

otiosus: at leisure

otium [leisure]: free time

ovis: a sheep

ovum: an egg

Oxoniensis (Oxon.): of Oxford

P

pabulum animi [food of the soul]: learning

pace [by leave of]: with all deference to

pace tua [by your leave]: with your approval

pacta conventa [the conditions agreed upon]: a diplomatic agreement

pactum (pl. **pacta**) [pact]: a contract or agreement

pactum illicitum: an unlawful or illegal contract or agreement

pactum vestitum: an enforceable contract or agreement

paganus: rustic; rural

pagina: a page of a book or letter

pallida mors: pale Death (Horace)

pallidus irae: pale with rage

pallium: a ceremonial mantle worn over the shoulders by a priest

panacea [a plant believed to heal all ailments]: a cure-all

panis: bread

panis cibarius: common or ordinary bread

pannis obsitus: in rags

papae!: wonderful!

papilio: a butterfly

par [equal]: a match

par est: it is appropriate

par oneri: equal to the task

par pari refero [I return like for like]: tit for tat

parabola: an application; a comparison

paralysis agitans: (med.) Parkinson's disease

parens: a parent or ancestor

parentalia: a festival honoring dead ancestors

pares cum paribus: equals with equals

pari passu [with equal pace]: equally and simultaneously; without partiality

pari ratione [for a like reason]: neither is acceptable; an impasse

pars adversa: the opposite party

pars pro toto: a part for the whole

partes aequales (p.ae.): equal parts

partes primae: the leading part in a story or play

particeps criminis: (leg.) an accomplice in the crime

participium (ptc.): a participle

partim (p.): in part

parum: too little; not enough

passim (pass.) [here and there]: throughout (as in references found throughout the pages of a book)

Passionale: a book containing the Acts of the Christian Martyrs

passis crinibus: with tossled hair

passus [a measure equal to five Roman feet]: in literature, a portion or division of a poem or story

pater: father

pater patriae: [father of his country]: a national hero

paterfamilias [father of a family]: head of a household

Paternoster or **Pater Noster** [Our Father]: the Lord's Prayer

patres: forefathers

patres conscripti (PP.C.) [conscript fathers]: a title of the Roman Senators

patria potestas [parental authority]: in ancient Rome, the power of a father over the members of his family

patriis virtutibus: by ancestral virtues

patrimonium: (leg.) inherited property

patris est filius [his father's son]: like father, like son

pauca dixit: he said little

paucis verbis: in or with few words

Pax [peace]: peace established by law

Pax Britannica: British peace

Pax Dei: Peace of God (i.e., the Church's protection of non-combatants during war)

Pax Ecclesiae: Peace of the Church (i.e., the Church's protection of non-combatants during war)

Pax Romana: Roman peace (referring to the period from the emperors Augustus to Commodus, ca. 27 B.C.E. to 192 C.E.)

pax in bello: peace in war

pax orbis terrarum [the peace of the world]: universal peace

pax regis: king's peace

peccavi (pl. **peccavimus**) [I have sinned]: a confession of guilt

pecunia mutua: a loan

pedalis: a foot long or wide

pedes: going on foot

pedes muscarum [flies' feet]: (mus.) a system of musical notation

pedibus [on foot]: by land

pedibus nudis: barefoot

pedilavium: ritual foot-washing (cf., St. John 13:2–17)

pedis digitus: a toe

peior or **pejor:** worse

penates: Roman household gods

pendente lite: (leg.) pending the suit

pendere filo: to hang by a thread

penes se esse: to be in one's senses

penetralia mentis [the inner chambers of the mind]: a person's innermost thoughts

penis: a tail

penna: a feather or a wing

per [by or through]: by means of; throughout

per accidens [by accident]: by chance

per acria belli: through the bitterness of war

per ambages [by circuitous ways]: indirectly

per annum (p.a.) [by the year]: annually

per capita [by heads]: for each individual

per centum (per cent. or **p.c.** or **pct.**): by the hundred

per contra: on the contrary

per curiam: (leg.) by the court *in toto*

per diem [by the day]: daily

per dolum: by craft

per essentiam [by essential means]: essentially

per eundem [by the judge]: (leg.) by the same judge

per extensum: at length

per fas et nefas [through right and wrong]: by fair means or foul

per gradus: step by step

per hominen stare: (leg.) occurring through the fault of someone

per impossibile: as is impossible

per incuriam: through carelessness

per infortunium: by accident

per interim: in the meantime

per jocum: in jest

per Jovem: by Jove

per ludibrium: in sport or in fun

per mare per terram: by sea and by land

per mensem [by the month]: monthly; for each month

per mese: by the month

per mille: by the thousand

per minas: by threats

per os: by mouth

per pares: (leg.) by one's peers

per procurationem (p.p. or **per. pro.**) [by proxy]: by the action of

per quod [through which]: by which

per recto et recto: forward and backward

per saltum [by a leap]: in a single bound

per saturam: indiscriminately

per se [by or in itself]: intrinsically

per se esse: to exist by its own being

per se nota: in logic, a proposition, derived by the principle of deduction, that is evident by the meaning of its own terms

per se subsistere: to subsist by itself

per somnum [asleep]: in a dream

per stirpes: (leg.) by families; by representation

per studium: partially

per totam curiam [by the entire court]: unanimously

per viam: by way of

per viam dolorosam: by the way of sorrows

per vias rectas [by the straight road]: directly

per vices [by retaliation]: reciprocally

per vivam vocem: by the living voice

perdiu: for a very long time

perdudum: a long time ago

peregrinatio [travelling abroad]: a foreign journey

peregrinatio sacra: a pilgrimage

perennis: lasting throughout the year

perfervidum ingenium: an ardent temperment

perfidia Punica: Punic treachery

perfidus: treacherous; faithless

perfugium [a shelter for fugitives]: a place of refuge

permissu: by permission

pernox [throughout the night]: lasting all night

perpetuum mobile: perpetual motion

perserverando: by perservering

persona [a mask worn by stage players]: a person or personality

persona ficta: a fictitious person

persona grata (p.g.): an acceptable person

persona gratissima: a most acceptable person

persona muta: a silent actor

persona non grata (p.n.g.) [an unacceptable person]: a diplomatic representative who is not welcome by the government to which he or she is assigned

persona prima: the hero or heroine in a play

pervagatus: widespread; well-known

pes or **pedis:** the foot

pessimi exempli: of a very bad example

pessimus: worst

pestis: plague or pestilence

petasus: a broad-brimmed hat

petitio principii: (rhet.) begging the question

phalanx: soldiers in close formation

pharmaceutria: a sorceress

pharmacopola: a druggist; also, a quack

phiala prius agitata: the bottle being first shaken

philologia [lover of learning]: philology

philosophia [lover of wisom]: philosophy

philosophia moralis [moral philosophy]: ethics

philosophia mundi: philosopher of the world

Philosophiae Baccalaureus (Ph.B.): Bachelor of Philosophy

Philosophiae Doctor (Ph.D.): Doctor of Philosophy

philtrum: a love potion

phrenesis: madness or frenzy

physica or **physiologia:** physics or natural science

pia fraus: a pious fraud (Ovid)

pictor: a painter

pictor ignotus: an unknown painter

pictura textilis: embroidery

pietas: piety or devotion

pietatis causa: for the sake of piety

pila: a ball

pilarius: a juggler

pilosus: hairy

pilula (pl. **pilulae**; **pil.**): (med.) a pill

pinxit (pinx. or **pxt.**): he or she painted it

pirum: a pear

pirus: a peartree

piscator: a fisherman or fishmonger

piscis: a fish

pistor: a baker

pistris: a sea-monster

pius: godly or devoted

placebo [I shall please]: (med.) a prescription given to please a patient; (Eccles.) the first antiphonal in the vespers for the dead

placet [it seems good]: it is agreed

placitum (pl. **placita**) [a decree]: (leg.) a decision

plaudite, cives [citizens, applaud]: a curtain call at the end of a performance

plebeius [of the people]: common

plebiscitum: a decree of the people of Rome

plebs: the common people

plectrum: a stick used to play a stringed instrument

plenilunium: a full moon

pleno jure: with full right or authority

pleno modio [in full measure]: abundantly

plenus: full or complete

plexus: braided or plaited

plumbum (pb.): lead

plumbum album [white lead]: tin

pluralis (pl.): plural

plus solito: more than usual

pluvia: rain

pocula ex auro: gold cups

poena damni [pain of the damned]: (theo.) refers to the anguish the damned
experience in hell as a result of their separation from God

poena sensus [pain of judgment]: (theo.) refers to the means by which humans will
be tortured in hell (e.g., Dante's *Inferno*)

poeta epicus: an epic poet

pollex: the thumb or big toe

pollice verso [with thumb turned]: the "thumb's down" signal by which spectators
indicated the judgment of death to a beaten gladiator

polus glacialis: the North Pole

pomarius: a fruit vendor

pompa: a solemn procession

pompa funebris: a funeral procession

pondere non numero: by weight not by number

pons (pl. **pontes**) [a bridge]: (anat.) a part connecting two parts

pons asinorum [ass's bridge]: a term applied to the fifth proposition of the first book
of Euclid, concepts difficult for the unlearned to grasp

pons Varolii: (zool.) in higher species of veterbrates, a band of traverse fibers on the
ventral surface of the brain

Pontifex Maximus [the high priest of the Roman cultus]: a papal appellation

pontifex: a priest

pontificalia [pontificals]: the vestments and insignia of a bishop

porca [pig]: a sow

porcus [pig]: a hog

portorium circumvectionis: port customs or transit duties

portus: a port or harbor

posse [to be able]: potential or possibility (as opposed to **esse**)

posse comitatus [the power of the county]: a sheriff's posse

posse videor [seem to be able]: I think I can

post bellum auxilium [aid after the war]: assistance offered too late

post Christum natum (P.Ch.N.): after Christ's birth

post cibum (p.c.): (med.) after meals

post diem: (leg.) after the appointed day

post hoc ergo propter hoc [after this, therefore, on account of this]: in logic, a
fallacy of cause and effect

post litem motam: (leg.) after litigation began

post meridiem (p.m.): after noon

post mortem (P.M.): after death

post obitum: after death

post partum: after birth

post postscriptum (PPS): an additional postscript

post terminum: after the conclusion

postpartor: an heir

postremo: at last

postremum: for the last time

postridie [the day after]: on the next day

postscriptum (PS): a postscript

postulata [postulates]: fundamental assumptions

postulatus: a legal complaint or suit

potestas est: it is possible

prae: in front of; before

prae quam: in comparison with

praecognitum (pl. **praecognita**) [something foreknown]: a branch of knowledge necessary to the understanding of something else

praecox: premature

praedium [land]: landed property; an estate

praefectus urbis: governor of the city of Rome

praenomen: first name

praesentia animi: presence of mind

praestat [it is better]: it is preferable

praeter: past, beyond, or beside

praeteriti anni: bygone years

praeterito anno: in the past year

praetexta: a toga with purple borders worn by magistrates

praetorius cohors: the bodyguard or military detail protecting a general

prandium: lunch or brunch

precibus infirmis: with ineffective prayers (Livy)

pretium: worth, value, price, or reward

pretium affectionis [the price of affection]: (leg.) the sentimental value of a thing as distinct from its market value

pretium periculi: an insurance premium

pretium puellae [the price of a maiden]: the marriage price demanded by a young woman's guardian

prex: a prayer

pridie: on the day before

prima facie [at first appearance]: a judgment based on the first impression

prima (or **primus**) **inter pares:** first among equals

prima luce [at first light]: early in the morning

prima lux [first light]: the break of day

primas partes: to play the leading part

primitus: for the first time

primo [in the first place]: first

primo intuitu: at the first glance

primo vere: in the beginning of spring

primordium: origin or first beginnings

primoribus labris: superficially

primum cognitum: the first thing known

primum mobile [the first moving thing]: in Ptolemaic astronomy, the prime source of the motion of the universe

principia rerum: the principle elements

priore anno: last year

privatim [privately]: in private life

pro: before

pro bono publico [for the public good]: without charge (also known as **pro bono**)

pro certo [for sure]: you bet!

pro certo habeo: I feel sure

pro confesso [for the confession]: (leg.) as if confessed

pro consule (or **proconsul**) [an officer in place of a consul]: the governor of a province

pro eo quantum [in proportion as]: proportionally

pro et contra: for and against

pro forma [for the sake of form]: as a matter of form

pro hac vice: for this occasion only

pro mea parte [for my part]: to the best of my ability

pro memoria [for memory]: for a memorial

pro meritis: deservedly

pro merito: according to merit

pro nunc: for now

pro rata [according to rate]: in proportion; proportionally

pro re: according to circumstance

pro re nata (p.r.n.): (med.) whenever necessary

pro sua parte: to the best of one's ability

pro tanto [for so much]: so far; to that extent

pro tempore (p.t. or **pro tem.)** [temporarily]: for the time being

pro verbo [according to the word]: literally

pro viribus [to the best of one's ability]: as well as can be done

pro virili parte [for a man's part]: to the best of one's ability

probatum est: it has been proven

procul dubio: without doubt

procurator: a viceroy

proelium justum: a pitched battle

profanum vulgus [the profane rabble]: the ungodly multitude

profanus: not sacred

progenitor: an ancestor

proletarius: a citizen of the lowest class

promotor fidei: promoter of the faith (opposite of **advocatus diaboli** in an ecclesiastical argument in favor of the beatification of a person)

propediem [at an early date]: very soon

propositi tenax: firm of purpose

propositio [a purpose]: in logic, the major premise of a syllogism

propria natura: individuality

propria quae maribus [things appropriate to males]: the rudiments of Latin

propria vis: the literal sense; proper meaning

proprio jure: of his own right

proprio motu [by its own motion]: spontaneously

proprio vigore [of its own strength]: independently; by its own power

propter: on account of; because of

propter hoc: on this account

prosit [may it do you good]: to your health!

prosit tibi: may it be well with thee!

prospectus: an outlook or view

provisio [foresight]: a provision

provocatio: (leg.) an appeal to a higher court

proxime accessit (pl. **accesserunt; prox. acc.**) [he/she came very near (to winning)]: the runner-up in a contest

proximo (prox.): in the following month

proximo mense (prox. m.): in the following month

proximum genus: the nearest kind

prudens futuri: thoughtful of the future

pruina: hoarfrost

publice: publicly

publicum juris: of the public right

pudet me: I am ashamed

puella: a female youth

puer: a male youth

pugil: a fighter

pugna navalis: a naval battle

pulex: a flea

pullus: a chick or chicken

pulmo (pl. **pulmones**): a lung

pulvis (pulv.): dust; powder

punctatim: point for point

puncto temporis: in an instant

punctum (pl. **puncta**): a point; a spot

punctum caecum: (anat.) the blind spot of the eye

punctum contra punctum [note against note]: counterpoint

punctum saliens: a salient point

punctum temporis: a point of time

punctum vegetationis: (bot.) the growing point of a plant

pupa: a little girl; a doll

purpuratus [clothed in purple]: a person of high rank

puto or **ut puto:** I suppose (said parenthetically)

pyorrhea alveolaris: (med.) Rigg's disease

Q

qua: as

quadra or **quadrum:** a square

Quadragesima [fortieth]: the forty-day period of fasting preceding Easter that begins on Ash Wednesday

quadriennium: a period of four years

quadrimus: four years old

Quadrivium [a crossroads]: the four principle subjects of advanced study in medieval universities (i.e., arithmetic, astronomy, geometry, and music), following the **Trivium**

quadrupes: four-footed

quadruplex: quadruple

quae cum ita sint: in these circumstances

quae est eadem: which is the same

quae summa est?: what does it amount to?

quae vide (qq.v.): (pl.) which see

quaere (qu.): a question or query

quaeritur [it is sought]: the question arises

quaesitum [that which is sought]: the solution to a problem

quaestio vexata (pl. **quaestiones vexatae**): a vexed or vexing question

quaestiones perpetuae: (leg.) standing courts of justice

qualibet: wherever you like; in any way you please

qualis: of what kind?

qualis ab incepto: such as from the beginning (Horace)

quam celerrime: as fast as possible

quam libet or **quamlibet:** as much as you please

quam maxime: as much as possible

quam primum or **quamprimum:** as soon as possible

quam proxime: as nearly as possible

quamvis [as much as you please]: ever so much

quantum (pl. **quanta**): a concrete quantity or specified amount

quantum [as much as]: how much

quantum in me est: as far as in me lies

quantum libet (**q.l.** or **q.lib.**) [as much as you please]: liberally

quantum meruit: as much as he or she deserved

quantum placet (**q.pl.** or **q.p.**): as much as you please

quantum satis: as much as is sufficient

quantum scio: as far as I know

quantum sufficit (**q.s.** or **quant. suff.**) [as much as suffices]: a sufficient quantity

quantum valeat: as much as it may be worth

quantum valebat: as much as it is worth

quantum vis (**q.v.**): as much as you will

quaque hora (**Q.H.**): (med.) every hour

quaque mane (**Q.M.**): (med.) every morning

quare impedit [why does he hinder?]: (leg.) a writ issued against the objector to a disputed right or claim

quarta pars: one quarter

quarto die (**q.i.d.**): on the fourth day

quartus: the fourth; the fourth hour

quasi [as it were; about]: a sort of

quasi dicat (**q.d.**): as if one should say

quasi dictum (**q.d.**): as if said

quasi dixisset: as if he had said

quater [four times]: again and again

quater in die (**q.i.d.**) (also **quater die**): four times a day

quaterni: four each

querela (pl. **querelae**) [bill of complaint]: (leg.) a court action

qui tam [who as well]: (leg.) action to recover (brought by an informer in conjunction with the State)

quia timet: because he fears

quid agis?: how do you do?

quid est rei?: what is the matter?

quid est veritas?: what is truth? (Pontius Pilate, St. John 18:38)

quid faciendum?: what is to be done?

quid hoc sibi vult?: what does this mean?

quid ni?: why not?

quid novi? [what news?]: what's new?

quid nunc?: what now?

quid pro quo [this for that]: something given in return for a favor

quid rides?: why do you laugh?

quid times [what do you fear?]: what are you afraid of?

quidam: a person known though unnamed (i.e., an unknown person)

quidditas [whatness]: the essence of a thing

Quinque Viae [The Five Ways]: the five arguments of St. Thomas Aquinas for the existence of God

quinquennis: five years old

quinquennium: a five year period

quo animo?: with what spirit or intention?

quo in genere: from this standpoint; from this point of view

quo jure?: by what right?

quo modo? or **quomodo?:** by what means?; in what way?

quo tendis?: where are you going?

quo vadis?: whither goest thou?

quoad [as to]: as regards; so far as

quoad hoc [as to this]: as regards this particular matter; as far as this goes

quoad minus: as to the lesser matter

quoad ultra: as regards the past

quocunque modo [in whatsoever manner]: in whatever way

quocunque nomine: under whatever name

quod abominor!: God forbid!

quod absurdum est: it is absurd

quod ad hoc [as far as this]: to this extent

quod ad me attinet: as far as I am concerned

quod bene notandum [which is to be well marked]: take especial notice

quod erat demonstrandum (Q.E.D.): which was to be demonstrated or shown

quod erat faciendum (Q.E.F.): which was to be done

quod est (q.e.): which is

quod hoc sibi vult?: what does this mean?

quod sciam: as far as I know

quod vide (q.v.): which see

quodlibet [what you please]: a subtle or debatable point

quomodo vales? [how do you fare?]: hello

quondam [former]: formerly; at times

quot annis or **quotannis:** every year

quota pars?: how large a part?

quotidianus or **quotidie:** daily

quousque tandem?: to what lengths? (Cicero)

quovis modo: in whatever manner

R

radicitus: by the roots

radix: a root or foundation

rana: a frog

raptor: a robber or plunderer

rara avis (pl. **rarae aves**) [a rare bird]: a prodigy

raro: seldom; rarely

rata [rate]: an individual share

ratio [a reckoning or reasoning out]: a calculation; a transaction

ratione domicilii: (leg.) by reason of domicile

ratione soli: (leg.) by reason of the land or soil

re: regarding or concerning

re infecta: the business being unfinished

re vera or **revera** [in truth]: in fact

rebus sic stantibus: things being the way they are

recessim: backwards

recitatio: a reading; a recitation

recta linea: a straight line

recta via: straight ahead

recte est: all is well

recto or **recto folio:** the right-hand page of a book (opposite of **verso**)

rector: a ruler; a director

rectus (pl. **recti**): straight or upright

rectus abdominis: (anat.) the abdominal muscles

rectus femoris: (anat.) the major thigh muscle surrounding the femur bone

rectus in curia [upright in court]: blameless

rectus musculus or **rectus:** (anat.) any of various straight muscles

redivivus [restored to life]: resuscitated; renewed

reductio ad absurdum [reduction to the absurd]: in logic, to prove the falsity of a proposition or conclusion by reducing it to the point of absurdity

reductio ad impossibile [reduction to the impossible]: in logic, an impossible conclusion

redux: a bringing back; a restoring

Regina Caeli [Queen of Heaven]: the Virgin Mary

regina (R.): a queen

regio meridiana: the south

regium donum: a royal gift or grant

rei publicae causa: for political reasons

religio illicita: in the Roman Empire, an unlawful or illegal religion

religio laici: a layperson's religion

religio licita: in the Roman Empire, a lawful or legal religion

religio loci: the sanctity of a place (Virgil)

reliquiae [the remains]: relics

remedium efficacissum: a sovereign remedy (i.e., an effective cure)

remisso animo [the mind relaxed]: listlessly

renes: the kidneys

renovato nomine: by a revived name

repertorium (pl. **repertoria**): a catalogue

repetatur (**rep.** or **repet.**): (med.) let it be repeated

requiem [rest]: a mass for the dead

requiescat in pace (pl. **requiescant; R.I.P.**): may he/she rest in peace

requiescit in pace (**R.I.P.**): he/she rests in peace

rerum natura [things of nature]: the natural world; the universe

rerum primordia: the first beginnings of things

rerum progressio: evolution

Res Tota Simul [the whole thing at the same time]: a medieval Christian definition of eternity (also **Totum Simul**)

res (pl. **res**): a thing, matter, or circumstance; a cause or action

res adjudicata [a matter already settled]: (leg.) a decided case

res adversae: misfortune

res alienae [things belonging to others]: debt

res bene gesta: a successful military campaign or exploit

res cogitans [a thinking thing]: the natural state of the mind without reference to space or time (Descartes)

res confecta est: the question is settled

res corporales [corporeal things]: tangible things

res discrepat: non agreement

res divina [divine things]: sacrificial service to the gods

res expedit: it is useful, expedient, or advantageous

res extensa [an extended thing]: the body in motion (i.e., the natural state of the body with reference to space and time is motion; Descartes)

res fessae: distress

res gesta: a deed

res gestae [things done]: deeds, transactions; (leg) the attendant circumstances; exploits in war

res hereditaria: an heirloom

res incorporales [things incorporeal]: nontangible things

res inter alios: a matter between others

res judicata [a matter already settled]: (leg.) a decided case

res judicata pro veritate accipitur: (leg.) a case decided is accepted as just

res militaris: (mil.) military strategy

res mobiles: movable things

res nihili [a none thing]: a nonentity

res nullius [a none thing]: a nonentity

res publica: the state

res repetundae: extortion

res rustica: a rural affair

res secundae: prosperity; success

respublica: commonwealth; republic

respublica forum: public life

resurgam: I shall rise again

rete (pl. **retia**) [a net]: (anat.) plexus of nerves; vascular network
retro: backwards
retro Satana!: Satan, behind!
reus: (leg.) an accused person
rex (**R.**): a king
rex regum: king of kings
rhombus: a magician's circle
rhythmus [measured motion]: rhythm
ridicula imitatio: a parody
rigor mortis [rigor of death]: the stiffening of the body after death
risus [a laugh]: laughter
rite: in proper form
rituale: a ritual manual for priests
rivus: a stream
Romae natus: a native of Rome
ros marinus: rosemary
rosa: a rose; a garland of roses
rosarium: a rose garden
rota: a wheel
rotula: a yo-yo
rotundus: circular or round
rubrica [red earth]: a law with its title written or printed in red ink
rudera [rubbish]: debris
rudis indigestaque moles: a rude and disorderly mass
ruri or **rure:** in the country
rus in urbe: the country in a city (Martial)

S

sacer or **sacra:** holy; consecrated
sacerdos: a priest
Sacrae Theologiae Baccalaureus (**S.T.B.**): Bachelor of Sacred Theology
Sacrum Romanum Imperium (**S.R.I.**): the Holy Roman Empire
saeculum [a century]: a generation or age
saga: a prophetess; a fortune-teller
sagitta: an arrow
sagittarius: an archer
sal: salt
sal amarus [bitter salt]: a cathartic (e.g., Epsom salt)
sal Atticum [Attic salt]: a keen wit (also **sal Atticus**)
sal catharticus: a cathartic (e.g., Epsom salt)
sal culinarius [cooking salt]: table salt

sal gemmae: rock salt

saltem [at least]: at all events

saltus ad funem: to play jump-rope

salus: health or welfare; safety or salvation

salus mundi: the salvation or welfare of the world

Salutem dicit! (**Sal.** or **S.**): Greetings!

salve! [may you be safe]: God's speed!

salvo jure: without prejudice; (leg) without infraction of law

salvo ordine: with due regard to one's rank

salvo pudore: without offense to modesty

salvo sensu: without violation of sense

sanae mentis esse: to be in one's right mind

sanctio: (leg.) a clause in a law defining a penalty for breach

sanctum sanctorum [holy of holies]: a private room; a place of retreat

sanctus: holy or consecrated

sane quam: exceedingly

sanguine suffusus: bloodshot

sanguis: blood

sapientia: wisdom; discernment

sarcophagus: a coffin; a grave

satis: enough

Saturnalia: the winter festival

Saturnia regna [the reign of Saturn]: the Golden Age (Virgil)

saxum: a rock or stone

saxum quadratum: hewn stone

scala: a ladder

scalae: a staircase

scandalum magnatum (pl. **scandala magnatum**; **scan. mag.**)
 [scandal of magnates]: defamation or slander of notable or high-ranking persons

scarabaeus: a beetle

scienter [knowingly]: willfully

scientia [knowledge]: science

scilicet (**sc.**) [that is to say]: namely

scintilla: a spark

scire facias (**sci. fa.**) [cause it to be known]: (leg.) a writ to enforce, annul, or vacate
 a judgment, patent, charter or other matter of record

scorpio: a scorpion

scribere scientes: skilled in writing

scripsit: he/she wrote (it)

scriptura: a composition or a piece of writing

sculpsit (**sc.** or **sculpt.**): he/she sculpted (it)

se defendendo: in defending him/herself

secunda mensa: dessert

secundo: secondly

secundo flumine: downstream

secundum (sec.): according to

secundum artem (sec. art.) [according to art]: scientifically; artificially

secundum formam statuti: (leg.) according to the form of the statute

secundum genera: according to classes

secundum legem (sec. leg.): according to law

secundum naturam (sec. nat.) [according to nature]: naturally

secundum ordinem [according to order]: in an orderly manner

secundum quid [according to some one thing]: with limitations

secundum regulam (sec. reg.): according to rule

secundum usum: according to usage

secundum veritatem [according to truth]: universally true

sedes: a seat or chair

selibra: half a pound

selpuchra: a cemetery

semel: once; one time only

semel pro semper: once for all

semen: seed

semihora: half an hour

seminex: half-dead

semis (s̄s̄): (med.) half or one half

semper: always

semper florens: perennials

sempiterna gloria [everlasting glory]: immortality

semuncia: half an ounce

Senatus Populusque Romanus (S.P.Q.R.): the Senate and People of Rome (motto of the Roman Republic)

senatus consultum: a decree of the Roman Senate

senior: older

seniores priores: elders' first

sensu bono: in a good sense

sensu malo: in a bad sense

sententia legis: the spirit of the law

sententiae judicum: (leg.) the finding of the jury

separatio a mensa et toro (or **thoro**) [separation from room and board]: legal separation

separatio a vinculo matrimonii [separation from the bond of marriage]: divorce

septemtriones or **septentrio:** the north or northwind

Septemviri epulones: a college of priests in charge of sacrificial feasts (previously **Tresviri epulones**)

septimana: a week

sepultus (S.): buried

sequens (seq.): the following

sequentia (seqq.): the following things

sequitur (seq.) [it follows]: a logical inference

seriatim [in a series]: point by point; also, one volume in a series of publications

serra: a saw

servare modum: to keep within the bounds

Servus Servorum Dei [Servant of the Servants of God]: a papal appellation

servus ad manum or **servus a manu:** a secretary; an amanuensis

sescenaris: a year and a half old

sescenti [six hundred]: countless

sesqui [one half more]: half as much again

sesquialter: one and a half

sesquihora: an hour and a half

sesquipedalia verba [words a foot and a half in length]: very long words

sexangulus: hexagonal

sexennis: six years old

sexennium: a period of six years

sextarius: a pint

sexus: sex (i.e., gender)

sexus muliebris: the female sex

sexus virilis: the male sex

si modo: if only

si opus sit (s.o.s.): (med.) if necessary

si placet [if it pleases]: please

si quis: if anyone

sic [thus]: usually found in brackets following a doubtful word in a quotation to indicate that the original passage is being followed *verbatim*

sic in originali: thus in the originals

sic jubeo: thus I command

sic passim [thus throughout]: here and there

sic totidem verbis: thus in as many words

sicarius: an assassin

sicut ante: as before

signa (S. or **Sig.)** [write]: (med.) that which is to be written on the label of a prescription

signum: a signet or seal

sigillum: a seal

silentio noctis: in the silence of night

silentium altum: deep silence

silex [a hard rock]: a flint stone

silva: a wood or forest

similiter: in like manner

similitudo Dei: the likeness of God

simpliciter [absolutely]: without reservation or reserve

simul [at once]: at the same time

simulare morbum: to feign illness

sincerus: genuine; pure

sine: without

sine anno (s.a.): without date

sine auxilio: unaided

sine controversia: indisputably

sine cortice natare [to swim without corks]: to need no assistance

sine cura [without care]: all the benefits of office without all the responsibilities

sine die (s.d.) [without a day]: without fixing a day for future action or meeting (e.g, indefinitely adjourned)

sine dolore: painless

sine dubio: without doubt

sine fraude [without deceit or offense]: honorably; without harm

sine fuco [without pretense]: frankly

sine ictu: without a blow

sine ira: without anger

sine invidia: without envy

sine joco [without jesting]: seriously

sine legitima prole (s.l.p.): without legitimate issue

sine loco (s.l.): without place

sine loco et anno (s.l.a.): without place and year

sine loco, anno, vel nomine (s.l.a.n.): without place, year, or name

sine maculis [without stain]: spotless

sine mascula prole (s.m.p.): without male issue

sine mora: without delay

sine nervis [without strength]: weak

sine nomine (s.n.) [without name]: anonymous

sine odio: without hatred

sine omni periculo: without any danger

sine ope: without help

sine praejudicio: without prejudice

sine proba causa: without approved cause

sine prole (s.p.): without issue

sine prole supersite (s.p.s.): without surviving issue

sine qua non [without which not]: something essential; an indispensible condition

sine sapore: tasteless

sine ulla dubitatione: without any hesitation

singillatim or **singulatim:** one by one

singularis (sg. or **sing.):** singular

singulis annis [year by year]: every year

singulis diebus [day by day]: every day

sinister: left

sinistra manu: with the left hand

sinus urbis: the heart of the city

Sirius: the Dog-Star

Sitio: I thirst (one of the Seven Last Words of Christ; St. John 19:29)

sobrius: sober or sober-minded

societas: a partnership or association

socius criminis: (leg.) an associate in crime

sodalis [a companion]: a member of a secret society

sodes [if you please]: with your leave

Sol Invictus [the Invincible Sun]: the Sun God of ancient Mithraism whose festival was celebrated on December 25th of each year

sol: the sun

sol occidens: setting sun

sol oriens: rising sun

sola fide: faith alone (a doctrine of Martin Luther)

sola gratia: grace alone (a doctrine of the Protestant Reformers)

sola scriptura: scripture alone (a doctrine of the Protestant Reformers)

solarium: a sundial; an open terrace

solea (pl. **soleae**): a sandal

solis defectio: a solar eclipse

solis occasus: sunset

solis ortus: sunrise

solstitium: the summer solstice

solus: by oneself

solutio (sol.): (med.) a solution

solvendo non esse: to be insolvent

somnium: a dream

somnus: sleep

sonus: sound

sonus dulcis: a sweet or pleasant sound (i.e., euphony)

sophia: wisdom

sorbilo [by sipping]: drop by drop

soror: a sister

sortes Biblicae [casting a fortune with the Book]: divination by the selection of random passages from the Christian Bible

sortes Homericae [casting a fortune with Homer]: divination by the selection of random passages from Homer

sortes Vergilianae (or **sortes Virgilianae**) [casting a fortune with Virgil]: divination by the selection of random passages from Virgil

soter: a savior

speciali gratia: by special favor

specimen: a model or an example

spectaculum: a spectacle or a show

spectator (fem. **spectatrix**): a spectator; an observer

speculum: a mirror

speculum aeterni Patris: mirror of the eternal Father (a reference to the Crucifixion as an image of the eternal love of God)

speravi: I have hoped

spes: hope

spina: a thorn

spinosus: thorny or prickly

spiritus: spirit

spiritus asper: in Greek grammar, rough breathing (i.e., asperated)

spiritus lenis: in Greek grammar, smooth breathing (i.e., nonasperated)

spolia opima [the richest spoils]: a supreme achievement (originally, the spoils taken from a vanquished general by a victorious general in a single contest)

spolia sua [from one's own spoils]: out of one's excess

sponte sua or **sua sponte** [of one's own accord]: unsolicited

sportula (pl. **sportulae**) [small basket]: a present, gratuity, or largesse

Stabat Mater [the Mother was standing]: Latin hymn inspired by the suffering of the Holy Virgin Mother at the Crucifixion

stadium [a measure of distance]: a race course

stannum (sn.): tin

stans pede in uno [standing on one foot]: a certain posture taken by orators during a speech (Horace)

statim (stat.) [immediately]: on the spot; at once

statu quo: as things were before

statua: a statue

status in quo [the state in which]: an existing condition or unchanged position

status quo [the state which]: an existing condition or unchanged position

status quo ante bellum: the state existing before the war

stella: a star

stella comans: a comet

stella crinita [long-haired star]: a comet

sterilis: barren; fruitless

stet [let it stand]: to leave as is (i.e., not to be changed or deleted)

stomachus: the stomach

stomachus bonus [good digestion]: good humor

stratum super stratum: layer upon layer

strena [a new year's gift]: a favorable omen

stricto sensu: in a strict sense (the opposite of **lato sensu**)

strictum jus [strict law]: the strict letter of the law

stultus: silly or foolish

sua sponte or **sponte sua** [of one's own accord]: unsolicited

sub: under or underneath

sub audi or **subaudi (sub.)** [to supply the missing word or words by subaudition]: to read between the lines

sub colore juris: under color of law

sub dio or **sub divo** [under the open sky]: in the open air

sub ferula: under the rod

sub finem: toward the end

sub initio: at the beginning

sub Jove [under Jupiter]: in the open air

sub Jove frigido [under cold Jupiter]: under the cold sky

sub judice [before the judge]: under judicial consideration

sub modo: in a qualified sense

sub noctem: at nightfall

sub poena: under penalty

sub quocunque titulo: under whatever title

sub rosa [under the rose]: confidentially

sub sigillo [under seal]: in the strictest confidence

sub silentio [in silence]: privately

sub spe rati: in the hope of a decision

sub specie: under the appearance of

sub verbo (s.v., pl. **s.vv.):** look under the word

sub vino: under the influence of wine

sub voce (s.v., pl. **s.vv.):** look under the word

subito: suddenly

subscriptio [a writing beneath]: a signature

subter or **subtus:** beneath or below

subterraneus: underground

suburbanus: near the city

succubus: a female spirit or demon believed to prey sexually on young men while they sleep

sufficit (pl. **sufficiunt**): it is enough

suffragium [a voting tablet]: the right to vote

suggestio falsi [suggestion of a falsehood]: an indirect lie or misrepresentation

sui generis [of its own kind]: unique; one of a kind; something in a class by itself

sui impotens: beside oneself

sui juris [in one's own right]: of full legal capacity

sulfur (s.): sulfur

Summa or **Summae:** a compendium of philosophical thoughts or theological conclusions, the most famous being the *Summa Theologica* of St. Thomas Aquinas

summa aestas: midsummer

summa aqua: the surface of the water

summa cum laude: with highest honors

summa gloria: the height of glory

summa pax: a great peace

summa res publica: the welfare of the state

summa summarum [the sum of sums]: the sum of all things

summa urbs: the highest point of the city

summa vitae: life span (also **vitae summa**)

summo loco natus: of noble origin

summum bonum: the highest or chief good

summum genus (pl. **summa genera**): in logic, the highest genus

summum jus: the highest law

summus collis: the brow of a hill or ridge

summus mons: the mountain summit

sumptibus publicis or **sumptu publico:** at the public expense

sumptio: in logic, the premise of a syllogism

suo jure: in one's own right

suo loco: in its proper place

suo Marte: by one's own prowess

suo motu: by its own motion

suo periculo: at one's own peril

suo tempore: at its own time

super: over or above

superas ad auras: to the light of day

supercilium [an eyebrow]: (fig.) arrogance

superiore anno: last year

supinus: lying face-up

supinus manus: lying on one's back with palms facing upwards

suppositio terminorum [substitution of terms]: in logic, the claim that an affirmative proposition is true only when the subject and predicate terms stand for the
same thing

suppressio veri [a suppression of the truth]: concealment of facts

supra (sup.): over, above, or on the top

supra vires: beyond one's powers

supremo vitae die: on one's last day

supremum vale: a last farewell

sursum deorsum [up and down]: backwards and forwards

sursum versus: upwards

suspensio per collum (sus. per col.) [suspension by the collar]: execution by
hanging

suspenso gradu: on tiptoe

suum cuique: to each his/her own

T

tabella (tab.): (med.) a tablet

tabellarius: a letter carrier

tabernaculum: a tent

tabernarius: a shopkeeper

tabula: a map, record book, or register

tabula rasa (pl. **tabulae rasae**) [a blank writing tablet]: the mind at birth (Locke)

tabulae publicae: public archives

tace!: be silent!

tacet [it is silent]: in music, a direction indicating that a certain instrument (or instruments) is not played during a particular section or movement of a piece

tacitus: silent; unmentioned

taedium: boredom

taedium vitae: weariness of life

talis qualis: such as it is

tamquam alter idem or **tanquam alter idem** [as if a second self]: a completely trustworthy person

tandem: at length

tandem denique: in the end

tangere ulcus: to touch a sore

Tantum Ergo [so great, therefore]: a Eucharistic hymn

tantum quantum: just as much as is required

taurus: a bull

Te Deum, Laudamus: We praise Thee, O God (an ancient Christian hymn)

Te Igitur [Thee, therefore]: part of the Eucharistic liturgy of the Latin mass

te judice [you being the judge]: in your judgment

tempestas: bad weather; a violent storm

templum: consecrated ground

tempora matutina: the morning hours

tempore (temp. or **t.):** in the time of

temporis causa: on the spur of the moment

temporis puncto: in the twinkling of an eye

tempus: time

tempus in ultimum: to the last extremity

tempus ludendi: the time for play

tenax propositi: tenacious of purpose

tendo calcaneus: (anat.) the Achilles tendon

tenebrae aeternae: (theo.) eternal darkness

tepidus: warm or lukewarm

ter [thrice]: three times

ter in die (t.i.d.): (med.) three times a day

tere bene: (med.) rub well

terminus a quo [the end from which]: the starting point

terminus ad quem [the end to which]: the finishing point; the destination

terra: the earth

terra firma [solid earth]: dry land; firm footing

terra incognita (pl. **terrae incognitae**) [an unknown land]: an unknown region or subject

terrae filius (pl. **terrae filii**) [son of the earth]: a person of lowly birth

terrae motus: an earthquake

terrestris: terrestrial

Tersanctus [thrice holy]: the Trisagion

tertia hora est: it is the third hour (i.e., 9 A.M.)

tertium: for the third time

tertium quid [a third something]: something in between two fixed points or positions; a third alternative or choice beyond two fixed choices

tertius: third

teste [by the evidence of]: a witness

testimonium internum (or **testimonium Spiritus Sanctus internum**) [internal testimony]: (theo.) the internal witness of the Holy Spirit that inspires faith within those who seek the truth of the Gospel

testis gravis: (leg.) an important witness

testis unus, testis nullus: (leg.) one witness is no witness

textor: a tailor or weaver

textus receptus (text. rec.): the received text (i.e., the scriptural tradition that has been handed down from generation to generation)

theologia crucis [theology of the cross]: the emphasis of Protestant reformers on the sacrificial death of Christ on the Cross (as opposed to **theologia gloriae**)

theologia gloriae [theology of glory]: Martin Luther's pejorative label for Church doctrines that did not lay proper stress on the sacrificial death of Christ on the Cross (as opposed to **theologia crucis**)

thermae: warm springs or baths

thesaurus: a store-house or treasury

thorax: a breastplate

thyrsus: a stalk of a plant, such as corn, symbolizing fertility

tibia: the shin-bone

tigris: a tiger

tintinnabulum: a bell

titulus: a label or inscription

toga candida [the white robe]: the white robe worn by Roman candidates for office

toga praetexta: a white robe bordered with purple and worn by Roman magistrates and freeborn children

toga virilis [the manly robe]: the toga worn by Roman freemen from ages fourteen and older

togata: a freed woman (sometimes, a prostitute)

totidem verbis [in so many words]: in these very words

toties quoties [as often as]: repeatedly or on each occasion

totis viribus: with all one's might

toto caelo [by the whole heaven]: by a great distance; diametrically opposite

Totum Simul [the whole at the same time]: a medieval Christian definition of eternity (also **Res Tota Simul**)

totum: the whole

toxicum: poison (usu. for arrows)

tractim [in managed bits]: by degrees

trans: across, over, or beyond

transfugium [going across]: desertion

transmarinus [from beyond the sea]: foreign

tremulus: trembling

Tresviri epulones: a college of priests who had charge of sacrificial feasts (later **Septemviri epulones**)

Treuga Dei (or **Treva Dei**) [Truce of God]: during the Middle Ages, the suspension of hostilities and private warfare during certain religious holidays, on pain of excommunication

triangulus [triangular]: three-cornered

tribuni plebis: tribunes or magistrates of the people

tributum: tax or taxation

triceps: having three heads or three points of origin

tricuspis: having three points

tridens: having three teeth or three prongs

triduum: a period of three days

triennia: a festival celebrated every three years

triennium (pl. **triennia**): a period of three years

trilibris: three pounds in weight

trinitas [trinity]: (theo.) the doctrine of the Christian Trinity (i.e., Father, Son, and the Holy Ghost)

trimus: three years old

tripartito: having three parts

tripedalis: three feet in length or width

tripes: having three feet

triplex munus [triple service]: (theo.) refering to Christ as fulfilling the triple roles of prophet, priest, and king

triplex or **triplus** [threefold]: triple

Trisagion: thrice holy

tristes kalendae (or **calendae**) [the unhappy calends]: the day interest on borrowed money was due to the lender

trium literarum homo [a man of three letters]: a thief (properly, **homo trium literarum**)

triumvir (pl. **triumviri**): a ruling board of three members (referring specifically to the first and second Roman triumvirs: Julius Caesar, Pompeius, and Crassus; and Octavian, Marcus Antonius, and Lepidus)

Trivium: the three principle subjects of basic study in medieval universities (i.e., dialectic, grammar, and rhetoric), followed by the **Quadrivium**

trivium: a junction where three roads meet

tu quoque [you as well]: (leg.) a statement accusing the accuser of the same charge

tuba: a straight war trumpet

tuebor: I will defend

tumor [a swelling]: a protuberance

tumulus: a burial mound

tunica: a sleeved garment

turris: a tower

tutamen (pl. **tutamina**) [protection]: a protective pact

tutor et ultor: protector and avenger

tuum [yours]: your property

tuum est: it is yours

tuum est?: is it yours?

tyrannis: an absolute ruler

U

uberrima fides [superabounding faith]: implicit trust

ubi gentium?: where in the world?

ubi supra (**u.s.**) [where above]: in the place mentioned above

ubique: everywhere

ultima forsan: perhaps the last [moment] (an inscription on clocks)

ultima ratio: the final argument (i.e., force)

ultima ratio regum [the last argument of kings]: a resorting to arms

ultima Thule [farthest Thule]: the utmost limit; an unknown region (Virgil)

ultimo (**ult.**): last month

ultimum: for the last time

ultimum vale: a last farewell

ultimus haeres [the last of the heirs]: the final heir (i.e., the Crown)

ultimus regum: the last of the kings

ultimus Romanorum: the last of the Romans

ultra: beyond

ultra licitum: beyond the legal limit

ultra valorem: beyond the value

ultra vires [beyond one's power]: transcending legal authority

ultro: to the far side

ultro citroque: to and fro

ultro et citro [up and down]: hither and thither

umbilicus: the navel

umbra: shade or shadow

umerus: the shoulder

una sancta [one holy]: a reference to the divine nature of the Christian Church

una voce [with one voice]: unanimously

unanimus: of one mind or spirit

uncia: one twelfth (i.e., one ounce)

unciatim: little by little

unicus: sole or unique

unigena [of the same race]: (theo.) only-begotten

unio mystica [mystical union]: (theo.) referring to the mystical union of the human consciousness with the divine consciousness

Unitas Fratrum [unity of brethren]: official name of the Moravian Church

unius diei: ephemeral

uno animo [with one spirit]: unanimously

uno consensu: unanimously

uno ictu: at one blow

uno ore [one mouth]: unanimously

uno saltu [in one leap]: in a single bound

uno tempore: at the same time

uno verbo: in a word

unus et alter: one or two

urbanus [of a city]: elegant; refined

urbs: a walled city

urbi et orbi [to the city and to the world]: words traditionally occurring in a special Papal benediction

urceus [an earthen jug]: urn

Ursa Major [Great Bear]: the Big Dipper

Ursa Minor [Little Bear]: the Little Dipper

usque a Romulo [ever since Romulus]: since the beginning of time

usque ad aras [even to the altars]: to the last extremity

usque ad nauseum [even to nausea]: to the point of disgust

usque Romam: as far as Rome

usu venit [it comes]: it happens

usus et fructus or **ususfructus:** (leg.) the use of the property of another

usus loquendi: usage in speaking

ut adsolet: as is usual

ut dictum (ut dict.): (med.) as directed

ut fata trahunt [as the fates pull]: at the mercy of fate

ut infra (ut i. or **ut inf.)** [as below]: as stated or cited below

ut pignus amicitiae: as a token of friendship

ut prosim [that I may be of service]: that I may do good

ut puto or **puto:** I suppose (said parenthetically)

ut solet: as usual

ut supra (ut sup. or **u.s.):** as above

ut videtur: apparently

uterlibet: whichever of the two you please

uterus: a womb

uti possidetis [as you possess]: (leg.) with the possessions held at the present time

utilis: useful

uva: a bunch of grapes

uxor (ux.): a wife

V

vacatio: freedom; immunity

vacca: a cow

vacuo: in a vacuum

vacuum: an empty place

vade mecum [go with me]: a companion; a reference volume

vadium mortuum [a dead pledge]: a mortgage

vagina: a sheath

vagitus: (med.) the first cry of a newborn child

vale or **valete:** farewell

valgus: a bow-legged person

varia lectio (pl. **variae lectiones**): a variant reading

varicus: straddling

variorum notae: notes of various commentators

vas (pl. **vasa**) [utensil]: a vessel or duct

vas deferens (pl. **vasa deferentia**): (anat.) the sperm duct

vasculum: a small vessel

velociter: quickly

vena (pl. **venae**): a vein

vena cava (pl. **venae cavae**): one of the large veins flowing into the heart

venire facias [to make to come]: (leg.) a writ from a judge ordering the sheriff to summon a jury

Venite [O, Come]: a musical setting of Psalm 95 which begins *Venite, exultemus Domino*

ventriculus: the belly or stomach

ventus adversus [winds fore]: an unfavorable wind

ventus Africus or **Africus:** the southwest wind

ventus secundus [winds aft]: a favorable wind

venus: love; a loved one

ver: spring

ver sacrum: an offering of the first fruits

vera causa: a true cause

verbatim et literatim [word for word and letter for letter]: exactly

verbatim et literatim et punctatim [word for word and letter for letter and point for point]: with the utmost accuracy

Verbi Dei Minister (V.D.M.): minister of the Word of God

verbi causa: for instance

verbo: in name only

verbosus: wordy

veri similis: probable

veritas: truth

veritas entis [truth of being]: metaphysical truth

veritas signi: the truth of a symbol

vermis: a worm or grub

verso or **verso folio** (**v.** or **vo.**) [reverse side]: the left-hand page of a book (opposite of **recto**)

versus (**v.** or **vs.**): towards; against

verte [turn]: turn the page over

veritas victrix: truth the conqueror

vertigo [whirling round]: dizziness or light-headedness

vesania: (med.) insanity

vesica piscis [a fish bladder]: the aura surrounding the heads of sacred figures in medieval and renaissance Christian art (also, **cum nimbus**)

vesper [evening]: the Evening Star

vesperi: in the evening

vestigia (pl. of **vestigium**) [vestiges]: footprints; traces

vestigia nulla retrorsum: no footsteps backward (i.e., no retreat)

vestigium Dei [vestige of God]: doctrine teaching that, despite the Fall, creation still reflects traces of its divine origins

veteranus: an old soldier

veterator: an experienced or skilled person (i.e., an old hand)

vexata quaestio: a vexed or disputed question (also **quaestio vexata**)

Via Dolorosa [the way of sorrows]: the route taken by Jesus on his way to crucifixion

via (pl. **viae**): a street or way

via affirmativa [the affirmative way]: (theo.) the way to knowledge of or union with God that is gained through affirmation of the positive aspects of the world (also known as **via positiva**)

via amicabili: in a friendly way

via compendiaria: a short cut

via eminentiae [the way of eminence]: (theo.) the positive way to knowledge of or union with God that is gained by affirming those perfections in the world that point to the eminence of God (St. Thomas Aquinas)

via illuminativa [the way of enlightenment]: (theo.) the way to God through illumination, whether mystical, inspirational, or relevatory

via Lactea: the Milky Way

via Matris: the Seven Sorrows of Mary, the Mother of God, en route to the crucifixion of Christ

via media: the middle way

via militaris: a military road

via negativa or **via negationes** [the negative way]: (theo.) the way to knowledge of or union with God that is gained through negation of the world (Maimonides)

via positiva [the positive way]: (theo.) the way to knowledge of or union with God that is gained through affirmation of the positive aspects of the world (also known as **via affirmativa**)

via purgativa [the way of purgation]: (theo.) the way to knowledge of or union with God that is gained through purification by ascetic practices

via strata: a street

via trita: a well-traveled road

via unitiva [the way of union]: (theo.) the way to knowledge of or union with God that is gained by perfection of the self

viator: a wayfarer

vice versa (**V.V.**) [with the meaning or order reversed]: conversely

victus cotidianus: daily bread

victus tenuis: a meager diet

vide (**v.**): see

vide ante: see before

vide infra (**v.i.**): see below

vide post: see after this

vide supra (**v.s.**): see above

vide ut supra [see as above]: see the above comment

videlicet (**viz.**): namely

videtur [it appears]: it seems

vigilantibus: to be watchful

villa: a country estate

vinarius: a vintner

vinculum matrimonii: the bond of marriage

vindex injuriae: an avenger of wrong

vinitor: a vinedresser

vir: a man

vir bonus dicendi peritus: a good man skilled in rhetoric

vir doctus: a scholar

vir et uxor: husband and wife

vir insignis: a celebrity

vir literatus or **vir litteratus** [a man of letters]: a scholar

vir privatus: a private person

viribus totis: with all one's strength

viribus unitis: with united strength

virago [a female warrior]: a heroine

vires corporis: bodily strength

virginibus puerisque: for young women and men

Virgo: the Virgin

Virgo Sapientissima: The Virgin Wisest of All

Virgo Sponsa Dei: the Virgin Bride of God

virgo: a maiden girl or virgin

virgo vestalis: a vestal virgin

viritim [man by man]: individually

virtus [manly excellence]: virtue or valor

vis (pl. **vires**): force, power, or strength

vis a fronte: a propelling force from in front

vis a tergo: a propelling force from behind

vis comica: comic genius

vis conservatrix: the preservative power

vis inertiae [power of inertia]: the power of passive resistance

vis insita [the innate force of matter]: an aspect of Newton's first law of motion

vis major [superior force]: (leg.) an inevitable accident (e.g., an act of God)

vis medicatrix: healing power

vis medicatrix naturae: the healing power of nature

vis mortua [dead force]: force that does not work

vis poetica: poetic genius

vis vitae: vital force

vis viva [living force]: kinetic energy

viscus (pl. **viscera**): internal organs (i.e., the guts)

vita: life

vita beata [the blessed life]: happiness

vita honesta: a virtuous life

vita occidens: the evening of life

vita privata: private life

vita turpis: an immoral life

vitae curriculum [course of life]: a résumé (also **curriculum vitae**)

vitae societas: social life

vitae summa: life span (also **summa vitae**)

vitellus: an egg yolk

vitium: a fault or crime

vitrum: a glass

viva voce [by a living voice]: orally (i.e., by oral examination)

vivarium [a fish pond]: an animal preserve

vivendi causa [cause of living]: the source of life

vivere parvo: to live on little

vivida vis animi: the living force of the mind

vixit . . . annos (v.a.): he lived . . . years

vocis imago: an echo

volenti non fit injuria: (leg.) no injury is done to consenting parties

voluntas: freewill

voluntas legis: the spirit of the law

voluptates corporis [the pleasures of the body]: sensual pleasures

vortex or **vertex:** a whirlpool

vox (pl. **voces**): voice

vox angelica: an organ stop producing a stringlike sound

vox barbara [strange or barbaric voice]: (gram.) an incorrectly formed word (e.g., a hybrid)

vox clandestina: a whisper

vox humana: an organ stop producing a sound like a human voice

vox populi (pl. **voces populi**): the voice of the people

vox stellarum [voice of the stars]: music of the spheres

vulgi opinio: public opinion

vulgo: commonly or generally

vulgus [the common people]: a mob

vulneribus confectus: weakened by battle wounds

vulnus: an injury or wound

vulpes: a fox

Z

zelotypus: jealousy

zephyrus: a warm westwind

zonam solvere [to untie the girdle]: to marry a maiden (during the Roman wedding ceremony, the woman's apron is untied and laid aside as a rite symbolizing her change of marital status)

DICTA
Common Phrases and Familiar Sayings

A

a cruce salus: salvation comes from the Cross

a Deo et rege: from God and the king

a Deo lux nostra: our light comes from God

a fronte praecipitium a tergo lupi [a precipice before (me), wolves behind (me)]: between a rock and a hard place

a verbis legis non est recedendum: (leg.) from the words of the law there is no departure

ab abusu ad usum non valet consequentia: the usefulness of something is not invalidated by the consequences of its abuse

ab actu ad posse valet illatio: it is possible to infer the future from the past

ab hoc et ab hac et ab illa [from this and from this and from that]: from here, there, and everywhere (i.e., confusedly)

ab Jove principium: from Jove is the beginning (of all things; Virgil)

ab ovo usque ad mala [from the egg to the apples]: from appetizer to the dessert (i.e., from beginning to end)

ab uno disce omnes [from one learn all]: from one sample we judge the rest

abeunt studia in mores: pursuits become habits (Ovid)

abi in malam crucem: (fig.) to the devil with you!

absens haeres non erit [the absent one will not be the heir]: out of sight, out of mind

abundans cautela non nocet: abundant caution does no harm

Acheruntis pabulum [food for Acheron]: marked for death (Plautus; referring to corrupt and depraved persons)

acta est fabula: the play is over (the dying words of Caesar Augustus)

actio personalis moritur cum persona: (leg.) a personal right dies with the person

actori incumbit onus probandi: (leg.) the burden of proof falls to the plaintiff

actum est de me [it is all over with me!]: all is lost!

actum est de nobis [it is all over with us!]: all is lost!

actum est de republica: [it is all over with the Republic!]: the Republic is lost!

actum ne agas [do not do what is done]: leave well enough alone (Terence)

actus Dei nemini facit injuriam: (leg.) acts of God do injury to no one

actus Dei nemini nocet: (leg.) acts of God bring harm to no one

ad astra per aspera: to the stars through adversities (motto of Kansas)

ad augusta per angusta: to honors through difficulties

ad instar omnium: in the likeness of all

ad kalendas (or **calendas**) **Graecas** [at the Greek calends]: never (the Greeks did not have a calends, only the Romans had)

ad majorem Dei gloriam (**A.M.D.G.**): to the greater glory of God (motto of the Society of Jesus, the Jesuits)

ad meliora vertamur: let us turn to better things

ad perpetuam rei memoriam: for the perpetual remembrance of the matter

ad praesens ova cras pullis sunt meliora [eggs today are better than chickens tomorrow]: a bird in the hand is worth two in the bush

adjuvante Deo labor proficit: with God's help, work prospers

adulescentia deferbuit: the fires of youth have cooled

adversus solem ne loquitor [neither speak against the sun]: do not dispute with what is obvious

aedificatum solo, solo cedit: (leg.) the thing built on the land goes with the land

aegrescit medendo [he grows worse with the treatment]: the remedy is worse than the disease (adapted from Virgil)

aequitas sequitur legem: equity follows the law

aeternum servans sub pectore vulnus: tending an eternal wound within the heart

age quod agis [do what you are doing]: attend to the work you have at hand

alea jacta est: the die is cast

alia tendanda via est: another way must be tried

alis volat propriis: she flies with her own wings (motto of Oregon)

alitur vitium vivitque tegendo [the taint is nourished and lives by being concealed]: vice lives and thrives by secrecy

alter ego est amicus: a friend is another self

alter ipse amicus: a friend is a second self

alteri sic tibi: do to another as to thyself

alterum alterius auxilio eget: one thing needs the help of another

altiora peto: I seek higher things

amantes amentes or **amantes sunt amentes:** lovers are lunatics (Terence)

amicus usque ad aras [a friend as far as the altar]: a friend in everything save religion

amo ut invenio: I love as I find

amor gignit amorem: love begets love

amor vincit omnia: love conquers all things

anguillam cauda tenes [you hold an eel by the tail]: you have caught a lion by the tail.

anima in amicis una: one mind among friends

animal bipes implume [a two-legged animal without feathers]: man (Plato's definition of man)

animis opibusque parati: prepared in minds and resources (a motto of South Carolina)

animo et fide: by courage and faith

animo non astutia: by courage, not by craft

animis opibusque parati [prepared in spirit and resources]: ready for anything

animus et prudentia: courage and discretion

animus hominis est anima scripti: (leg.) the intention of the person is the intention of the written instrument

animus non deficit aequus [a well-balanced mind is not wanting]: equanimity does not fail us

annona cara est [corn is dear]: the cost of living is high (also **annonae caritas**)

annuit coeptis: He (God) has favored our undertaking (a motto of the United States of America)

ante tubam trepidat [he trembles before the trumpet sounds]: he cries before he is hurt (Virgil)

apage Satanus!: away with you, Satan!

apage!: be off!

aperto vivere voto [to live with unconcealed desire]: to live life as an open book (Persius)

appetitus rationi pareat: let your desires be governed by reason (Cicero)

aqua profunda est quieta: still water runs deep

aquila non capit muscas: an eagle does not catch flies

arbitrium est judicium: (leg.) an award is a judgment

arma pacis fulcra: arms are the props of peace

arma tuentur pacem: arms maintain peace

arma virumque cano: sing of arms and of a man (the opening lines of Virgil's epic poem *The Aeneid*)

armat spinat rosas: the thorn arms the rose

ars est celare artem: true art is to conceal art

ars est longa, vita brevis: art is long, life is short

ars gratia artis: art for art's sake (motto of Metro-Goldwyn-Mayer)

arte magistra: by the aid of art (Virgil)

arte perire sua [to perish by one's own trickery]: to be caught in one's own trap

artes honorabit: he will adorn the arts

artes, scientia, veritas: arts, science, truth (motto of the University of Michigan)

asinus ad lyram [an ass at the lyre]: to be all thumbs

asinus asino, et sus sui pulcher: as an ass is beautiful to an ass so a is pig to a pig

asinus asinum fricat [the ass rubs the ass]: one fool rubs another fool's back (i.e., mutual praise)

astra castra, numen lumen: the stars my camp, the divine Spirit my light

at spes non fracta: but hope is not broken

Athanasius contra mundum [Athanasius against the world]: referring to the stand made by St. Athanasius against heresy in the early fourth century C.E.

auctor pretiosa facit: the giver makes the gifts precious (adapted from Ovid)

audaciter at sincere: boldly and frankly

audax et celer: bold and swift

aude sapere: dare to be wise

audemus jura nostra defendere: we dare to defend our rights (motto of Alabama)

audentes (or **audaces**) **fortuna juvet:** fortune favors the bold

audi alteram partem: (leg.) hear the other side (the right of the defendant to answer a charge or to speak in his or her own defense)

audita et altera pars: let the other side be heard as well

aureo hamo piscari [to fish with a golden hook]: gold is the surest of lures

auri sacra fames: accursed craving for gold

auribus teneo lupum [I have a wolf by the ears]: I am in desparate trouble

auro quaeque janua panditur: a golden key opens any door

aurora musis amica est: Dawn is the friend of the muses

auspicium melioris aevi [an omen of a better age]: a pledge of better times (motto of the Order of St. Michael and St. George)

Austriae est imperare orbi universo (A.E.I.O.U.): all the world is to be ruled by Austria (motto of Frederick III)

aut bibat aut abeat: either drink or go away

aut Caesar aut nihil [either Caesar or nothing]: either first or not at all

aut disce aut discede: either learn or depart

aut inveniam viam aut faciam: I will either find a way or make one

aut mors aut victoria: either death or victory

aut non tentaris, aut perfice: either do not try it or go through with it

aut vincere aut mori: either to conquer or to die

auxilium ab alto: help from on high

ave atque vale: hale and farewell

ave, Caesar, morituri te salutamus!: Hail, Caesar, we who are about to die salute you (salutation of the gladiators to the Roman emperors)

avi memorantur avorum [my ancestors recall their ancestors]: my ancestral line is long

avito viret honore [he flourishes upon ancestral honors]: his honor is not of his own doing

B

barbae tenus sapientes [men are wise as far as their beards]: referring to those who pretend to have knowledge they do not in fact possess

basis virtutum constantia: constancy is the foundation of virtue

beati pacifici: blessed are the peacemakers

beati pauperes spiritu: blessed are the poor in spirit

bella, detesta matribus: war, the horror of mothers

bella, horrida bella: wars, horrid wars

bene est tentare: it is as well to try

bene orasse est bene studuisse: to have prayed well is to have striven well

bene qui latuit bene vixit [well has he lived who has lived a retired life]: he who has lived in obscurity has lived in security (Ovid)

beneficium accipere libertatem est vendere: to accept a favor is to sell one's liberty

bibere venenum in auro: to drink poison from a golden cup

bis dat qui cito dat: he gives twice who gives quickly

bis peccare in bello non licet: it is not permitted to err twice in war

bis pueri senes: old men are twice children

bis repetita placent: that which pleases is twice repeated

bis vincit qui se vincit in victoria: he conquers twice who conquers himself in victory (Publius Syrus)

bis vivit qui bene vivit: he lives twice who lives well

blandae mendacia linguae: the lies of a flattering tongue

bona fide polliceor: I promise in good faith

boni judicis est lites dirimere: (leg.) a good judge is one who prevents litigation

bonis nocet quisquis pepercerit malis: whoever spares the bad injures the good (Publius Syrus)

bonis quod bene fit haud perit: whatever is done for good men is never done in vain (Plautus)

bonum vinum laetificat cor horminis: good wine makes men's heart rejoice

brevis esse haboro, obscurus fio: in trying to be concise, I become obscure (Horace)

C

caeca invidia est: envy is blind

caeli enarrant gloriam Dei: the heavens are telling the glory of God

caelitus mihi vires: my strength is from heaven

candide et constanter: frankly and firmly

candor dat viribus alas: sincerity gives wings to strength

cane pejus et angue: worse than a dog or a snake

cantabit vacuus coram latrone viator: the penniless man has nothing to lose (Juvenal)

cantilenam eandem canis: he sings the same old song (Terence)

capiat qui capere possit [let him take who can]: catch as catch can

captantes capti sumus [we catchers have been caught]: the biter is bitten

captus nidore culinae: caught by the odor of the kitchen

caput inter nubia condo: I hide my head among the clouds (i.e., fame; Virgil)

caret initio et fine: it lacks beginning and end

carpe diem [seize the day]: enjoy today; make the most of the present

carpe diem, quam minimum credula postero: seize the day, trusting little in tomorrow (Horace)

carpent tua poma nepotes: your descendants will pick your fruit

carpere et colligere: to pick and gather

cassis tutissima virtus [virtue is the safest helmet]: an honest person need not fear a thing

castigat ridendo mores: it corrects manners by laughing at them (i.e., comedy)

causa latet, vis et notissima: the cause is hidden but its strength is well noted (Ovid)

cave canem: beware of the dog

cave ignoscas: take care not to overlook (or forgive)

cave ne cadas [take heed you do not fall]: beware of falling from your high position

cave quid dicis, quando et cui: beware what you say, when and to whom

caveat actor: let the doer beware

caveat emptor: let the buyer beware

caveat venditor: let the seller beware

caveat viator: let the traveler beware

cavendo tutus: safe by taking heed

cedant arma togae [let arms yield to the toga]: let the military yield power to civil authority (Motto of Wyoming)

cede Deo: submit to God

celeritas et veritas: swiftness and truth

certum est quia impossibile est: it is true because it is impossible (Tertullian)

certum scio: I know for certain

certum voto pete finem: set a definite limit to your desire (Horace)

cessante causa, cessat effectus: when the cause ceases, the effect ceases

Christi crux est mea lux: the cross of Christ is my light

Christo et Ecclesiae: for Christ and for the Church

cineri gloria sera est: glory paid to ashes comes too late (Martial)

cito maturum, cito putridum: soon ripe, soon rotten

civilitas successit barbarum: civilization succeeds barbarism (territorial motto of Minnesota)

civis Romanus sum: I am a citizen of Rome

clarior ex obscuro: (I shine) more brightly from out of obscurity

clarior ex tenebris: (I shine) more brightly from out of the darkness

clarum et venerabile nomen: an illustrious and venerable name

classicum canit: the trumpet sounds attack

coelitus mihi vires: my strength is from heaven

coetus dulces valete [happy meetings]: fare you well (Catullus)

cogito ergo sum: I think, therefore I am (Descartes)

colubrem in sinu fovere: to hold a snake in one's bosom

comes jucundus in via pro vehiculo est: a pleasant companion on the road is as good as a vehicle (Publius Syrus)

commune periculum concordiam parit: a common danger begets unity

communis error facit jus: (leg.) sometimes common error makes law

compendia dispendia: short cuts are round-abouts

compesce mentem: control your temper

confido et conquiesco: I trust and I am at rest

conscia mens recti: a mind conscious of integrity (Ovid)

conscientia mille testes: conscience is as a thousand witnesses

consensus facit legem: consent makes law

consensus tollit errorem: (leg.) consent takes away error

consequitur quodcunque petit: he attains whatever he attempts

consilia et facta: by thoughts and deeds

consilio et animis: by wisdom and courage (also **consilio et animo**)

consilio et prudentia: by wisdom and prudence

consilio manuque: by work and wisdom

consilio, non impetu: by wisdom, not impulse

constantia et virtute: by constancy and courage

consuetudo quasi altera natura: habit is as second nature (Cicero)

consule Planco [when Plancus was consul]: in my younger days (Horace)

consummatum est: it is finished (one of the Seven Last Words of Christ on the Cross: St. John 19:30)

cor unum, via una: one heart, one way

corda serata fero: I carry a heart locked up

corpora lente augescunt cito extinguuntur: bodies are slow in growth, rapid in decay (Horace)

corruptio optimi pessima: the corruption of the best is the worst

corruptissima re publica plurimae leges: in the most corrupt state exist the most laws (Terence)

crambe repetita [warmed-over cabbage]: the same old thing (Juvenal)

cras credemus, hodie nihil: tomorrow we will believe, not today

credat Judaeus Apella [let Apella the Jew believe it]: only the credulous believe it (Horace)

crede quod habes, et habes: believe that you have it, and you have it

credite posteri: believe it, posterity (Horace)

credo quia absurdum (est): I believe it because it is absurd

credo quia impossibile (est): I believe it because it is impossible

credo ut intelligam [I believe so that I might understand]: belief precedes knowledge (St. Augustine)

credula res amor est: a credulous thing is love (Ovid)

crescere ex aliquo: raising oneself through the fall of another

crescit eundo: it grows as it goes (motto of New Mexico)

crescit sub pondere virtus: virtue grows under oppression

crescite et multiplicamini: increase and multiply (motto of Maryland)

cribro aquam haurire: to draw water with a sieve

cruce, dum spiro, fido: while I have breath, I trust in the Cross

crux mihi ancora: the Cross is my anchor

cucullus non facit monachum: the cowl does not make the monk

cui Fortuna ipsa cedit: to whom Fortune herself yields (Cicero)

cuilibet in arte sua perito credendum est: every skilled man is to be trusted in his own art

cujus regio, ejus religio [whose region, his religion]: the faith of the people is determined by their king

culpam poena premit comes: punishment presses hard upon the heels of crime (Horace)

cum tacent, clamant [when they are silent they cry loudest]: silence speaks louder than words

cuneus cuneum trudit: wedge drives wedge

cura facit canos: care brings grey hairs

curae leves loquuntur, ingentes stupent: light griefs find utterance, great ones hold silent (Seneca)

curiosa felicitas: nice felicity of expression (Petronius)

currus bovem trahit [the cart draws the ox]: to put the cart before the horse

curta supellex [scanty supply of furniture]: meager stock of knowledge

D

da fidei quae fidei sunt: give to faith that which belongs to faith

da locum melioribus: give place to your betters (Terence)

dabit Deus his quoque fine: God will put an end to these troubles as well (Virgil)

dabit qui dedit: he will give who gave

damna minus consulta movent: losses to which one grows accustomed affect one much less (Juvenal)

damnant quod non intelligunt: they condemn what they do not understand

damnum sentit dominus: (leg.) the master suffers the loss

damnum sine injuria esse potest: (leg.) loss without injury is deemed possible

dare cervices [give the neck]: submit to the executioner

dare pondus idonea fumo [fit only to give weight to smoke]: utterly worthless (Persius)

data fata secutus: following what is decreed by faith (Virgil)

date obolum Belisario: give alms to Belisarius (a Roman general who, according to legend, was reduced to poverty)

date, et dabitur vobis: give and it shall be given to you (St. Luke 6:38)

Davus sum, non Oedipus [I am Davus, not Oedipus]: I am a simple man, not a genius

de asini umbra disceptare [to argue about the shadow of an ass]: to argue over trifling matters

de duobus malis, minus est semper eligendum: of two evils, always choose the lesser (Thomas à Kempis)

de fumo in flammam [out of the smoke into the flame]: out of the frying pan and into the fire

de gustibus non est disputandum (or **de gustibus non disputandum**): there is no disputing about tastes

de minimis non curat lex: the law does not concern itself with trifles

de minimis non curat praetor: a magistrate does not concern himself with trifles

de mortuis nil nisi bonum: of the dead say nothing but good

de nihilo nihil: from nothing nothing can come (Persius)

de omni re scibili et quibusdam aliis [of all things knowable and certain others]: a "know it all"

de omnibus rebus et quibusdam aliis [of all things and of certain others]: a book that rambles on and on

de similibus idem est judicium: (leg.) in similar cases, the judgment is the same

de te fabula narratur: the story relates to you (Horace)

debellare superbos: to overthrow the proud (Virgil)

debile fundamentum fallit opus: a weak foundation destroys the work upon which it is built

decies repetita placebit: though repeated ten times, it is still pleasing (Horace)

decipimur specie recti: we are deceived by the semblance of what is right (Horace)

decipit frons prima multos: the first appearance deceives many

decori decus addit avito: he adds honor to his ancestral honor

decus et tutamen: honor and defense

deficit omne quod nascitur: everything which is born passes away (Quintilian)

degeneres animos timor arguit: fear betrays ignoble souls (Virgil)

Dei gratia: by the grace of God

Dei gratias: thanks be to God

Dei irati: the wrath of God

Dei memor, gratus amicus: mindful of God, grateful to friends

delectando pariterque monendo: by giving pleasure and at the same time instructing (Horace)

delegatus non potest delegare: a delegate cannot delegate

delenda est Carthago [Carthage must be destroyed]: the war must be carried on to the bitter end

deliciae humani generis: the delight of mankind (a reference to the Emperor Titus)

delphinum natare doces: you are teaching a dolphin to swim

delphinum silvis appingit, fluctibus aprum [he portrays a dolphin in the woods and a boar in the waves]: he introduces objects unsuited to the scene (Horace)

deme supercilio nubem [remove the clouds from your brow]: come down from your cloud

denique caelum: heaven at last (Crusaders' battle cry)

dente superbo: with a disdainful tooth (Horace)

Deo adjuvante non timendum: with God's help, nothing need be feared

Deo date: give unto God

Deo duce, ferro comitante: with God as my leader and a sword as my friend

Deo et regi fidelis: loyal to God and king

Deo favente [with God's favor]: by the grace of God

Deo gratias: thanks be to God

Deo juvante: with God's help (motto of Monaco)

Deo monente [with God's warning]: a warning from God

Deo volente (D.V. or **d.v.):** God willing

deo dignus vindice nodus [a knot worthy of a god to unlose]: a great dilemma

Deo, non fortuna: from God, not chance

Deo, Optimo, Maximo (D.O.M.): to God, the Best, the Greatest (motto of the Benedictine order)

Deo, patriae, amicus: for God, homeland, and friends

deorum cibus est: it is food for the gods

deos fortioribus adesse: the gods are said to aid the stronger (Tacitus)

deprendi miserum est: it is wretched to be found out

desipere in loco [to act foolishly at the proper time]: to unwind occasionally (Horace)

detur digniori: let it be given to those more worthy

detur pulchriori: let it be given to those more beautiful

Deum cole, regem serva: worship God, serve the king

Deum esse credimus: we believe in the existence of God

Deus avertat!: God forbid!

Deus det!: God grant!

Deus est regit qui omnia: there is a God who rules all things

Deus est summum bonum: God is the greatest good

Deus est suum esse: God is his own being

Deus gubernat navem: God pilots the ship

Deus misereatur: God be merciful

Deus nobis haec otia fecit: a god has given us this place of rest (Virgil)

Deus nobiscum, quis contra?: God with us, who can be against us?

Deus providebit: God will provide

Deus sive natura: God or nature (Spinoza)

Deus vobiscum: God be with you

Deus vult: God wills it (the rallying cry of the First Crusade)

di meliora: god forbid!

di or **dii pia facta vident:** the gods see virtuous deeds (Ovid)

dicamus bona verba: let us speak words of good omen (Terence)

dictis facta suppetant: let deeds suffice for words

dictum ac factum [said and done]: no sooner said than done

dictum sapienti sat est: a word to the wise is sufficient

diem perdidi [I have lost a day]: I have done nothing of worth (attributed to Titus)

difficilia quae pulchra: things that are beautiful are difficult to attain

dimidium facti qui coepit habet: a work that is begun well is already half done (Horace)

dirige nos Domine: direct us, O Lord

dirigo: I direct (motto of Maine)

dis aliter visum: it seemed otherwise to the gods

dis bene juvantibus: with the help of the gods

dis ducibus: under the direction of the gods

disce pati: learn to endure

discere docendo: to learn through teaching

disjecti membra poetae: limbs of a dismembered poet (Horace)

ditat Deus: God enriches (motto of Arizona)

divide et impera: divide and rule

divinitus accidit: it happened miraculously

divitiae virum faciunt: riches make the man

dixit Dominus: the Lord has spoken it

doce ut discas: teach that you may learn

docendo discimus: we learn by teaching

docta ignorantia: learned ignorance (Nicolas of Cusa)

dolium volvitur: an empty cask is easily rolled

domi militiaeque: at war and at peace

Domine, dirige nos: O Lord, direct us (motto of the city of London)

Domine, illuminatio mea: O Lord, my light!

Domino, Optimo, Maximo (D.O.M.): the Lord, the Best, the Greatest (an alternate rendering of the motto of the Benedictine Order)

Dominus illuminatio mea: the Lord is my light (motto of Oxford University)

Dominus providebit: the Lord will provide

Dominus vobiscum: the Lord be with you

domus et placens uxor: home and a pleasing wife (Horace)

donec eris felix multos numerabis amicos: as long as you are prosperous you will have many friends (Ovid)

dormitat Homerus [even Homer nods off]: sometimes even the best of us are caught napping (Horace)

duabus sellis sedere: to sit in two saddles

ducit amor patriae: love of country leads me

dulce bellum inexpertis: war is sweet to those not acquainted with it

dulce est desipere in loco: it is sweet to unwind upon occasion (Horace)

dulce et decorum est pro patria mori: sweet and seemly it is to die for one's country

dulce quod utile: what is useful is sweet

dulce sodalicium [sweet society]: what a sweet thing is companionship

dulces moriens reminiscitur Argos: as he died he remembered Argos (the home of his youth) (Virgil)

dulcis amor patriae: sweet is the love of one's homeland

dum fortuna fuit: while fortune lasted

dum loquor, hora fugit: time is flying while I speak (Ovid)

dum spiro, spero: while I breathe, I hope (a motto of South Carolina)

dum tacent clamant [though they are silent, they cry aloud]: their silence speaks loudly

dum vita est, spes est: while there is life, there is hope

dum vitant stulti vitia in contraria current: in shunning one kind of vice, fools run to the opposite extreme (Horace)

dum vivimus, vivamus: while we live, let us live

duplici spe uti: to have a double hope

dura lex, sed lex: the law is hard, but it is the law

durate et vosmet rebus servate secundis: carry on and preserve yourselves for better times (Virgil)

dux femina facti: the leader of the action was a woman (Virgil)

E

e flamma petere cibum [to snatch food out of the flame]: to live by desperate means (Terence)

e pluribus unum: out of many one (motto of the United States of America)

Ecce Agnus Dei: Behold the Lamb of God!

ecce iterum Crispinus [here's that Crispin again]: here's that bore again

Ecclesia non moritur: the Church does not die

ego et rex meus [my king and I]: I and my king (as rendered by Cardinal Wolsey)

ego spem pretio non emo [I do not purchase hope for a price]: I do not buy a pig in a poke (Terence)

egomet mihi ignosco: I myself pardon myself (Horace)

eheu! fugaces labuntur anni: alas! the fleeting years slip by (Horace)

elephantem ex musca facis: you are making an elephant out of a fly (i.e., making a mountain out of molehill)

empta dolore docet experientia: experience bought with pain teaches effectually

ense et aratro: with sword and plow

ense petit placidam sub libertate quietem: by the sword she seeks peaceful quiet under liberty (motto of Massachusetts)

Epicuri de grege porcus [a hog from the drove of Epicurus]: a glutton (Horace)

epulis accumbere divum: to recline at the feast of the gods (Virgil)

equis virisque [with horse and foot]: with all one's might

errare humanum est: to err is human

errores Ulixis: the wanderings of Ulysses

erubuit; salva res est: he blushed; the affair is safe (Terence)

esse est percipi: to be is to be perceived (Berkeley)

esse quam videri: to be rather than to seem (motto of North Carolina)

est ars etiam male dicendi: there is even an art of maligning

est deus in nobis: there is a god within us (Ovid)

est mihi honori: it reflects well on me

est modus in rebus: there is a method in all things (Horace)

est quaedam flere voluptas: there is a certain pleasure in weeping (Ovid)

esto perpetua [be thou eternal]: may she be everlasting (motto of Idaho)

esto perpetuum: let it be everlasting

esto quod esse videris: be what you seem to be

et campos ubi Troja fuit: and the fields where once was Troy (Virgil)

et cum spiritu tuo: and with thy spirit (liturgical response to **Dominus vobiscum,** the Lord be with you)

et decus et pretium recti: both the ornament and the rewards of virtue

et ego in Arcadia [I too have been to Arcadia]: I know all about it

et genus et formam regina pecunia donat: like a queen, money bestows both rank and beauty (Horace)

et nos quoque tela sparsimus [we too have hurled javelins]: we are also veterans

et sceleratis sol oritur: the sun shines even on the wicked (Seneca)

et tu, Brute [and you too, Brutus!]: last words of Caesar indicating betrayal by a trusted ally (Shakesphere's *Julius Caesar*)

etiam periere ruinae [even the ruins have perished]: there is nothing left (Lucan)

etiam quod esse videris: be what you seem to be

eventus stultorum magister: experience is the teacher of fools

ex Africa semper aliquid novi: out of Africa there is always something new

ex desuetudine amittuntur privilegia: it is out of disuse that rights are lost

ex facto jus oritur: the law goes into effect after the fact

ex fide fortis: strong through faith

ex granis fit acervus: many grains make a heap

ex malis moribus bonae leges natae sunt: from bad usages, good laws have sprung (Coke)

ex nihilo nihil fit [from nothing, nothing is made]: nothing produces nothing

ex ore parvulorum veritas: out of the mouth of little children comes truth

ex ungue leonem [from a claw, the lion]: the lion is known by its claws (i.e., from a part one can determine the whole)

ex uno disce omnes [from one learn all]: from one we judge the rest

excelsior: ever higher (motto of New York State)

exceptio probat regulam: the exception establishes the rule (i.e., gives greater definition)

excitari, non hebescere: to be spirited, not sluggish

exegi monumentum aere perennius: I have raised a monument more lasting than bronze (Horace)

exempla sunt odiosa: examples are odious

exercitatio optimus est magister: practice is the best teacher

exitus acta probat [the ending proves the deeds]: all's well that ends well

expende Hannibalem: weigh the dust of Hannibal (Juvenal)

experientia docet: experience teaches

experientia docet stultos: experience teaches fools

experto crede or **experto credite:** believe one who has had experience

expertus dico: I speak from experience

expertus loquitur: he speaks from experience

expertus metuit [having had experience, he is afraid]: once burnt, twice shy (Horace)

explorant adversa viros: misfortune tries men

extinctus amabitur idem: (though hated in life), the same man will be loved after he is dead (Horace)

F

fabas indulcet fames [hunger sweetens beans]: hunger makes everything taste good

faber est quisque fortunae suae: everyone is the architect of his or her own fortune (Sallust)

facere non possum quin: I cannot but

facile est inventis addere: it is easy to add to things already invented

facile largiri de alieno: it is easy to be generous with what is another's

facilis descensus Averno: the descent to hell is easy (Virgil)

facit indignatio versum [indignation produces verse]: righteous anger flames into verse (Juvenal)

facta non verba: deeds not words

faenum habet in cornu, longe fuge: flee far from the danger; beware, he is vicious (Horace)

fallentis semita vitae: the narrow path of an unnoticed life (Horace)

falsus in uno, falsus in omnibus: false in one thing, false in everything

fama fert: rumor runs away

fama malum quo non aliud velocius ullum: there is no evil swifter than a rumor (Virgil)

fama nihil est celerius: nothing is swifter than rumor

fama semper vivat!: may his/her fame live forever!

fama volat: the report or rumor flies (Virgil)

famam extendere factis: to spread abroad his fame by deeds (Virgil)

fames optimum condimentum: hunger is the best of seasonings

fare fac: speak and act

fari quae sentiat: to say what one feels (Horace)

fas est ab hoste doceri: it is allowable to learn even from an enemy (Ovid)

Fata obstant: the Fates oppose (Virgil)

Fata viam invenient: the Fates will find a way (Virgil)

Fata volentem ducunt, nolentem trahunt: the Fates lead the willing and drag the reluctant

fatetur facinus qui judicium fugit: to flee the law is to confess one's guilt

favete linguis [favor with your tongues]: be silent (Horace)

fax mentis incendium gloriae: the passion for glory is the torch of the mind

felicitas multos habet amicos: happiness (or prosperity) has many friends

felix qui nihil debet: happy is the one who owes nothing

felix qui potuit rerum cognoscere causas: happy is the one who understands the causes of all things (Virgil)

ferrum ferro acuitur: iron is sharpened by iron

fervens difficili bile tumet jecur: my hot passion swells with savage wrath (Horace)

fervet olla, vivit amicitia: while the pot boils, friendship lives (or endures)

fervet opus: the work boils (Virgil)

festina lente: make haste slowly

fiat Dei voluntas: God's will be done

fiat experimentum in corpore vili: let the experiment be done upon a worthless body (or object)

fiat justitia, ruat caelum: let justice be done, though the heavens fall

fiat lux: let there be light (Genesis 1:3)

fiat voluntas tua: Thy will be done (Matthew 6:10)

fictio cedit veritati: fiction yields to truth

fide et amore: by faith and love

fide et fiducia: by faith and confidence

fide et fortitudine: by faith and fortitude

fide, non armis: by faith, not by arms

fide, sed cui vide: trust, but be careful whom

fidei coticula crux: the Cross is the touchstone of faith

fideli certa merces: to the faithful one, reward is certain

fidelis ad urnam [faithful to the urn]: true till death

fides ante intellectum: faith before understanding

fides et justitia: faith and justice

fides facit fidem [faith creates faith]: confidence begats confidence

fides non timet: faith does not fear

fides probata coronat: faith approved confers a crown

fides Punica [Punic faith]: treachery

fides quaerens intellectum or **fidens quaerens intellectum** [faith seeking under-
standing]: belief before understanding (St. Augustine)

fides servanda est: faith must be protected

fidus Achates [faithful Achates]: a trustworthy friend

fidus et audax: faithful and courageous

finem respice [look to the end]: consider the outcome

finis coronat opus: the end crowns the work

finis finem litibus imponit: (leg.) the end put an end to litigation

finis unius diei est principium alterius: the end of one day is the beginning of
another

fit via vi: a way is made by force

flamma fumo est proxima [flame is close to smoke]: where there is smoke, there is
fire

flectere si nequeo superos, Acheronta movebo: if I cannot bend heaven then I'll
stir hell (Virgil)

flecti, non frangi: to be bent, not broken

floreat Etona: may Eton flourish (motto of Eton College)

flores curat Deus: God takes care of the flowers

flosculi sententiarum: flowerets of thought

fluctuat nec mergitur: she is tossed by the waves but she does not sink (motto of
Paris, which has a ship as its emblem)

fons et origo: the source and origin

forensis strepitus: the clamor of the forum

forma bonum fragile est: beauty is a transitory blessing (Ovid)

forma flos, fama flatus: beauty is a flower, fame is a breath

forte scutum, salus ducum: a strong shield is the safety of leaders

fortem posce animum: pray for a strong will (Juvenal)

fortem te praebe: be brave!

fortes fortuna [ad]juvat: fortune favors the strong

forti et fideli nihil difficile: to the brave and faithful, nothing is difficult

fortis cadere, cedere non potest: the brave may fall, but they cannot yield

fortis et fidelis: brave and faithful

fortiter et recte: bravely and uprightly

fortiter geret crucem: he will bravely bear the cross

fortiter in re, suaviter in modo [strongly in deed, gently in manner]: resolute in deed, but gentle in manner

fortiter, fideliter, feliciter: fearlessly, faithfully, felicitously

fortitudine et prudentia: by courage and prudence

fortuna caeca est: fortune is blind

fortuna favet fatuis: fortune favors fools

fortuna favet fortibus: fortune favors the brave

fortuna mea in bello campo: the fortune is mine in a fair fight

fortuna meliores sequitur: fortune follows the better man (Sallust)

fortuna multis dat nimium, nulli satis: to many fortune gives too much, to none does it give enough (Publius Syrus)

fortuna sequatur: let fortune follow

fortunae cetera mando: I commit the rest to fortune

fortunae filius: a child of fortune (Horace)

fortunae objectum esse: abandoned to fate

fortunae vicissitudines: the vicissitudes of fortune

fossoribus orti [sprung from ditch diggers]: from humble origins

frangas, non flectes: you may break, you will not bend (me)

frons est animi janua: the forehead is the door of the mind (Cicero)

fronti nulla fides: there is no trusting appearances (Juvenal)

fructu non foliis arborem aestima: judge a tree by its fruit, not by its leaves (Phaedrus)

fruges consumere nati: born merely to consume the fruits of the earth (Horace)

frustra laborat qui omnibus placere studet: he labors in vain who tries to please everybody

fugaces labuntur anni: the fleeting years glide by

fugit hora: the hour flies (Ovid)

fugit irreparabile tempus: irretrievable time flies (Virgil)

fuimus Troes [we were once Trojans]: our day is over (Virgil)

fuit Ilium [Troy once was]: its day is over (Virgil)

fulmen brutum [a harmless thunderbolt]: an empty threat

fumum et opes strepitumque Romae: the smoke, the wealth, the din of Rome (Juvenal)

fundamentum justitiae est fides: the fountain of justice is good faith (Cicero)

furiosi absentis loco est: a madman is like a man who is absent

furiosi solo furore punitur: (leg.) a madman is to be punished by his madness alone

furor arma ministrat: rage supplies arms (Virgil)

G

gaudeamus igitur (juvenes dum sumus): let us be joyful (while we are young)

gaudet tentamine virtus: virtue rejoices in trial

genus est mortis male vivere: to live an evil life is a type of death (Ovid)

genus irritabile vatum: the irritable race of poets (Horace)

Gloria Tibi, Domine: Glory be to Thee, O Lord

gloria virtutis umbra: glory is the shadow of virtue

gradatim vincimus: we conquer by degrees

gradu diverso, una via [with different pace, but on the same road]: the same way by different steps

Graeculus esuriens [hungry young Greek]: a parasite (Juvenal)

grammatici certant, et adhuc sub judice lis est: the grammarians quibble and still the question is unresolved (Horace)

grata testudo: the pleasing lyre

gratia Dei: by the grace of God

gratia gratiam parit: kindness produces kindness

gratia placendi: the grace of pleasing

Gratias agimus tibi: we give Thee thanks

graviora manent [more grievous perils remain]: the worst is yet to come

graviora quaedam sunt remedia periculis: some remedies are worse than the disease (Publius Syrus)

gravis ira regum est semper: the wrath of kings is always heavy (Seneca)

gravissimum est imperium consuetudinis: the power of custom is most weighty (Publius Syrus)

gutta cavat lapidem, non vi, sed saepe cadendo: the drop hollows the stone, not by force but by constant dripping

H

habemus confitentem reum: (leg.) we have an accused person who pleads guilty

habent sua fata libelli: books have their own destiny (attributed to Horace)

habere et dispertire: to have and to distribute

habere, non haberi: to hold, not to be held

habet et musca splenem: even a fly gets angry

hac mercede placet: I accept the terms

hac urgent lupus hac canis: on one side a wolf menaces, on the other, a dog (Horace)

hae nugae in seria ducent mala: these trifles will lead to serious evils (Horace)

haec generi incrementa fides: this faith will bring increase to our race

haec olim meminisse juvabit: it will be a pleasure to remember these things hereafter (Virgil)

haec tibi dona fero: these gifts I bear to thee (motto of Newfoundland)

haerent infixi pectore vultus: his face is graven on her heart (Virgil)

Hannibal ad portas [Hannibal is at the gate]: the enemy is close at hand (adapted from Cicero)

haud ignota loquor [I speak of things by no means unknown]: I speak of well-known events

heroum filii: sons of heroes (motto of Wellington College)

heu pietas! heu prisca fides: alas for piety! alas for the ancient faith! (Virgil)

hic domus, haec patria est [here is our home]: this is our country (Virgil)

hic est enim sanguis meus novi testamenti: this is the new covenant in my blood (St. Matthew 26:28)

hic et ubique terrarum: here and everywhere throughout the world (motto of the University of Paris)

hic finis fandi [here was an end of the speaking]: here the speech ended (Virgil)

hic funis nihil attraxit [this line has taken no fish]: this scheme has failed

hic jacet lepus [here lies the hare]: here lies the difficulty

hiems subest: winter is at hand

hinc illae lacrimae: hence these tears (Terence)

hinc lucem et pocula sacra: from hence we receive light and sacred drafts (motto of Cambridge University)

hoc certum est: this much is certain

hoc erat in more majorum: this was in the manner of our ancestors

hoc erat in votis [this was among my wishes]: this was one of my desires (Horace)

hoc est corpus meum: this is my body (St. Matthew 26:26)

hoc genus omne: all of this class (Horace)

hoc habet! [he has it!]: he is hit! (the cry of the spectators at gladiatorial contests)

hoc indictum volo [I wish this unsaid]: I withdraw the statement

hoc opus, hic labor est [this is the task, this is the toil]: there's the rub (Virgil)

hoc opus, hoc studium: this work, this pursuit (Horace)

hoc sustinete, majus ne veniat malum: endure this evil, lest a greater come upon you (Phaedrus)

hoc tibi est honori: this reflects well on you

hoc volo, sic jubeo, sit pro ratione voluntas: this I write, thus I command, let my will stand for reason

hodie mecum eris in paradiso: Today, you shall be with me in Paradise (one of the Seven Last Words of Christ; St. Luke 23:43)

hodie mihi, cras tibi [today for me, tomorrow for thee]: my turn today, your turn tomorrow

hodie, non cras: today, not tomorrow

hominem quaero: I am looking for a man (Phaedrus)

hominis est errare: to err is human

homo antiqua virtute ac fide: a man of the old-fashioned virtue and loyalty

homo doctus in se semper divitias habet: a learned person always has wealth within

homo homini aut deus aut lupus: to man, man is either a god or a wolf (Erasmus)

homo homini lupus: man is a wolf to man

homo mensura [man is the measure]: man is the measure of all things (Protagoras)

homo sum; humani nihil a me alienum puto: I am a man; nothing that relates to man do I deem alien to me (Terence)

homo unius libri: a man of one book (Thomas Aquinas's definition of a learned man)

homo vitae commodatus non donatus: a man is lent, not given, to life (Publius Syrus)

homunculi quanti sunt: what insignificant creatures we men are (Plautus)

honesta mors turpi vita potior: an honorable death is better than a base life (Tacitus)

honesta quam splendida [honorable things rather than brilliant ones]: reputable rather than showy

Honor est a Nilo: honor is from the Nile (anagram for **A**dmiral **H**oratio **N**elson, who won the Battle of the Nile)

honor virtutis praemium: honor is the reward of virtue

honores mutant mores: honors alter mannners

honos alit artes: honor nourishes the arts (Cicero)

honos habet onus [honor has its burdens]: honor carries responsibilty

hora fugit: the hour flies

horas non numero nisi serenas: I number none but shining hours (an inscription on a sun dial)

horresco referens: I shudder to relate it

horror ubique: terror everywhere (motto of the Scots Guards)

hos ego versiculos feci, tulit alter honores: I wrote these lines, another has taken the credit (Virgil)

hostis honori invidia: envy is the foe of honor

hostis humani generis: an enemy of the human race

humani nihil alienum: nothing that relates to man is alien to me (Terence)

humanum est errare: to err is human

hunc tu, Romane, caveto: of him, Romans, do thou beware (Horace)

hypotheses non fingo [I frame no hypothesis]: I deal entirely with the facts (Sir Isaac Newton)

I

idem velle atque idem nolle: to like and dislike the same things (Sallust)

idoneus homo [a fit man]: a man of proved ability

Iesus Nazarenus, Rex Iudaeorum (I.N.R.I.) [Jesus of Nazareth, King of the Jews]: the title placard appended to the Cross of Christ by Pontius Pilate at the Crucifixion (St. John 19:20)

ignavis semper feriae sunt: to the indolent it is always a holiday

ignis fatuus (pl. **ignes fatui**): a delusive hope

ignorantia legis neminem excusat: ignorance of the law excuses no one

ignorantia judicis est calamitas innocentis: the ignorance of a judge is calamitous to an accused person

ignoscito saepe alteri nunquam tibi: forgive others often, yourself never

ignoti nulla cupido [no desire is felt for what is unknown]: ignorance is bliss

ignotum per ignotius: the unknown explained by the unknown

Ilias malorum: an Iliad of woes

illaeso lumine solum: an undazzled eye to the sun

imitatores, servum pecus: ye imitators, servile herd (Horace)

impavidum ferient ruinae [ruins strike him without dismay]: nothing can shatter the steadfastness of an upright man (Horace)

imperat aut servit collecta pecunia cuique: money is either our master or our slave (Horace)

imperium et libertas: empire and liberty

imperium in imperio: an empire within an empire (motto of Ohio)

imponere Pelion Olympo: to pile Pelion on Olympus

impunitas semper ad deteriora invitat: impunity is always an invitation to a greater crime

in aqua scribis [you are writing in water]: it is without effect

in arena aedificas [you are building on sand]: it will not last (i.e., it is in vain)

in beato omnia beata: with the blessed, all things are blessed (Horace)

in caelo quies: in heaven is rest

in caelo salus: in heaven is salvation

in cauda venenum [in the tail is poison]: beware of danger

in Christi nomine: in Christ's name

in cruce spero: I hope in the Cross

in Deo speravi: in God have I trusted

in ferrum pro libertate ruebant: for freedom they rushed upon the sword

in generalibus latet error: in generalities lies error

in hoc salus: there is safety in this

in hoc signo spes mea: in this sign is my hope (a reference to the Cross of Christ)

in hoc signo vinces: by this sign you will conquer (Emperor Constantine's vision before the Battle of the Milvian Bridge, 312 C.E., which, according to Eusebius, inspired the Chi-Rho [XP] monogram, the labarum)

in lumine tuo videbimus lumen: in your light we shall see the light (motto of Columbia University)

in manus tuas commendo spiritum meum: into Thy hands I commend my spirit (one of the Seven Last Words of Christ; Luke 23:46)

in maxima potentia, minima licentia: in the greatest power exists the least liberty

in medio tutissimus ibis: safety is in going the middle course

in necessariis unitas, in dubiis libertas, in omnibus caritas: in things essential unity, in things doubtful liberty, in all things love (a motto of the Christian Church, Disciples of Christ)

in nocte consilium [in the night is counsel]: sleep on it

in nomine Domini: in the name of the Lord

in nomine Patris et Filii et Spiritus Sancti: in the name of the Father, the Son, and the Holy Spirit

in omnibus caritas: in all things love

in perpetuam rei memoriam: in everlasting remembrance of the event

in silvam ligna ferre: to carry wood to the forest

in solo Deo salus: in God alone is salvation

in te omnia sunt: everything depends on you

in te, Domine, speravi: in thee, O Lord, have I put my trust

in vino veritas [in wine is truth]: under wine's influence, the truth is told

incessu patuit dea: by her gait the goddess was revealed (Virgil)

incredulus odi: being skeptical, I detest it (Horace)

incudi reddere [to return to the anvil]: to revise or retouch (Horace)

inde irae et lacrimae: hence this anger and these tears (Juvenal)

index animi sermo est: speech is an indicator of thought

indignante invidia florebit justus: the just man will flourish in spite of envy

indocilis pauperiem pati: one that cannot learn to endure poverty (Horace)

industriae nil impossibile: to industry, nothing is impossible

inest clementia forti: clemency belongs to the brave

inest sua gratia parvis: even little things have a charm of their own

infandum renovare dolorem: to renew an unspeakable grief (adapted from Horace)

infecta pace: without effecting a peace (Terence)

infixum est mihi [I have firmly resolved]: I am determined

ingens telum necessitatis: necessity is an enormous weapon

injuria non excusat injuriam: one wrong does not justify another

inopem me copia fecit: abundance made me poor (Ovid)

inopiae desunt multa, avaritiae omnia: poverty is the lack of many things, but avarice is the lack of all things

insanus omnis furere credit ceteros: every madman thinks all others insane (Publius Syrus)

integer vitae scelerisque purus: blameless of life and free from crime (Horace)

integra mens augustissima possessio: a sound and vigorous mind is the highest possession

integros haurire fontes: to drink from pure fountains

integrum est mihi: I am at liberty

intelligenti pauca: to the understanding, few words suffice

intentio caeca mala: a hidden intention is an evil one

inter arma leges silent: in time of war, the laws are silent (Circero)

inter canem et lupum [between dog and wolf]: twilight

inter malleum et incudem: between the hammer and the anvil

inter spem et metum: between hope and fear

interdum vulgus rectum videt: sometimes the common folk see correctly

intra verba peccare: to offend in words only

invictus maneo: I remain unconquered

invita Minerva [Minerva being unwilling]: lacking inspiration

invitum sequitur honor: honors follow him unsolicited

io Triumphe! [Hail, god of Triumph]: the shout of the Roman soldiers and
populace on the occasion of a procession of a victorious general

ipsa quidem pretium virtus sibi: virtue is its own reward

ipse dixit Dominus: the Lord himself has spoken it

ira furor brevis est: anger is a brief madness (Horace)

irritabis crabones: you will stir up the hornets

ita lex scripta est [thus the law is written]: such is the law

ite missa est: go, the mass is over

J

jacta est alea or **jacta alea est:** the die is cast (words attributed to Julius Caesar upon
crossing the Rubicon)

jam redit et Virgo: now returns the Virgin (the return of Astraea, goddess of Justice,
was thought by Romans to be a signal for the return of the Golden Age)

jejunus raro stomachus vulgaria temnit: a hungry stomach rarely despises
common things (Horace)

Joannes est nomen ejus: his name is John (St. Luke 1:63; the Motto of Puerto Rico)

Jubilate Deo: rejoice in God

jucundi acti labores: [the memory of] past labors are pleasant (Cicero)

judex damnatur cum nocens absolvitur: the judge is condemned when the guilty
are acquitted (Publius Syrus)

judex est lex loquens: a judge is the law speaking

judicium parium aut leges terrae: judgment of one's peers or else the laws of the
land (Magna Carta)

juncta juvant: union is strength

juniores ad labores: the younger men for labors

jus est ars boni et aequi: law is the art of the good and the just

jus summum saepe summa malitia est: extreme law is often extreme wrong
(Terence)

justitia omnibus: justice for all (motto of the District of Columbia)

justitiae soror fides: faith is the sister of justice

justum et tenacem propositi virum: one who is upright and firm of purpose (Horace)

juvante Deo: God helping

L

labor ipse voluptas [work itself is a pleasure]: labor is its own reward

labor omnia vincit: labor conquers all things (motto of Oklahoma)

laborare est orare: to work is to pray

labore et honore: by labor and honor

laborum dulce lenimen: the sweet solace of my labors (Horace)

labuntur et imputantur: the moments slip away and are entered into our account (a popular saying for a sundial)

lacrimae rerum: the tears of things

lacrimae simulatae [simulated tears]: crocodile tears

lacrimus oculos suffusa nitentis: her glittering eyes filled with tears (Virgil)

lateat scintillula forsan: perchance a little spark of life may lie hidden (motto of the Royal Humane Society, founded in 1774 for the rescue of drowning persons)

latet anguis in herba: a snake lies hid in the grass

laudari a laudato viro: to be praised by a man of praise (Cicero)

laudator temporis acti [a praiser of times past]: one who prefers the good old days (Horace)

laudem virtutis necessitati damus: we give to necessity the praise of virtue

laudumque immensa cupido [and a immense desire for praise]: passion for praise (Virgil)

laus Deo: praise be to God

laus propria sordet: self-praise is base

lege, quaeso: I beg you read (a note appended to the top of student papers inviting tutors to read their work)

leges mori serviunt: laws are subservient to custom

legimus, ne legantur: we read that others may not read (Lactantius, referring to censors and reviewers)

leone fortior fides: faith is stronger than a lion

leve fit quod bene fertur onus: light is the load that is cheerly borne (Ovid)

liberavi animam meam: I have freed my soul

libertas et natale solum: liberty and native land

libertas in legibus: liberty under the laws

libertas sub rege pio: liberty under an upright king

libido dominatur: the passions have gained control

ligonem ligonem vocat [he calls a hoe a hoe]: to call a spade a spade

limae labor et mora [the toil and delay of polishing]: the tedious revising of a literary work before publication (Horace)

linguae verbera: lashings of the tongue

lis litem generat: strife begets strife

litem lite resolvere [to settle strife by strife]: to clarify one's obscurity by another

litem quod lite resolvit: resolving one controversy by creating another (Horace)

longe aberrat scopo [he wanders far from the goal]: to be wide of the mark

longe absit [far be it from me]: God fobid

longe lateque: far and wide

longinquae nationes: distant tribes or nations

longo sed proximo intervallo: the next, but after a long interval (Virgil)

luce lucet aliena: it shines with a borrowed light (e.g., the moon)

lucernam olet: it smells of a lamp

ludere cum sacris: to trifle with sacred things

ludibrium fortunae: the plaything of Fortune

lumenque juventae purpureum [the light of purple youth]: the radiant bloom of youth (Virgil)

lupum auribus tenere [to hold a wolf by its ears]: to catch a Tartar (i.e., to oppose someone stronger than oneself)

lupus est homo homini: man is a wolf to his fellow man

lupus in fabula [the wolf in the fable]: speak of the devil

lupus pilum mutat, non mentem: the wolf changes its coat, not its disposition

lux: light (motto of the University of Northern Iowa)

lux et veritas: light and truth (motto of Yale University)

lux in tenebris: light in darkness

lux venit ab alto: light comes from above

M

magis mutus quam piscis: quieter than a fish

magistratus indicat virum: the office shows the man

magna civitas, magna solitudo: great city, great solitude

magna est veritas et praevalebit: truth is mighty and will prevail

magna est vis consuetudinis: great is the force of habit (Cicero)

magna servitus est magna fortuna: a great fortune is a great slavery (Seneca)

magnae multae pecuniae: large sums of money

magnae spes altera Romae [another hope of mighty Rome]: a youth of promise

magnas inter opes inops: poor amid great riches (Horace)

magni nominis umbra: the shadow of a great name

magnificat anima mea Dominum [my soul magnifies the Lord]: the Hymn of the Virgin at the Annunciation (St. Luke 1:46)

magno conatu magnas nugas [a great effort for great trifles]: so much for so little

magnum in parvo: a great amount in a small space

magnum vectigal est parsimonia: economy is a great revenue (Cicero)

magnus ab integro saeculorum nascitur ordo: the mighty cycle of the ages begins its turn anew (Virgil)

major e longinquo reverentia [greater reverence from afar]: no one is a hero in his or her own city

majores pennas nido [wings greater than the nest]: to rise above the position in which one is born (Horace)

male parta male dilabuntur [things ill-gotten are ill lost]: ill-gotten, ill-spent; easy come, easy go (Cicero)

malesuada fames: hunger that impels the crime (Virgil)

mali principii malus finis: the bad end of a bad beginning

malignum spernere vulgus: to scorn the wicked rabble

malo mori quam foedari: I had rather die than be dishonored

manet alta mente repostum: it remains stored deep in the mind (Virgil)

manibus pedibusque [with hands and feet]: with might and main

manu e nubibus [a hand from the clouds]: help from above

manus haec inimica tyrannis: this hand is an enemy to tyrants

margaritas ante porcos: pearls before swine

Mars gravior sub pace latet: a more grievous war lies beneath peace

mater artium necessitas [necessity is the mother of the arts]: necessity is the mother of invention

materiam superabat opus: the workmanship surpassed the material (Ovid)

matre pulchra filia pulchrior: a daughter more beautiful than her beautiful mother

maturato opus est: there is need of haste (Livy)

maxima debetur puero reverentia: the greatest respect is due to a child (Juvenal)

maximus in minimis [greatest in the least]: very great in little things

me, me adsum qui feci: it is I, here before you, who did the deed (Virgil)

mea nihil interest: it is all the same to me

mea virtute me involvo: I wrap myself up in my virtue (Horace)

medice, cura te ipsum: physician, heal thyself (St. Luke 4:23)

medio tutissimus ibis: a middle course will be safest (Ovid)

mediocria firma [the middle course is most secure]: moderation is safer than extremes

medium tenuere beati: blessed are they who have kept a middle course

medius fidius!: so help me God!

meliores priores [the better, the first]: the better ones first

memor et fidelis: mindful and faithful

mendacem memorem esse oportet: a liar should have a good memory

mens aequa in arduis: [a mind undisturbed in adversities]: equanimity in difficulties

mens agitat molem [mind moves the mass]: mind moves matter (Virgil)

mens conscia recti: a mind conscience of uprightness

mens invicta manet: the mind remains unconquered

mens sana in corpore sano: a sound mind in a healthy body

mens sibi conscia recti [a mind conscious of its own uprightness]: a good conscience

mentis gratissimus error: a most delightful hallucination (Horace)

meret qui laborat: he is deserving who is industrious

merum sal [pure salt]: genuine Attic wit

metus autem non est, ubi nullus irascitur: there is no fear where none is angry (Lactantius)

mihi cura futuri: my care is for the future

mihi non constat: I have not made up my mind

mihi persuasum est [I am persuaded]: I firmly believe

militat omnis amans: every lover serves as a soldier (Ovid)

militiae species amor est: love is a kind of military service (Ovid)

minima de malis [the least of evils]: choose the lesser of two evils

minor jurare non potest: (leg.) a minor cannot swear (i.e., serve on a jury)

misce stultitiam consiliis brevem: mix a little foolishness with your wisdom (Horace)

miscebis sacra profanis: you will mix sacred things with profane (Horace)

miseris succurrere disco: I am learning to help the distressed (Virgil)

moderata durant: things used in moderation endure

mole ruit sua [it falls down of its own bulk]: it is crushed under its own weight (Horace)

mollia tempora fandi: favorable occasions for speaking (a misquotation of Virgil)

mollissima fandi tempora: the most favorable occasions for speaking (Virgil)

Montani semper liberi: mountaineers are always free (motto of West Virginia)

monumentum aere perennius: a monument more lasting than brass (Horace)

morituri morituros salutant: those about to die salute those about to die

morituri te salutamus: we who are about to die salute thee

mors janua vitae: death is the gate of life

mors omnia solvit: death dissolves all things

mors omnibus communis: death is common to all persons

mors tua, vita mea [your death, my life]: you die that I might live

mors ultima linea rerum est: death is the final goal of things (Horace)

mortui non mordant [the dead do not bite]: dead men tell no tales

mortuo leoni et lepores insultant: even hares insult a dead lion

mox nox in rem: night is approaching, let's get on with the matter

multa acervatim frequentans: crowding together a number of thoughts

multa docet fames: hunger teaches us many things

multa fidem promissa levant: many promises weaken faith (Ovid)

multa gemens: with many a groan (Virgil)

multa petentibus desunt multa: to those who seek many things, many things are lacking (Horace)

multa tulit fecitque: much has he suffered and done

multi sunt vocati, pauci vero electi: many are called but few are chosen (St. Matthew 22:14)

multum demissus homo: a very modest or unassuming man (Horace)

multum, non multa: much, not many (Pliny)

munditiis capimur: we are captivated by neatness (Ovid)

mundus vult decipi: the world wishes to be deceived

munus Apolline dignum: a gift worthy of Apollo (Horace)

murus aeneus conscientia sana: a sound conscience is a wall of brass

mutare vel timere sperno: I scorn to change or to fear

mutato nomine, de te fabula narratur [the name being changed, the story is told of you]: with only the change of a name, the story applies to you (Horace)

mutum est pictura poema: a picture is a silent poem

N

nam et ipsa scientia potesta est: for knowledge is itself power (Francis Bacon)

nam tua res agitur, paries cum proximus ardet: (fig.) you too are in danger when your neighbor's house is on fire

nascentes morimur: from birth we begin to die

natio comoeda est: it is a nation of comics (Juvenal, referring to the Greeks)

natura abhorret a vacuo: nature abhors a vacuum

natura appetit perfectum: nature desires perfection

natura non facit saltum [nature makes no leaps]: there are no gaps in nature

naturae vis maxima: the greatest force is that of nature

Ne Aesopum quidem trivit [neither has he encountered Aesop]: he knows nothing

ne cede malis: neither yield to evils

ne fronti crede: trust not to appearances

ne Juppiter quidem omnibus placet: not even Jupiter can please everyone

ne puero gladium: do not entrust a sword to a boy

ne quid detrimenti respublica capiat: (fig.) take care to protect the republic from harm

ne quid nimis [not anything too much]: avoid excess

ne tentes, aut perfice [attempt not, or accomplish]: do not attempt what you do not intend to accomplish

ne teruncius quidem: not a penny!

ne vile fano: bring no vile thing to the temple

ne vile velis: incline to nothing base

nec amor nec tussis celatur: neither love nor a cough can be hidden

nec aspera terrent: not even hardships deter us

nec habeo, nec careo, nec curo: I have not, I want not, I care not

nec male notus eques [a knight of no stigma]: a knight of good repute

nec placida contentus quiete est: nor is he content with calm repose

nec pluribus impar [not equal to many]: a match for the whole world (motto of Louis XIV of France)

nec prece nec pretio: neither by entreaty nor by bribery

nec quaerere nec spernere honorem: neither to seek nor to shun honors

nec scire fas est omnia: nor is it permitted to know all things (Horace)

nec tecum possum vivere, nec sine te: neither can I live with you nor without you

nec temere nec timide: neither rashly nor timidly

nec timeo nec sperno: I neither fear nor despise

necessitas non habet legem [necessity has no law]: necessity knows no law

nemo bis punitur pro eodem delicto: no one is punished twice for the same crime

nemo dat quod non habet: no one can give what he does not have

nemo malus felix: no bad person is happy

nemo me impune lacessit: no one attacks me with impunity

nemo mortalium omnibus horis sapit: no mortal is wise all the time

nemo repente fuit turpissimus [no one ever was suddenly base]: no one ever became a villain all at once (Juvenal)

nemo solus satis sapit [no one is sufficiently wise alone]: two heads are better than one (Plautus)

nemo tenetur se ipsum accusare: no one is bound to accuse himself

nervi belli pecunia infinita: war's strength lies in an unlimited supply of money

nescit vox missa reverti: the word once spoken can never be recalled

nihil amori injuriam est: there is no wrong that love will not forgive

nihil dat qui non habet: a person gives nothing who has nothing

nihil est ab omni parte beatum [nothing is blessed in all its parts]: there is no perfect happiness

nihil ex nihilo: nothing comes from nothing

nihil quod tetigit non ornavit: he touched nothing which he did not adorn

nihil sub sole novum: there is nothing new under the sun

nil admirari: to wonder at nothing (Horace)

nil consuetudine majus: nothing is greater than custom (Ovid)

nil desperandum [nothing must be despaired of]: never despair

nil magnum nisi bonum: nothing is great unless it is good

nil mortalibus arduum est: nothing is too difficult for mortals

nil nisi bonum [nothing unless good]: say nothing but good about the dead

nil nisi Cruce: nothing except by the Cross

nil novi sub sole: there is nothing new under the sun

nil sine Deo: nothing without God

nil sine magno vita labore debit mortalibus: life has given nothing great to mortals without labor

nil sine numine: nothing without divine will (motto of Colorado)

nimium ne crede colori [trust not too much in a beautiful complexion]: trust not too much in appearances

nisi Dominus frustra: except the Lord [build it, those who build it build] in vain (motto of Edinburgh after Psalm 127)

nitor in adversum: I strive against opposition (Ovid)

nobilitas sola est atque unica virtus: only nobility is the one virtue above all (Juvenal)

nobilitatis virtus non stemma character: virtue, not pedigree, is the mark of the most noble

nocet empta dolore voluptas: pleasure bought by pain is injurious

noli irritare leones: do not provoke the lions

noli me tangere: touch me not (St. John 20:17)

nomina stultorum parietibus haerent [fool's names stick to the walls]: fools' names and fools' faces are always found in public places

nominis umbra: the shadow of a name

non Angli sed angeli: not Angles but angels (Pope Gregory the Great, upon seeing English youths for sale in the slave market at Rome)

non cuivis homini contingit adire Corinthum [not all men are fortunate enough to go to Corinth]: not everyone is blessed with an easy and luxurious life

non datur tertium [no third is given]: there is no third choice

non decipitur qui scit se decipi: the one who knows he/she has been deceived is not deceived

non deficiente crumena [the purse not failing]: while the money holds out (Horace)

non est vivere, sed valere, vita: life is not mere living but the enjoyment of health

non generant aquilae columbas: eagles do not begat doves

non ignara mali, miseris succerrere disco: not unacquainted with misfortune, I learn to give aid to those in misery (Virgil)

non inferiora secutus: having followed nothing inferior (Virgil)

non licet omnibus adire Corinthum [not everyone is permitted to go to Corinth]: we cannot all be wealthy

non mihi, non tibi, sed nobis: not for you, not for me, but for us

non mihi sed Deo et regi: not for myself but for God and the king

non multa, sed multum: not many things, but much

non nobis solum nati sumus: not for ourselves alone are we born (Cicero)

non nobis, Domine: not to us, Lord (Psalm 115:1)

non nova sed nove: not new but a new way

non olet: it has not a bad smell (i.e., money, no matter its source)

non omne licitum honestum: not every lawful thing is honorable

non omnia possumus omnes: we cannot all do all things (Virgil)

non omnis moriar: not all of me shall die (Horace, referring to his works)

non passibus aequis: not with equal steps (Virgil)

non possidentem multa vocaveris recte beatum: you cannot correctly call happy the one who possesses many things (Horace)

non pugnat sed dormit: instead of fighting, he sleeps

non quis sed quid: not who but what

non quo sed quomodo: not by whom but how

non revertar inultus: I shall not return unavenged

non semper erit aestas: it will not always be summer (Hesiod)

non semper erunt Saturnalia [it will not always be Saturnalia]: the carnival will not last forever

non sibi sed omnibus: not for himself but for all

non sibi sed patriae: not for himself but for his country

non sine numine: not without divine aid

non subito delenda: not to be hastily destroyed

non sum qualis eram: I am not what I once was (Horace)

non tali auxilio: not for such aid as this (Virgil)

non vobis solum: not for you alone

nonum(que) prematur in annum: let it be kept back from publication until the ninth year (Horace)

nos duo turba sumus: we two are a multitude (Ovid)

nosce te ipsum or **nosce teipsum:** know thyself

noscitur a sociis: he is known by his companions

novus ordo seclorum: a new order for the ages (a motto of the United States)

nox senatum dirimit [night breaks upon the session]: the meeting is called on account of darkness

nugis addere pondus: to add weight to trifles (Horace)

nugis armatus: armed with trifles

nulla dies sine linea [no day without a line]: no day without something done

nulli desperandum, quamdiu spirat: (fig.) while there is life there is hope

nullo meo merito: I had not deserved it

nullum quod tetigit non ornavit: he touched nothing which he did not adorn

numini et patriae asto: I stand on the side of God and my country

Nunc Dimittis (servum tuum, Domine): Lord, now let thy servant depart
(Simeon's holy prayer of rejoicing at the sight of the Christ child; St. Luke 2:29)

nunc est bibendum: now is the time for drinking

nunquam dormio [I never sleep]: I am always on guard

nunquam minus solus quam cum solus: never less alone than when alone (Cicero)

nunquam non paratus [never unprepared]: always ready

nusquam tuta fides: nowhere is there true honor (Virgil)

O

O dea certe!: O Thou, who are a goddess surely! (Virgil)

O fama ingens, ingentior armis!: great in fame, greater still in deeds

O imitatores, servum pecus [O servile herd of imitators!]: miserable apes! (Horace)

O laborum dulce lenimen: O sweet solace of labors (Horace, in reference to
Apollo's lyre)

O mihi praeteritos referat si Juppiter annos: O that Jupiter would give me back
the years!

O Salutaris Hostia: O saving Victim (first words of the hymn used at the beginning
of the Benediction of the Blessed Sacrament)

O sancta simplicitas!: O sacred simplicity

O si sic omnis [O, if all things were thus!]: O that he had always done or spoken thus!

O tempora! O mores!: O times! O customs!

O ubi campi! [O, where are those fields]: O for life in the country! (Virgil)

obscuris vera involvens: shrouding truth in darkness (Virgil)

obscurum per obscurius: explaining an obscure thing by something more obscure

obsta principiis: resist the beginning (more properly, **principiis obsta**)

occasio furem facit: opportunity makes the thief

occasionem cognosce: know your opportunity

occupet extremum scabies: Plague, take the hindmost (Horace)

occurrent nubes: clouds will intervene

oderint dum metuant: let them hate, so long as they fear (Cicero)

odi et amo: I hate and I love (Catullus)

odi profanum vulgus et arceo: I detest the ungodly rabble and keep them at a
distance

odora canum vis: the strong scent of the hounds

ohe! jam satis est: hey there!, that is enough (Horace)

olet lucernam [it smells of the lamp]: it bears the mark of nightly toil

oleum addere camino [to pour oil onto the fire]: add fuel to the flame (i.e., to
make things worse)

omne bonum desuper: all good is from above

omne ignotum pro magnifico (est): all things unknown are thought to be magnificant (Tacitus)

omne solum forti patria: to a brave man, all soil is his homeland

omne trinum perfectum: every perfect thing is threefold

omne vivum ex ovo: everything living thing comes from an egg

omnem movere lapidem: to leave no stone unturned

omnia ad Dei gloriam: all things for the glory of God

omnia bona bonis: to the good all things are good

omnia desuper or **omnia de super:** all things are from above

omnia mea mecum porto: everything that is mine I carry with me

omnia mors aequat: death levels all things

omnia munda mundis: to the pure all things are pure

omnia mutantur, nos et mutamur in illis: all things change and we change with them

omnia praeclara rara: all excellent things are rare (Cicero)

omnia suspendens naso: turning up his nose at everything

omnia tuta timens: fearing all things, even those that are safe (Virgil)

omnia vanitas: all is vanity

omnia vincit amor: love conquers all things

omnia vincit labor: labor overcomes all things

omnibus hoc vitium est: all have this vice (Horace)

omnibus invideas, livide, nemo tibi: you may envy everyone, envious one, but no one envies you

omnis amans amens: every lover is demented

omnium rerum principia parva sunt: the beginnings of all things are small (Cicero)

onus segni impone asello: lay the burden on the lazy ass

ope et consilio: with help and counsel

opera illius mea sunt: his works are mine

operae pretium est [there is a reward for work]: it is worth doing (Terence)

operose nihil agunt: they are busy about nothing (Seneca)

opinione asperius est: it is harder than I thought

optima mors Parca quae venit apta die: the best death is that which comes on the day that Fate determines (Propertius)

optimi consiliarii mortui: the best counselors are the dead

optimum obsonium labor [work is the best of relishes]: work is the best means to eating

opum furiata cupido: frenzied lust for wealth (Ovid)

opus artificem probat [the work proves the craftsman]: the worker is known by his work

ora et labora: pray and work

ora pro nobis: pray for us

orando laborando: by prayer and by toil (motto of Rugby School, England)

orator fit, poeta nascitur: the orator is made, the poet is born

osculo Filium hominis tradis?: you betray the Son of Humanity with a kiss? (St. Luke 22:48)

otia dant vitia: leisure begats vices

otiosa sedulitas: leisurely zeal

otium cum dignitate [leisure with dignity]: dignified leisure (Cicero)

otium sine dignitate: leisure without dignity

otium sine litteris mors est: leisure without literature is death

P

pabulum Acheruntis [food for Acheron]: one deserving of death (Plautus)

pace tanti viri [by leave of so great a man]: if so great a man will pardon me (said ironically)

palmam qui meruit ferat: let him bear the palm who has deserved it (motto of Lord Nelson and the University of Southern California.)

panem et circenses [bread and the games of the circus]: food and amusement (according to Juvenal, the sole interests of the ancient Roman plebeian class)

par in parem imperium non habet: an equal has no authority over an equal

par negotiis, neque supra: equal to his business and not above it (Tacitus)

par nobile fratrum [a noble pair of brothers]: two people just alike (Horace)

parce, parce, precor: spare me, spare me, I pray

parcere subjectis, et debellare superbos: to spare the vanquished and subdue the proud (Virgil)

parem non fert: he endures no equal

parendo vinces: you will conquer by obedience

paritur pax bello: peace is produced by war

Parthis mendacior: more mendacious than the Parthians

parva componere magnis: to compare small things with great

parva leves capiunt animas: little minds are caught up with little things (Ovid)

parvum parva decent: small things benefit the small (Horace)

Pater, in manus tuas commendo spiritum meum: Father, into Your hands I commend my spirit (one of the Seven Last Words of Christ; St. Luke 23:46)

patria cara, carior libertas: the nation is dear, but liberty is dearer

patriae infelici fidelis [faithful to my misfortunate homeland]: (fig.) It is my country, wrong or right

pauca sed bona [few things, but good]: quality, not quantity

paulo majora canamus: let us sing of somewhat greater things (Virgil)

paupertas omnium artium repertrix: poverty is the inventor of all the arts

pax huic domui: peace be to this house

pax paritur bello: peace is produced by war

pax potior bello: peace is more powerful than war

pax quaeritur bello: peace is sought by war (motto of the Cromwell family)

pax vobiscum: peace be with you

pectus est quod disertos facit: it is the heart that makes one eloquent (Quintillan)

pecunia non olet: money does not smell

pecunia obediunt omnia: all things are obedient to money

Pelio imponere Ossam: to pile Ossa on Pelion

Pelion imposuisse Olympo: to have piled Pelion on Olympus (Horace)

per angusta ad augusta: through adversity to honor

per ardua ad astra: through difficulties to the stars (motto of the R.A.F.)

per aspera ad astra: a variation of **ad astra per aspera** (motto of Kansas)

per deos immortales!: for heaven's sake!

per tot discrimina rerum: through all manner of calamitous events (Virgil)

per viam dolorosam: by the way of sorrows

pereunt et imputantur: the hours pass away are reckoned against us (a saying used for a sundial)

periculum fortitudine evasi: by courage I have escaped danger

periculum in mora: there is danger in delay

perjuria ridet amantum Juppiter: Jupiter laughs at lovers' deceits

permitte divis caetera: leave the rest to the gods

persta atque obdura: be steadfast and endure

pessimum genus inimicorum laudantes: flatters are the worst type of enemies

Pia Desideria: the desire after things religious (motto of the Pietistic movement)

piscem natare docere: to teach a fish how to swim

plures crapula quam gladius: drunkenness kills more than the sword

plus aloes quam mellis habet [he has more aloes than honey]: the bitter outweighs the sweet (Juvenal)

plus salis quam sumptus [more of good taste than expense]: more tasteful than costly (Nepos)

poesis est vinum daemonum: poetry is the wine of demons

poeta nascitur, non fit: a poet is born, not made

populus me sibilat, at mihi plaudo: the people boo me, but I applaud myself (Horace)

populus vult decipi, ergo decipiatur: the people wish to be deceived, therefore let them be deceived

porro unum est necessarium: there is still one necessary thing

possunt quia posse videntur: they can because they think they can

post cineres gloria sera venit [glory comes after one is reduced to ashes]: fame comes too late for one to enjoy it

post equitem sedet atra cura [behind the horseman sits dark cares]: even the nobleman cannot escape his worries

post factum nullum consilium: counsel is of no effect after the fact

post festum venisti: you have come after the feast

post nubila, Phoebus: after the clouds, the sun

post proelia praemia: after battles come rewards

post tenebras lux: after darkness, light

post tot naufragia portum: after so many shipwrecks, then the harbor

potestas vitae necisque: power over life and death

potius mori quam foedari: rather to die than to be dishonored

praefervidum ingenium Scotorum: the fervently serious disposition of the Scots

praemonitus, praemunitus: forewarned, forearmed

praestat sero quam nunquam: better late than never

praesto et persto: I stand in front and I stand firm

presto maturo, presto marcio: soon ripe, soon rotten

pretiosum quod utile: what is useful is valuable

pretium laborum non vile: no cheap reward for the labors (motto of the Order of Golden Fleece)

primus inter pares: first among his equals

principia, non homines: principles, not men

principibus placuisse viris non ultima laus est: to have won the approval of important people is not the lowest of praise (Horace)

principiis obsta [resist the beginnings]: nip the evil at the bud (Ovid)

prior tempore, prior jure [first by time, first by right]: first come, first served

pristinae virtutis memores: mindful of the courage of earlier times

pro aris et focis [for our altars and our hearths]: for civil and religious liberty

pro Deo et Ecclesia: for God and the Church

pro Ecclesia et Pontifice: for Church and Pope

pro libertate patriae: for the liberty of my country

pro mundi beneficio: for the benefit of the world (motto of Panama)

pro patria [for the country]: for one's country

pro patria et rege: for country and king

pro pelle cutem: the hide for the sake of the fir (motto of the Hudson Bay Company)

pro rege et patria: for king and country

pro rege, lege, et grege [for king, law, and the people]: for ruler, rule, and ruled

pro salute animae: for the welfare of the soul

probitas laudatur et alget: honesty is praised and is left to freeze to death

probitas verus honor: honesty is true honor

probum non poenitet: the honest man does not repent

prodesse quam conspici [to be of service instead of being stared at]: Get busy!

proh pudor!: for shame! (properly **pro pudor**)

proprie communia dicere: to speak commonplace things as if they were original

proximus ardet Ucalegon: Ucalegon's house, the one next door, is on fire (Virgil)

prudens quaestio dimidium scientiae: half of science is putting forth the right questions (Bacon)

pugnis et calcibus [with fists and heels]: with all one's might

pulvis et umbra sumus: we are but dust and shadow (Horace)

Punica fides [Punic faith]: treachery

Q

quae amissa salva: things lost are safe

quae fuerunt vitia mores sunt: what were once vices are now customary

quae nocent docent: that which hurts teaches

quae sursum volo videre: I desire to see the things that are above

quaere verum: seek after truth

qualis artifex pereo: what an artist dies in me (Nero, shortly before his death)

qualis pater, talis filius: like father, like son

qualis rex, talis grex: like king, like people

qualis vita, finis ita: as is the life, so is the end

quam parva sapientia mundus regitur!: with how little wisdom the world is governed!

quam te Deus esse jussit: what God commanded you to be

quamdiu se bene gesserit: so long as he conducts himself well

quandoque bonus dormitat Homerus: sometimes even good Homer nods off (Horace)

quanti est sapere!: what a great thing it is to be wise! (Terence)

quanti fama?: at what price fame?

quantum mutatus ab illo!: how changed from what he once was (Virgil)

quem di diligunt adolescens moritur: the one whom the gods esteem dies young

quem Juppiter vult perdere, prius dementat: the one whom Jupiter desires to destroy is first driven insane

qui bene amat bene castigat: the one who loves well chastises well

qui capit ille facit [if the hat fits, put it on]: if the shoe fits, wear it

qui desiderat pacem, praeparet bellum: the one wishing peace must prepare for war

qui docet discit: he who teaches learns

qui facit per alium facit per se: a man is responsible for the deeds he does through another

qui invidet minor est: he who envies is the lesser of the two

qui laborat orat: he who labors prays

qui nimium probat nihil probat: he who proves too much proves nothing

qui non improbat, approbat: the one who does not disapprove, approves

qui non proficit deficit: he who does not make progress loses ground

qui scribit bis legit: the one who writes reads twice

qui stat, caveat ne cadat: let the one who stands be careful lest he or she fall (1 Corinthians 10:12)

qui tacet consentit: he who is silent consents

qui timide rogat docet negare: he who asks timidly courts denial

qui transtulit sustinet: he who transplanted sustains (motto of Connecticut)

qui uti scit ei bona: one should profit who knows how to use it

quicunque vult servari: whoever will be saved (the beginning of the Creed of Athanasius, or the Quicunque Vult)

quid leges sine moribus vanae proficiunt?: what good are laws when there are no morals?

quid opus est verbis: what need is there for words?

quid sit futurum cras, fuge quaerere: avoid asking what the future will bring (Horace)

quid verum atque decens: what is true and becoming

quidquid agas prudenter agas: whatever you do, do so with caution

quieta non movere [not to move quiet things]: (fig.) let sleeping dogs lie

quis custodiet ipsos custodes?: who shall guard the guards? (Juvenal)

quis fallere possit amantem: who can deceive a lover? (Virgil)

quis separabit?: who shall separate? (motto of the Order of St. Patrick; referring to Britain and Ireland)

quisque sibi proximus: everyone is nearest to himself

quisque suos patimur manes: everyone suffers from the spirits of his or her own past

Quo Vadis, Domine?: whither goest Thou, Lord?

quo celerius eo melius: the faster the better

quo fas et gloria ducunt: where duty and glory lead

quo Fata vocant: whither the Fates call

quo pax et gloria ducunt: where peace and glory lead

quo spinosior fragrantior: the more thorns, the greater the fragrance

quod avertat Deus! [which may God avert!]: God forbid!

quod Deus bene vertat!: may God grant success!

quod dixi dixi: what I have said I have said

quod non legitur non creditur: what is not read is not believed

quod scripsi scripsi: what I have written I have written (Pontius Pilate)

quorum pars magna fui: of which things I was an important part (Virgil)

quot homines tot sententiae: so many men, so many opinions (Terence)

quot servi tot hostes: so many servants, so many enemies

R

radit usque ad cutem: he shaves down to the skin

radix omnium malorum est cupiditas: the love of money is a root to all evil

raram facit misturam cum sapientia forma: rarely are beauty and wisdom found together

rari nantes [swimming here and there]: one here and another there (Virgil)

ratio est legis anima: reason is the spirit and soul of the law

ratio est radius divini luminis: reason is a ray of divine light

recte et suaviter: justly and mildly

redintegratio amoris: the renewal of love

redire ad nuces [to return to the nuts]: resume childish interests

redolet lucerna or **redolet lucernam:** it smells of the lamp (a reference to a literary work whose labor was great)

regnant populi: the people rule (motto of Arkansas)

relata refero: I tell it as it was told to me

rem acu tetigisti [you have touched the thing with a needle]: you have hit the nail on the head

remis velisque [with oars and sails]: with all one's might

renovate animos: renew your courage

rerum cognoscere causas: to understand the cause of all things (motto of the London School of Economics and Political Science)

res accedent luminis rebus: one light shines upon others

res age, tute eris: be busy and you will be safe (Ovid)

res angusta domi: in straitened circumstances at home (Juvenal)

res est ingeniosa dare: giving requires good sense (Ovid)

res est sacra miser: (fig.) a person in misery is a sacred matter

res est solliciti plena timoris amor: love is full of anxious fears (Ovid)

res in cardine est [the matter is on the hinge]: the matter is hanging in the balances

res integra est: the matter is still undecided

res ipsa loquitur: the thing speaks for itself

res mihi integra est [I have not decided the matter]: I am still undecided

res mihi probatur: it meets my approval

res non posse creari de nilo: it is not possible to create matter from nothing

res perit suo domino: (leg.) the loss falls upon its owner

respice, adspice, prospice: examine the past, examine the present, examine the future (motto of the City University of New York)

respice finem [look to the end]: consider the result

respondeat superior [let the superior answer]: (leg.) let the principal answer for the actions of his agent

revocate animos: recover your courage (Virgil)

rex bibendi [king of drinkers]: king of the revelers

rex non potest peccare: the king can do no wrong

rex nunquam moritur: the king never dies

rex regnat sed non gubernat: the king reigns but does no govern

ride si sapis: laugh, if you are wise

ridentem dicere verum quid vetat?: what prevents a person from speaking the truth while laughing? (Horace)

ridere in stomacho [to laugh inwardly]: to laugh up one's sleeve

ridiculus mus: a ridiculous mouse (Horace)

risum teneatis, amici?: could you help laughing, friends? (Horace)

rixatur de lana saepe caprina [he often quarrels about goat's wool]: he argues about everything, whether right or wrong (Horace)

ruat caelum [though the heavens fall]: let the heavens fall!

S

saepe stilum vertas [often turn the stylus]: correct freely, if you want to write anything of merit

saeva indignatio: fierce wrath (Virgil)

saevus tranquillus in undis: calm amid the raging waters

sal sapit omnia: salt seasons everything

salus per Christum Redemptorem: salvation through Christ the Redeemer

salus populi est suprema lex: the welfare of the people is the supreme law

salus populi suprema lex esto: let the welfare of the people be the supreme law (motto of Missouri)

salus ubi multi consiliarii: there is safety in many advisors

salva conscientia [the conscience being preserved]: without compromising one's conscience

salva dignitate: without compromising one's dignity

salva fide: without compromising one's word

salva res est: the matter is safe (Terence)

salvam fac reginam, O Domine: God save the queen

salvum fac regem, O Domine: God save the king

sancte et sapienter: with holiness and wisdom

sapere aude: dare to be wise (Horace)

sapiens dominabitur astris: the wise will rule the stars

Sartor Resartus: the tailor retailored (title of a book by Thomas Carlyle)

sat cito, si sat bene: soon enough, if but well enough (Cato)

sat pulchra, si sat bona [beautiful enough, if she is good enough]: beauty is as beauty does

satis eloquentiae, sapientiae parum: enough eloquence but too little wisdom

satis quod sufficit: what suffices is enough

satis superque [enough and too much]: enough and some to spare

satis verborum [enough of words]: enough said

scientia est potentia: knowledge is power

scio enim cui credidi: I know in whom I have believed (2 Timothy 1:12)

scribere est agere: to write is to act

scribere jussit amor: love bade me write (Ovid)

scribimus indocti doctique: learned and unlearned, we all write (Horace)

scuto amoris Divini: with the shield of divine love

scuto bonae voluntatis tuae coronasti nos: with the shield of Thy good will you have surrounded us

securus judicat orbis terrarum: the whole earth judges in safety (i.e., unswayed by fear; St Augustine)

sed haec hactenus: but so much for this

seditio civium hostium est occasio: the dissatisfaction of the citizenry gives occasion to the enemy

semel abbas, semper abbas: once an abbot, always an abbot

semel et simul: once and together

semel insanivimus omnes: we have all been mad once

semper ad eventum festinat: he always hastens to the crisis (Horace)

semper avarus eget: the greedy are always in need

semper eadem: always the same (motto of Queen Elizabeth I)

semper et ubique: always and everywhere

semper felix [always happy]: ever fortunate

semper fidelis (pl. **semper fideles**): always faithful (motto of the U.S. Marine Corps)

semper idem: always the same

semper paratus: always ready

semper timidum scelus: crime is always fearful

semper vivit in armis: he lives ever in arms

senex bis puer: an old man is twice a boy

sequiturque patrem non passibus aequis: he follows his father but not with equal steps

sequor non inferior: I follow, but I am not inferior

sero sapiunt Phryges: the Phrygians became wise, but too late

sero sed serio: late, but in earnest

sero venientibus ossa [only bones for all those who come late]: first come, first served

serus in caelum redeas [late may you return to heaven]: long may you live

serva jugum [preserve the yoke]: preserve the bond of love

servabo fidem: I will keep faith

servata fides cineri: faithful to the memory of my ancestors

si componere magnis parva mihi fas est: if I may be allowed to compare small things with great (Ovid)

si Deus nobiscum, quis contra nos?: if God be with us, who shall be against us?

si Deus pro nobis, quis contra nos?: if God is for us, who is against us? (Romans 8:31)

si dis placet or **si diis placet:** if it pleases the gods

si fallor, sum: if I am deceived, then I exist (St. Augustine's refutation of skepticism through one's self-awareness of deception)

si fecisti nega: if you did it, deny it

si finis bonus est, totum bonum erit: if the end is good, all will be good

si fortuna juvat: if fortune favors

si monumentum requiris, circumspice: if you seek his monument, look around you (epitaph of Sir Christopher Wren, architect of London)

si parva licet componere magnis: if it be allowable to compare small things to great (Virgil)

si peccavi, insciens feci: if I have sinned, I have done so unknowingly (Terence)

si post fata venit gloria, non propero: if glory comes after death, then I am in no hurry

si quaeris peninsulam amoenam, circumspice: if you seek a pleasant peninsula, look around you (motto of Michigan)

si sic omnes!: if all did thus!

si sit prudentia: if there be prudence

si vis amari ama: if you want to be loved, then love (Seneca)

si vis pacem para bellum: if you desire peace, then prepare for war

sic eunt fata hominum: so go the destinies of men

sic itur ad astra [thus is the way to the stars]: such is the way to immortal fame

sic me servavit Apollo: thus Apollo preserved me (Horace)

sic semper tyrannis: thus always to tyrants (motto of Virginia)

sic transit gloria mundi: thus passes away the glory of the world

sic volo sic jubeo: thus I will, thus I command (Juvenal)

sic vos non vobis [thus do ye, but not for yourselves]: you do the work, another takes the credit (Virgil, as a challenge to Bathyllus who claimed authorship of a set of verses that Virgil himself had composed)

sicut meus est mos: as is my habit (Horace)

sicut patribus, sit Deus nobis: as with our fathers, may God also be with us (motto of Boston)

sile et philosophus esto: be silent and you will pass for a philosopher

silent leges inter arma: the laws are silent during war

similia similibus curantur: like cures like

simplex munditiis: elegant in simplicity (Horace)

sine cruce, sine luce: without the Cross, without light

sine ira et studio: without anger and without partiality

sis pacem, para bellum: if you want peace, then prepare for war

siste, viator!: stop, traveler!

sit pro ratione voluntas: let goodwill stand for reason

sit tibi terra levis: may the earth lie lightly upon you

sit ut est, aut non sit: let it be as it is, or let it not be

sit venia verbis: pardon my words

sol lucet omnibus: the sun shines on all

sola juvat virtus: virtue alone assists

sola nobilitas virtus: virtue alone is true nobility

sola salus servire Deo: our only salvation is in serving God

sola virtus invicta: virtue alone is invincible

solem quis dicere falsum audeat?: who would dare to call the sun a liar? (Virgil)

soli Deo gloria: to God alone be glory

solitudinem faciunt, pacem appellant [they make a solitude and call it peace]: they crush a rebellion by killing the population (Tacitus)

solventur risu tabulae [the bills of indictment are dismissed with a laugh]: the case breaks down and you are laughed out of court (Horace)

solvitur ambulando [it is solved by walking]: the problem is solved by action (i.e., the theory is proven by practice)

spargere voces in vulgam ambiguas: spreading ambiguous rumors among the common crowd (Virgil)

spectemur agendo: let us be judged by our actions

spem pretio non emo: I do not give money for mere hopes (Terence)

sperat infestis, metuit secundis: he hopes in adversity and fears in prosperity (Horace)

spero meliora: I hope for better things (Cicero)

spes bona: good hope (motto of Cape Colony)

spes gregis: the hope of the flock or the common herd (Virgil)

spes mea Christus: my hope is in Christ

spes mea in Deo: my hope is in God

spes sibi quisque [let each be a hope unto himself]: each must rely on him/herself alone

spes tutissima coelis: the safest hope is in heaven

Spiritus Sanctus in corde: the Holy Spirit in the heart

splendide mendax [nobly mendacious]: untruthful for a good purpose (Horace)

spretae injuria formae: the insult to her slighted beauty (Virgil)

sta, viator, heroem calcas: stop, traveler, you trample upon a hero

stare super antiquas vias: to stand on the old ways

stat fortuna domus virtute: the fortune of the household stands by its virtue

stat magni nominis umbra: he stands, the shadow of a great name

stat pro ratione voluntas: goodwill stands for reason

stat promissa fides: the promised faith remains

stemmata quid faciunt: what do pedigrees matter? (Juvenal)

stet fortuna domus: may the fortune of the house endure

stet pro ratione voluntas: let goodwill stand for reason

stillicidi casus lapidem cavat: a constant drip hollows a stone

strenua inertia: energetic idleness (Horace)

studiis et rebus honestis: by honorable pursuits and studies (motto of the University of Vermont)

studium immane loquendi: an insatiable desire for talking (Ovid)

sua cuique sunt vitia: everyone has his or her own vices

sua cuique utilitas: to everything its own use (Tacitus)

sua cuique voluptas: everyone has his or her own pleasures

sua munera mittit cum hamo: he sends his gift with a hook attached

suave mari magno: how pleasant when on a great sea (Lucretius)

suaviter et fortiter: gently and firmly

suaviter in modo, fortiter in re: gentle in manner, resolute in deed

sub cruce candida: under the pure white Cross

sub cruce salus: salvation under the Cross

sub hoc signo vinces: under this sign you will conquer (variation of **in hoc signo vinces**)

sub lege libertas: liberty under the law

sub specie aeternitatis: under the aspect of eternity (Spinoza)

sub tegmine fagi: beneath the canopy of the spreading beech (Virgil)

sublata causa, tollitur effectus: when the cause is removed, the effect ceases

sublato fundamento cadit opus: remove the foundation and the structure falls

sublimi feriam sidera vertice: with head lifted, I shall strike the stars (Horace)

suis stat viribus: he stands by his own strength

summa petit livor: it is the highest things that envy attacks

summa sedes non capit duos: the highest seat does not hold two

summo studio: with the greatest zeal (Cicero)

summum jus, summa injuria [extreme law, extreme injury]: (fig.) the law, strictly interpreted, may be the greatest of injustices (Cicero)

sumptus censum ne superet: let not your spending exceed your income

superstitio mentes occupavit: superstition has taken hold of their minds

superstitione tollenda religio non tollitur: religion is not abolished by abolishing superstition (Cicero)

suppressio veri suggestio falsi: suppression of the truth is the suggestion of falsehood

surgit amari aliquid [something bitter rises]: no joy without alloy (Lucretius)

sursum corda: lift up your hearts

suspendens omnia naso: turning up one's nose at everything (Horace)

suspiria de profundis: sighs from the depths of the soul

sutor, ne supra crepidam [cobbler, stick to your last sandal]: mind your own business

suum cuique pulchrum: to each one's own beauty

suus cuique mos [everyone has his/her own custom]: different strokes for different folks

T

tacent satis laudant: their silence is praise enough

tacitum vivit sub pectore vulnus: the unuttered wound lies deep within the breast (Virgil)

taedet me: I am bored

tam facti quam animi: as much in action as in intention

tam Marte quam Minerva [as much by Mars as by Minerva]: as much by war as by wisdom

tandem fit surculus arbor: a shoot at length becomes a tree

tantae molis erat [so vast a work it was]: so great was the difficulty of the undertaking

tantaene animis caelestibus irae?: can so great a wrath abide in celestial minds?

tantas componere lites: to settle such great disputes

tantus amor scribendi: so great a passion for writing (Horace)

tarde venientibus ossa [to all that come late go the bones] first come, first served

te hominem esse memento: remember that you are a man

te nosce: know thyself

telum imbelle sine ictu [a feeble spear thrown to no effect]: a weak and ineffectual argument (Virgil)

templa quam dilecta!: how lovely are Thy temples!

tempora mutantur, nos et mutamur in illis: times change and we change with them

tempori parendum: one must move with the times

temporis ars medicina fere est: time is the best of the healing arts

tempus abire tibi est: it is time for you to depart (Horace)

tempus anima rei: time is the essence of the thing

tempus edax rerum: time, the devourer of all things (Ovid)

tempus fugit: time flies

tempus omnia revelat: time reveals all things

tempus rerum imperator: time is sovereign over all things

tenax et fideles: steadfast and faithful

tenere lupum auribus [to hold a wolf by the ears]: to take the bull by the horns

tentanda via est: the way must be tried (Virgil)

ter quaterque beatus: thrice and four times blest (Virgil)

teres atque rotundus [smooth, polished, and rounded]: a polished and complete person (Horace)

terra es, terram ibis: you are dust, and to dust you will return (Genesis 3:19)

tetigisti acu [you have touched it with a needle]: you have hit the nail on the head (Plautus)

tibi seris, tibi metis [you sow for yourself, you reap for yourself]: as you sow, so shall you reap (Cicero)

time Deum, cole regem: fear God, honor the king

timeo Danaos et dona ferentes: I fear the Greeks, even when they bear gifts (Virgil)

timeo hominem unius libri: I fear the man of one book (St. Aquinas)

timet pudorem: he fears shame

timor addidit alas: fear gave him wings (Virgil)

timor mortis morte pejor: the fear of death is worse than death

tot homines quot sententiae: so many men, so many opinions (after Terence)

totum in eo est: all depends on this

totus in toto, et totus in qualibet parte: wholly complete and complete in every part (i.e., the human heart)

totus teres atque rotundus [entire, smooth, and round]: complete in itself

trahit sua quemque voluptas [each one is drawn by his own delight]: each is led by his or her own tastes (Virgil)

transeat in exemplum: let it become an example or a precedent

tria juncta in uno: three joined in one (motto of the Order of the Bath)

tristis eris si solus eris: (fig.) you will be sad if you keep company with only yourself (Ovid)

triumpho morte tam vita: I triumph in death as in life

Troja fuit: Troy was

truditur dies die: one day is urged on by another day

Tu solus sanctus: Thou alone art holy

tu est Christus, filius Dei vivi: you are the Christ, the son of the living God (St. Matthew 16:16)

tu ne cede malis, sed contra audentior ito: do not surrender to evil but go boldly against it (Virgil)

tu, Domine, gloria mea: Thou, O Lord, are my glory

U

ubi amici, ibi opes: where there are friends, there is wealth

ubi bene, ibi patria: where it is well with me, there is my country

ubi homines sunt, modi sunt: where there are persons, there are manners

ubi jus ibi remedium: where there is law there is remedy

ubi jus incertum, ibi jus nullum: where the law is uncertain, there is no law

ubi lapsus? quid feci?: where have I fallen into error? what have I done?

ubi libertas, ibi patria: where there is liberty, there is my country

ubi mel, ibi apes: where there is honey, there are bees

ubi sunt qui ante nos fuerunt? (or **ubi sunt?**): where are those who lived before us?

ubique patriam reminisci: everywhere to remember our country

ultra posse nemo obligatur: no one is obligated to do more than he or she is able

una et eadem persona: one and the same person

unguibus et rostro [with claws and beak]: tooth and nail

unguis in ulcere [a claw in the wound]: a knife in the wound

uni aequus virtuti, atque ejus amicis: equally a friend to virtue and to the friends of virtue

unica virtus necessaria: virtue is the only thing necessary

unius dementia dementes efficit multos: the madness of one makes many mad

unus vir, nullus vir [one man, no man]: two are better than one

urbem latericiam invenit, marmoream reliquit: he found the city brick and left it marble (Suetonius, referring to the emperor Augustus)

urbs in horto: a city in a garden (motto of the city of Chicago)

usus est optimum magister: experience is the best teacher

usus est tyrannus: custom is a tyrant

usus me docuit: experience has taught me

usus promptos facit: use makes one ready

ut ameris, amabilis esto: to receive love, be lovable (Ovid)

ut amnis vita labitur: like a brook, life flows away

ut apes geometriam: as bees practice geometry

ut homo est, ita morem geras: as the man is, thus adapt your conduct (Terence)

ut mos est: as the custom is (Juvenal)

ut nunc res se habet [as things are now]: as things stand

ut pictura poesis: poetry is like a painting (Horace)

ut quocunque paratus: prepared on every side

utcumque placuerit Deo: as it shall please God

uti non abuti: to use, not to abuse

utile dulci: the useful with the delightful (Horace)

utinam noster esset: would that he were ours

utrum horum mavis accipe: take whichever you prefer

V

vacuus cantat coram latrone viator: the traveler who has nothing sings before the robber

vade in pacem: go in peace

vade post me, satana: Get thee behind me, you satan! (St. Matthew 16:23)

vade retro me, Satana: Get thee behind me, Satan

vae soli: woe to the solitary person (Ecclesiastes 4:10)

vae victis: woe to the conquered

valeat quantum valere potest: let it pass for what it is worth

valet ancora virtus: virtue is a strong anchor

valete ac plaudite: farewell and applaud (the final line given by Roman actors at the end of a performance)

vanitas vanitatum, omnia vanitas: vanity of vanities, all is vanity (Ecclesiastes 1:2)

varium et mutabile semper femina: a woman is ever a fickle and changeable thing (Virgil)

vectigalia nervos esse rei publicae: taxes are essential to the strength of the republic (Cicero)

vehimur in altum: we are carried out into the depths

vel caeco appareat: it would be obvious to the blind

vel prece vel pretio [with either prayer or price]: for either love or for money

velis et remis [with sails and oars]: with all possible strength

velut aegri somnia: like the dreams of the sick (Horace)

veluti in speculum: even as in a mirror

venalis populus venalis curia patrum [the people and the senators are equally venal]: everyone has his or her price

vendidit hic auro patriam: this man sold his country for gold

venenum in auro bibitur: poison is drunk from a golden cup (Seneca)

veni, vidi, vici: I came, I saw, I conquered (Julius Caesar's message to the Roman Senate declaring his victory over the king of Pontus in Asia Minor)

venia necessitati datur: (fig.) necessity knows no law

venienti occurrite morbo: (fig.) prevention is better than cure

ventis secundis [winds aft]: with favorable winds

vento intermisso: the wind having died down

verba volant, scripta manent: spoken words fly away, written ones remain

verbera, sed audi: whip me, but hear me

verbis ad verbera: from words to blows

verbum sapienti (verb. sap.): a word to the wise

verbum sat sapienti (verb. sat.): a word to the wise is sufficient

veritas nihil veretur nisi abscondi: truth fears nothing save concealment

veritas nimium altercando amittitur: truth is lost through too much altercation

veritas nunquam perit: truth never dies

veritas odium parit: truth begats hatred

veritas omnia vincit: truth conquers all things

veritas praevalebit: truth will prevail

veritas temporis filia: truth is the daughter of time

veritas victrix: truth the conqueror

veritas vincit: truth conquers

veritas vos liberabit: the truth shall make you free (motto of Johns Hopkins University)

veritatem dies aperit: time reveals the truth

veritatis simplex oratio est: the language of truth is simple (Seneca)

vestigia morientis libertatis: the footsteps of dying liberty

vestigia nulla retrorsum: no footsteps backward (i.e., no retreat)

vestigia terrent: the footprints frightened me (Horace)

veteris vestigia flammae: the traces of my former flame (Virgil)

vi et armis [by strength and by arms]: by force of arms

via crucis, via lucis: the way of the Cross is the way of light

via trita est tutissima: the beaten path is the safest one

via trita, via tuta: the beaten path, the safe path

vicarius non habet vicarium: a vicar cannot have a vicar

vicisti, Galilaee: You have conquered, O Galilean (the dying words of Julian the Apostate)

victi vicimus: conquered, we conquer

victis honor: honor to the vanquished

victoria concordia crescit: victory is increased by concord

victoriae gloria merces: glory is the reward of victory

victrix fortunae sapientia: wisdom is the victor over fortune

vide et crede: see and believe

video meliora proboque deteriora sequor: I see and approve the better things but I follow the worse things

vidit et erubit lympha pudica Deum: the modest water saw God and blushed (a reference to Christ's first miracle, the turning of water into wine, St. John 2: 1–11)

vigilate et orate: watch and pray

vilius argentum est auro, virtutibus aurum: as silver is cheaper than gold, so gold than virtue

vincam aut moriar: I will conquer or die

vincere aut mori: to conquer or die

vincit amor patriae [love of homeland conquers]: (fig.) in the end, love of country wins out

vincit omnia veritas: truth conquers all things

vincit qui patitur: he conquers who endures

vincit qui se vincit: he conquers who conquers himself

vincit veritas: truth conquers

vino tortus et ira: tormented by wine and anger

vir sapit qui pauca loquitur: wise is the person who talks little

vires acquirit eundo: it gathers strength as it goes along (i.e., fame; Virgil)

virescit vulnere virtus: virtue flourished from a wound

viret in aeternum: it flourishes forever

Virgilium vidi tantum: so far I have only seen Virgil (Ovid)

viri infelicis procul amici: friends stay far away from an unfortunate person

virtus ariete fortior: virtue is stronger than a battering ram

virtus est militis decus: valor is the soldier's honor

virtus in actione consistit: virtue consists in action

virtus in arduis: virtue in difficulties

virtus incendit vires: virtue kindles one's strength

virtus laudatur et alget: virtue is praised and is left out to freeze

virtus millia scuta: virtue is a thousand shields (also **virtus milia scuta**)

virtus nobilitat: virtue ennobles

virtus non stemma: virtue, not pedigree

virtus post nummas: virtue after money

virtus probata florescit: virtue flourishes in trial

virtus semper viridis [virtue is always green]: virtue never fades

virtus sola nobilitat: virtue alone can ennoble

virtus vincit invidium: virtue overcomes envy

virtute et armis: by valor and arms (motto of Mississippi)

virtute et fide: by virtue and faith

virtute et labore: by virtue and toil

virtute et opera: by virtue and hard work

virtute fideque: by virtue and faith

virtute officii: by virtue of office

virtute quies: by virtue there is tranquility

virtute securus: secure through virtue

virtute, non astutia: by virtue, not by craft

virtute, non verbis: by virtue, not by mere words

virtute, non viris: by virtue, not by men

virtuti nihil obstat et armis: nothing can stand against valor and arms

virtuti non armis fido: I trust to virtue not to arms

virtutis amore: from love of virtue

virtutis avorum praemium: the reward of the valor of my ancestors

virtutis fortuna comes: fortune is the companion of valor (motto of the Duke of Wellington)

virum volitare per ora [to fly through the mouths of men]: to spread like wildfire

vis consilii expers mole ruit sua: force lacking judgment collapses under its own weight (Horace)

vis unita fortior: union is strength

vita brevis, ars longa: life is short, art is long

vita sine litteris mors est: life without literature is death

vitae via virtus: virtue is the way of life

vitam impendere vero: to risk one's life for the truth (Juvenal)

vitiis nemo sine nascitur: no one is born without faults

viva vox: living voice (the "still small voice" of 1 Kings 19:12)

vivamus atque amemus: let us live and love one another

vivant rex et regina: long live the king and queen

vivat regina: long live the queen

vivat respublica: long live the republic

vivat rex: long live the king

vive hodie: live for today

vive memor leti: live mindful of death (Persius)

vive ut vivas: live that you may truly live

vive, vale: long life to you, farewell (Horace)

vivere est cogitare: to live is to think (Cicero)

vivere sat vincere: to conquer is to live enough

vivit post funera virtus: virtue lives on after the grave (Tiberias Caesar)

vix ea nostra voco: with difficulty do I call these things ours

vixere fortes ante Agamemnona: there lived great men before Agamemnon
(Horace)

volat hora per orbem: time flies through the world

volens et potens: willing and able

volens et valens: willing and able

volente Deo: God willing

volenti non fit injuria: (leg.) one cannot claim injury for an act that is willingly done

volo, non valeo: I am willing but unable

voluntas habetur pro facto: the will is taken for the deed

volventibus annis [with revolving years]: as the years roll on

vota vita mea: my life is devoted

vox audita perit, litera scripta manet: the voice that is heard perishes, the letter
that is written remains

vox clamantis in deserto: the voice of one crying in the desert (St. John 1:23)

vox et praeterea nihil [a voice and nothing more]: sound without sense

vox faucibus haesit [the voice stuck in throat]: dumbfounded

vox populi, vox Dei: the voice of the people is the voice of God

vulgus amicitias utilitate probat: the common crowd seeks friendships for their
usefulness

vulneratus non victus: wounded but not conquered

vultus est index animi: the face is the index of the soul

Z

zonam perdidit [he has lost his moneybelt]: he is ruined (Horace)

ABBREVIATIONS

A

A.B. or **B.A.** [Artium Baccalaureus]: Bachelor of Arts

ab init. [ab initio]: from the beginning

abs. re. [absente reo]: (leg.) the defendant being absent

A.C. [ante Christum]: before Christ

a.c. [ante cibum]: (med.) before meals

A.Ch.N. [ante Christum natum]: before Christ's birth

A.D. [anno Domini]: in the year of our Lord

a.d. [ante diem]: before the day

ad (med.): up to; so as to make

adi. or **adj.** [adiectivum]: adjective

ad. or **add.** [adde]: (med.) let there be added (i.e., add)

ad eund. [ad eundem (gradum)]: to the same (degree or standing)

ad fin. [ad finem]: finally

ad inf. or **ad infin.** [ad infinitum]: to infinity (i.e., forever)

ad init. [ad initium]: at the beginning

ad int. [ad interim]: in the meantime; meanwhile; temporarily

ad loc. [ad locum]: to or at the place

ad lib. [ad libitum]: at will (i.e., improvise)

ad us. [ad usum]: according to usage

ad val. [ad valorem]: according to value

ads. [ad sectam]: (leg.) at the suit of

adv. [adversus]: against

A.E.I.O.U. [Austriae est imperare orbi universo]: all the world is to be ruled by Austria

aet. or **aetat.** [aetatis; anno aetatis suae]: of the age; in his/her lifetime

ag. [argentum]: silver

agit. [agita]: (med.) shake

A.H. [anno Hebraico]: in the Hebrew year (see also **A.M.**)

A.H. [anno Hegirae]: in the year of the Hegira (Muhammad's sacred flight to Medina)

a.h.l. [ad hunc locum]: at this place

A.H.S. [anno humanae salutis]: in the year of humanity's redemption

a.h.v. [ad hanc vocem]: at this word

A.M. [anno mundi]: in the year of the world since its creation

A.M. or **a.m.** [ante meridiem]: before noon

A.M. or **M.A.** [Artium Magister]: Master of Arts

A.M.D.G. [ad majorem Dei gloriam]: to the greater glory of God (motto of the Jesuits)

A.P.C.N. [anno post Christum natum]: in the year after the birth of Christ

A.P.R.C. [anno post Roman conditam]: in the year after the building of Rome (ca. 753 B.C.E.)

aq. [aqua]: water

aq. bull. [aqua bulliens]: boiling water

aq. dest. [aqua destillata]: distilled water

A.R. [anno regni]: in the year of the reign

A.S. [aetatis suae]: of his/her age or lifetime

A.S. [anno salutis]: in the year of redemption

A.A.S. [anno aetatis suae]: in the year of his/her age

au. [aurum]: gold

a.u.c. [ab urbe condita]: from the founding of the city

A.U.C. [anno urbis conditae]: in the year or from the time of the founded city (Rome, founded about 753 B.C.E.)

a.v. [ad valorem]: according to the value

a.v. [annos vixit]: he/she lived (so many years)

B

b.i.d. [bis in die]: (med.) twice a day

B.M. [beatae memoriae]: of blessed memory

B.M. or **B.V.** [Beata Maria or Beata Virgo]: the Blessed Virgin (also **B.V.M.**: the Blessed Virgin Mary)

b.p. [bonum publicum]: the common good

b.v. [bene vale]: farewell

C

c̄ [cum]: (med.) with

c. [congius]: (med.) gallon

c. or **ca.** [circa]: about

c. or **circ.** [circiter]: about

c. or **circ.** [circum]: about

Cantab. [Cantabrigiensis]: of Cambridge

cap. [capiat]: (med.) take

c.a.v. [curia advisari vult]: the court wishes to be advised or to consider

cent. [centum]: hundred

cet. par. [ceteris paribus]: other things being equal

cf. [confer]: compare

coch. [cochleare]: (med.) a spoonful

coch. mag. [cochleare magnum]: a tablespoonful
coch. parv. [cochleare parvum]: a teaspoonful
con. [conjunx]: wife
con. [contra]: against
cont. bon. mor. [contra bonos mores]: contrary to good manners
C.R. [custos rotulorum]: the principle justice of the peace in an English county
cuj. [cuius or cujus]: of which
cur. adv. vult [curia advisari vult]: the court wishes to be advised or to consider
c.v. [curriculum vitae]: a résumé

D

d. [da]: (med.) give
d. [decretum]: a decree or an ordinance
D.B. [Divinitatis Baccalaureus]: Bachelor of Divinity
D.D. [Divinitatis Doctor]: Doctor of Divinity (an honorary degree)
d.d. [dono dedit]: given as a gift
de d. in d. [de die in diem]: from day to day
del. [delineavit]: he/she drew it
dil. [dilue]: (med.) dilute or dissolve
D.O.M. [Deo, Optimo, Maximo]: to God, the Best, the Greatest
D.O.M. [Domino, Optimo, Maximo]: the Lord, the Best, the Greatest
D.P. or **Dom. Proc.** [Domus Procerum]: the House of Lords
dram. pers. [dramatis personae]: the cast of characters in a play
d.s.p. [decessit sine prole]: died without issue
D.T. [delirium tremens]: an acute delirium caused by alcohol poisoning
D.V. or **d.v.** [Deo Volente]: God willing

E

e.g. [exempli gratia]: for example
e.o. [ex officio]: by virtue of office
et al. [et alibi]: and elsewhere
et al. [et alii or et aliae]: and others
etc. [et cetera]: and so forth
et conj. [et conjunx]: and spouse (either husband or wife)
et seq. [et sequens]: and the following
et seq. [et sequentes]: and what follows
et ux. [et uxor]: and wife
exc. [excudit]: he/she fashioned it
ex. gr. [exempli gratia]: for example

F

f. [femininum]: feminine
F.D. [fidei defensor]: Defender of the Faith
fe. [ferrum]: iron
fec. [fecit]: he/she made or did it
ff. [fecerunt]: they made or did it
fict. [fictilis]: made of potter's clay
fid. def. [fidei defensor]: Defender of the Faith
fi. fa. [fieri facias]: cause it to be done
fl. [flores]: flowers
fl. or **flor.** [floruit]: flourished
fldxt. [fluidum extractum]: (med.) fluid extract
f.r. [folio recto]: on the front of the page (i.e., the right-hand page)
ft. [fiat]: (med.) let it be made
ft. haust. [fiat haustus]: let a draught be made
ft. mist. [fiat mistura]: let a mixture be made
ft. pulv. [fiat pulvis]: let a powder be made
f.v. [folio verso]: on the back of the page (i.e., the left-hand page)

G

gr. [granum]: (med.) a grain
gtt. [guttae]: (med.) drops

H

H. [hora]: (med.) hour
h.a. [hoc anno]: in this year
hab. corp.: (leg.) a writ of habeas corpus
haust. [haustus]: (med.) a draught
her. [heres]: heir
H.I. [hic iacet or hic jacet]: here lies
H.I.S. [hic iacet sepultus]: here lies buried
h.l. [hoc loco]: in this place
h.m. [hoc mense]: in this month
H.M.P. [hoc monumentum posuit]: he/she erected this monument
hor. decub. [hora decubitus]: (med.) at bedtime
h.q. [hoc quaere]: look for this
H.S. [hic sepultus]: here [lies] buried
h.s. [hoc sensu]: in this sense

h.t. [hoc tempore]: at this time
h.t. [hoc titulo]: under this title

I

i.a. [in absentia]: in absence
ib. or **ibid.** [ibidem]: in the same place (e.g., in a book)
id. [idem]: the same as above
i.e. [id est]: that is
ign. [ignotus] : unknown
in d. [in dies]: (med.) daily
inf. [infra]: below
infra dig. [infra dignitatem]: beneath one's dignity
init. [initio]: in or at the beginning (referring to a passage in a book)
in lim. [in limine]: in the beginning
in pr. [in principio]: in the beginning
I.N.R.I. [Iesus Nazarenus Rex Iudaeorum]: the title placard appended to the Cross
    of Christ by Pontius Pilate at the Crucifixion (St. John 19:20)
in trans. [in transitu]: in transit; on the way
inv. [invenit]: he/she designed it
i.p.i. [in partibus infidelium]: a titular bishop whose title is that of an extinct Roman
    Catholic see
i.q. [idem quod]: the same as

J

J.D. [Juris or Jurum Doctor]: Doctor of Law (a professional degree)
J.U.D. [Juris Utriusque Doctor]: Doctor of both Canon and Civil laws

L

l. or **lib.** [libra; pl. libri]: a book
L.B. [lectori benevolo]: to the gentle reader
lb. [libra]: a pound in weight (also *libra pondo*)
l.c. [loco citato]: in the place cited
L.H.D. [Litterarum Humaniorum Doctor]: Doctor of Humanities
Lit. Hum. [Litterae Humaniores]: the Humanities (e.g., the ancient Classics)
Litt.D. [Litterarum Doctor]: Doctor of Letters
LL.B. [Legum Baccalaureus]: Bachelor of Laws
LL.D. [Legum Doctor]: Doctor of Laws
loc. cit. [loco citato]: in the place cited

loc. laud. [loco laudato]: in the place cited with approval

loq. [loquitur]: he/she speaks

lot. [lotio]: (med.) a lotion

L.S. [locus sigilli]: the place of the seal

l.s.c. [loco supra citato]: in the place cited before

M

m. [masculinum]: masculine

m. or **M.** [meridies]: noon

M.A. [Magister Artium]: Master of Arts

M.D. [Medicinae Doctor]: Doctor of Medicine

m.m. [mutatis mutandis]: with the necessary changes being made

mob. [mobile vulgus]: the fickle masses (i.e., the mob)

mod. praesc. [modo praescripto]: (med.) as prescribed or directed

MS [manuscriptus]: manuscript

MSS [manuscripta]: manuscripts

N

n. [natus]: born

n. [neutrum]: neuter

n. [nocte]: at night

N.B. or **n.b.** [nota bene]: note well

n.l. [non licet]: it is not permitted

n.l. [non liquet]: it is not clear; it is not proven

nol. pros. [nolle prosequi]: an entry into court records indicating a stay or discontinuance of proceedings, either wholly or in part

non obs. [non obstante]: notwithstanding

non pros. [non prosequitur]: a legal judgment where the plaintiff does not appear

non seq. [non sequitur]: it does not follow

O

o. [octarius]: (med.) a pint

ob. [obiit]: he/she died

ob. [obiter]: incidentally

ob.s.p. [obiit sine prole]: he/she died without issue

o.c. [opere citato]: in the work cited

o.d. [oculus dexter]: right eye

o.h. [omni hora]: every hour
ol. [oleum]: (med.) oil
o.n. [omni nocte]: every night
op. [opus]: a musical compostion
op. cit. [opere citato]: in the work cited
o.q.h. [omni quadranta hora]: every fifteen minutes
o.s. [oculus sinister]: left eye
Oxon. [Oxoniensis]: of Oxford

P

p. [partim]: in part
p.a. [per annum]: by the year
p.ae. [partes aequales]: equal parts
pass. [passim]: throughout; here and there
pb. [plumbum]: lead
p.c. [post cibum]: (med) after meals
P.Ch.N. [post Christum natum]: after Christ's birth
pct. [per centum]: by the hundred
per cent. or **p.c.** [per centum]: by the hundred
per. pro. [per procurationem]: by proxy; by the action of
p.g. [persona grata]: an acceptable or welcome person
Ph.B. [Philosophiae Baccalaureus]: Bachelor of Philosophy
Ph.D. [Philosophiae Doctor]: Doctor of Philosophy
pil. [pilula; pl. pilulae]: (med.) a pill
pinx. [pinxit]: he/she painted this
pl. [pluralis]: plural
p.m. [post meridiem]: after noon
P.M. [post mortem]: after death
p.n.g. [persona non grata]: an unacceptable or unwelcome person
p.o. [post office]: see above entry
p.p. [per procurationem]: by proxy; by the action of
PP.C. [patres conscripti]: a title of the Roman Senators
PPS [post postscriptum]: an additional postscript
p.r.n. [pro re nata]: (med) whenever necessary or as the situation demands
pro tem. [pro tempore]: temporarily
prox. [proximo]: of or in the following month
prox. acc. [proxime accessit]: he/she came very near (to winning)
prox. m. [proximo mense]: in the next month
PS [postscriptum]: a postscript
p.t. [pro tempore]: temporarily
ptc. [participium]: a participle

pulv. [pulvis]: (med.) a powder
pxt. [pinxit]: he/she painted this

Q

q.d. [quasi dicat]: as if one should say
q.d. [quasi dictum]: as if said
q.e. [quod est]: which is
Q.E.D. [quod erat demonstrandum]: which was to be demonstrated or proven
Q.E.F. [quod erat faciendum]: which was to be done
Q.H. [quaque hora]: every hour
q.i.d. [quater in die]: (med) four times a day
q.l. or **q.lib.** [quantum libet]: liberally
Q.M. [quaque mane]: every morning
q.p. or **q.pl.** [quantum placet]: as much as you please
qq.v. [quae vide]: (pl.) which see
q.s. or **quant. suff.** [quantum sufficit]: as much as suffices
qu. [quaere]: a question or query
q.v. [quantum vis]: as much as you will
q.v. [quod vide]: (sing.) which see

R

R. [regina]: queen
R. [rex]: king
rep. or **repet.** [repetatur]: let it be repeated
R.I.P. [requiescat in pace]: may he/she rest in peace
R.I.P. [requiescit in pace]: he/she rests in peace

S

S. [sepultus]: buried
S. or **Sig.** [signa]: (med.) that which is to be written on the label of a prescription
s [sine]: (med.) without
s. [sulfur]: sulfur
s.a. [sine anno]: without date
Sal. or **S.** [Salutem dicit!]: Greetings!
sc. [scilicet]: that is to say; namely
sc. or **sculpt.** [sculpsit]: he/she sculpted [it]

scan. mag. [scandalum magnatum; pl. or scandala magnatum]: the defamation of notables or of high ranking persons

sci. fa. [scire facias]: (leg.) a writ to enforce, annul, or vacate a judgment, patent, charter or other matter of record

s.d. [sine die]: indefinitely

sec. [secundum]: according to

sec. art. [secundem artem]: scientifically; artificially

sec. leg. [secundum legem]: according to law

sec. nat. [secundum naturam]: naturally

sec. reg. [secundum regulam]: according to rule

seq. [sequens]: (sing.) the following

seq. [sequitur]: it follows

seqq. [sequentia]: (pl.) the following [things]

sg. or **sing.** [singularis]: singular

s.l. [sine loco]: without place

s.l.a. [sine loco et anno]: without place and year

s.l.a.n. [sine loco, anno vel nomine]: without place, year, or name

s.l.p. [sine legitima prole]: without legitimate issue

s.m.p. [sine mascula prole]: without male issue

s.n. [sine nomine]: anonymous

sn. [stannum]: tin

sol. [solutio]: (med.) a solution

s.o.s. [si opus sit]: (med.) if necessary

s.p. [sine prole]: without issue

S.P.Q.R. [Senatus Populusque Romanus]: The Senate and the People of Rome (motto of Rome)

s.p.s. [sine prole supersite]: without surviving issue

S.R.I. [Sacrum Romanum Imperium]: the Holy Roman Empire

ṧṧ [semis]: (med.) one half

stat. [statim]: immediately; on the spot

S.T.B. [Sacrae Theologiae Baccalaureus]: Bachelor of Sacred Theology

sub. [subaudi]: to read between the lines

sup. [supra]: above

sus. per col. [suspensio per collum]: execution by hanging

s.v. (pl., **s.vv.**) [sub verbo or sub voce]: look under the word

T

t. or **temp.** [tempore]: in the time of

tab. [tabella]: (med.) a tablet

text. rec. [textus receptus]: the received text

t.i.d. [ter in die]: (med) three times a day

U

ult. [ultimo]: last month
u.s. [ubi supra]: in the place mentioned above
ut dict. [ut dictum]: (med) as directed
ut inf. or **ut i.** [ut infra]: as stated or shown below
ut sup. or **u.s.** [ut supra]: as above
ux. [uxor]: wife

V

v. or **vo.** [verso]: reverse side
v. or **vs.** [versus]: against
v. [vide]: see
v.a. [vixit . . . annos]: he lived . . . years
V.D.M. [Verbi Dei Minister]: minister of the Word of God
verb. sap. [verbum sapienti]: a word to the wise
verb. sat. [verbum sat sapienti]: a word to the wise is sufficient
v.i. [vide infra]: see below
viz. [videlicet]: namely
v.s. [vide supra]: see above
V.V. or **v.v.:** [vice versa]: conversely

MISCELLANEOUS

THE CALENDAR YEAR
(Mensis)

Januarius: January
Februarius: February
Martius: March
Aprilis: April
Maius: May
Iunius: June
Quinctilis or **Iulius** (after Julius Caesar): July
Sextilis or **Augustus** (after Augustus Caesar): August
September: September
October: October
November or **Novembris:** November
December: December

THE CALENDAR MONTH

Idus [the Ides]: the fifteenth day in March, May, July, and October; the thirteenth day in all other months
Kalendae or **Calendae** [the Calends]: the first day of a Roman month
Nonae [the Nones]: the seventh day in March, May, July, and October; the fifth day in all other months

THE DAYS OF THE WEEK
(dies)

Dominica: Sunday
Lunae: Monday
Martis: Tuesday
Mercurii: Wednesday
Iovis: Thursday
Veneris: Friday
Saturni: Saturday

PRIMARY AND SECONDARY COLORS

albus: white
caeruleus: blue
caesius: blue-grey
flavus: yellow
fulvus: brown
glaucus: green-grey
niger: black
puniceus: pink
purpureus: purple
ruber: red
viola: violet
viridis: green

THE SEVEN HILLS OF ROME

Collis Quirinalis
Collis Viminalis
Mons Aventinus
Mons Caelius
Mons Capitolinus
Mons Esquilinus
Mons Palatinus

COUNTRIES AND REGIONS

Aegyptus: Egypt
Aethiops: Ethiopia
Africa: north Africa
Alpes: the Alps
Ancyra: Ankara
Antipodes: the Antipodes
Aquincum: Budapest
Arelate: Arles
Augusta Treverorum: Trier
Augusta Vindelicorum: Augsburg
Augustodunum: Autun
Batavia: Holland
Bononia: Bologna
Britannia: Britain

Burdigala: Bourdeaux
Caesar Augusta: Saragossa
Camulodunum: Colchester
Carthago: Carthage
Caledonia: Scotland
Carales: Cagliari
Colonia Agrippina: Cologne
Creta: the Island of Crete
Danuvius: the Danube river
Deva: Chester
Eboracum or **Eburacum:** York
Emerita Augusta: Merida
Etruria: Tuscany (i.e., the land of the Etruscans)
Florentia: Florence
Gades: Cadiz
Gallia: France
Genua: Genoa
Germania: Germany
Graecia: Greece
Helvetia: Switzerland
Hiberia: Spain
Hibernia: Ireland
Hispalis: Seville
Hispania: Spain
Ilium: Troy
Illyricum: the region of the former Yugoslavia
Italia: Italy
Iudea: Palestine
Lacus Lemannus: Lake Geneva
Latium: central Italy (i.e., Rome and its environs)
Lindum: Lincoln
Londinium: London
Lugdunum: Lyons
Lusitania: Portugal
Lugdunum Batavorum: Leiden
Lutetia: Paris
Malaca: Malaga
Mare Caspium: the Caspian Sea
Mare Inferum or **Mare Tyrrhenum:** the Tyrrhenian Sea
Mare Internum or **Mare Nostrum:** the Mediterranean Sea
Mare Superum or **Mare Adriaticum:** the Adriatic Sea
Massilia or **Massillia** or **Massuia:** Marseilles
Mazaca Caesarea: Kayseri

Mediolanum : Milan
Melita: Malta
Moguntiacum: Mainz
Neapolis: Naples
Nemausus: Nimes
Nilus: the Nile
Oceanus Germanicus: The North Sea
Olisipo: Lisbon
Panormus: Palermo
Patavium: Padua
Pontus Euxinus: the Black Sea
Portus Dubris: Dover
Pygmaei: the Pygmies of Africa
Regiones Torrides: the Tropics
Rhenus: the Rhine river
Rhodanus: the Rhone river
Roma: Rome
Salmantica: Salamanca
Sarmatia: Russia
Scotia: Scotland
Sequana: the Seine
Seres: China (or the Chinese)
Sicilia: the Island of Sicily
Sinus Arabicus: the Red Sea
Tamesa or **Tamesis:** the Thames
Tanais: the Don river
Thessalonica: Salonika
Tiberis: the Tiber river
Tibur: Tivoli
Toletum: Toledo
Tolosa: Toulouse
Transalpinus: southern France
Trinacria: Sicily
Tridentum: Trent
Tros: a Trojan
Valentia: Valencia
Via Appia: the Appian Way
Vindobona: Vienna

ROMAN NUMERALS

CARDINALS

unus (I): one
duo (II): two
tres (III): three
quattuor (IV): four
quinque (V): five
sex (VI): six
septem (VII): seven
octo (VIII): eight
novem (IX): nine
decem (X): ten
undecim (XI): eleven
duodecim (XII): twelve
tredecim (XIII): thirteen
quattuordecim (XIV): fourteen
quindecim (XV): fifteen
sedecim (XVI): sixteen
septemdecim (XVII): seventeen
duodevinginti/octodecim (XVIII):
  eighteen
undeviginti/novemdecim (XIX):
  nineteen
viginti (XX): twenty
unus et viginti (XXI): twenty-one
duoetviginti (XXII): twenty-two
duodetriginta (XXVIII): twenty-eight
undetriginta (XXIX): twenty-nine
triginta (XXX): thirty
duodequadraginta (XXXVIII):
  thirty-eight
undequadraginta (XXXIX):
  thirty-nine
quadraginta (XL): forty
duodequinquaginta (XLVIII): forty-eight

undequinquaginta (XLIX):
  forty-nine
quinquaginta (L): fifty
sexaginta (LX): sixty
septuaginta (LXX): seventy

ORDINALS

primus: first
secundus: second
tertius: third
quartus: fourth
quintus: fifth
sextus: sixth
septimus: seventh
octavus: eighth
nonus: ninth
decimus/decumus: tenth
undecimus: eleventh
duodecimus: twelfth
tertius decimus: thirteenth
quartus decimus: fourteenth
quintus decimus: fifteenth
sextus decimus: sixteenth
septimus decimus: seventeenth
duodevicesimus/octavusdecimus:
  eighteenth
undevicesimus/novemdecimus:
  nineteenth
vicesimus: twentieth
unetvice(n)simus: twenty-first
duoetvice(n)simus: twenty-second
duodetriginta: twenty-eighth
undetrice(n)simus: twenty-ninth
trice(n)simus: thirtieth
duodequadrage(n)simus:
  thirty-eighth
undequadrage(n)simus:
  thirty-ninth
quadrage(n)simus: fortieth
duodequinquage(n)simus: forty-
  eighth
undequinquage(n)simus:
  forty-ninth
quinquage(n)simus: fiftieth
sexage(n)simus: sixtieth
septuage(n)simus: seventieth

octoginta (LXXX): eighty

nonaginta (XC): ninety

centum (C): one hundred

centum (et) unus (CI):
one hundred and one

ducenti (CC): two hundred

trecenti (CCC): three hundred

quadringenti (CD): four hundred

quingenti (D): five hundred

sescenti (DC): six hundred

septingenti (DCC): seven hundred

octingenti (DCCC): eight hundred

nongenti (DM): nine hundred

mille (M): one thousand

duo milia/millia (MM): two thousand

octoge(n)simus: eightieth

nonage(n)simus: ninetieth

centesimus: hundredth

centesimus (et) primus:
one hundred and first

ducentesimus: two hundredth

trecente(n)simus: three hundredth

quadringente(n)simus:
four hundredth

quingente(n)simus: five hundredth

sescente(n)simus: six hundredth

septingente(n)simus:
seven hundredth

octingente(n)simus:
eight hundredth

nongente(n)simus: nine hundredth

mille(n)simus: one thousandth

bis mille(n)simus: two thousandth

ENGLISH-LATIN INDEX

A

a nobody: **natus nemo**

a word to the wise is sufficient: **dictum sapienti sat (est)**

above: **supra**

absence of justice: **jus nullum**

absolute power: **imperium singulare**

absolutely: **in absoluto**

abuse does not take away use: **abusus non tollit usum**

acceptable: **nihil obstat**

accomplice in the crime: **particeps criminis**

according to: **secundum**

according to circumstance: **pro re**

according to custom: **ad usum** or **ex more**

according to law: **secundum legem**

according to merit: **pro merito**

according to nature: **secundum naturam**

according to rule: **ad amussim** or **secundum regulam**

according to the law: **in jure**

according to the value: **ad valorem**

according to truth: **secundum veritatem**

according to usage: **secundum usum**

across: **in transversum** or **trans**

act of God: **actus Dei**

action: **actus**

add: **adde**

add fuel to the flame: **oleum addere camino**

add to this: **adde huc**

adjourned indefinitely: **sine die**

afresh: **de integro**

after birth: **post partum**

after death: **post mortem** or **post obitum**

after dinner: **cenatus**

after litigation began: **post litem motam**

after meals: **post cibum**

after noon: **post meridiem**

after the appointed day: **post diem**

after the conclusion: **post terminum**

after the fact: **ex post facto**

after the fashion of: **ad instar**

after the manner of: **ad modum** or **more**

against: **adversus** or **contra** or **versus**

against my will: **me invito**

against the peace: **contra pacem**

against the stream: **adverso flumine**

against the world: **contra mundum**

aged: **grandis natu**

agreement: **consensus**

alcohol: **aqua vitae**

all is well: **recte est**

all kidding aside: **extra jocum** or **sine joco**

all right: **bene habet**

all that sort: **id genus omne**

all things being equal: **caeteris paribus** or **ceteris paribus**

all thumbs: **asinus ad lyram**

all-powerful: **omnipotens**

almighty God: **omnipotentia Dei**

alone: **solus**

aloud: **magna voce**

already enough: **jam satis**

also: **et**

alternately: **alternus** or **in vicem** or **in vices**

altogether: **in toto**

always: **semper**

among equals: **inter pares**

among other persons: **inter alios**

among other things: **inter alia**

among the goods: **in bonis**

among the living: **inter vivos**

among us: **inter nos**

and: **et**

and elsewhere: **et alibi**

and from the Son: **filioque**

and husband: **et vir**

and others: **et alii**

and so forth: **et cetera**

and spouse: **et conjunx**

and the following: **et sequens**

and the like: **et similia**

and what follows: **et sequentes** or **et sequentia**

and wife: **et uxor**

anew: **ab integro** or **de novo**

annually: **anniversarius** or **per annum**

annuity: **annua pecunia**

anonymous: **sine nomine**

archer: **sagittarius**

aristocratic: **optimas**

armed: **cum telo**

around: **circa**

art of love: **ars amandi**

as: **qua**

as a matter of form: **pro forma**

as a matter of law: **ex lege**

as a token of friendship: **ut pignus amicitiae**

as a warning: **in terrorem**

as above: **ut supra**

as directed: **more dicto** or **ut dictum**

as far as I know: **quantum scio** or **quod sciam**

as far as in me lies: **quantum in me est**

as far as possible: **in toto caelo** or **quam celerrime**

as if confessed: **pro confesso**

as if said: **quasi dictum**

as is impossible: **per impossibile**

as is usual: **ut adsolet**

as it were: **quasi**

as matters stand: **e re nata**

as much as is sufficient: **quantum satis**

as much as it is worth: **quantum valebat**

as much as it may be worth: **quantum valeat**

as much as possible: **quam maxime**

as much as required: **tantum quantum**

as much as suffices: **quantum sufficit**

as much as you please: **quam libet** or **quamlibet** or **quantum placet**

as much as you will: **quantum vis**

as nearly as possible: **quam proxime**

as regards the past: **quoad ultra**

as soon as possible: **quam primum** or **quamprimum**

as stated below: **ut infra**

as to the lesser matter: **quoad minus**

as usual: **ut solet**

as well as can be done: **pro viribus**

ashore: **in litus** or **in litore**

asleep: **in somno** or **per somnum**

at: **ad**

at a high price: **magna pretio** or **magni pretii**

at a moment's notice: **in promptu**

at bedtime: **hora decubitus**

at chambers: **in camera**

at dead of night: **nocte intempesta**

at first glance: **primo intuiti**

at first light: **prima luce**

at frequent intervals: **haud longis intervallis**

at full length: **in extenso**

at hand: **ad manum**

at high tide: **aestu incitato**

at home: **domi**

at its own time: **suo tempore**

at leisure: **otiosus**

at length: **per extensum** or **tandem**

at my own risk: **meo periculo**

at night: **nocte**

at nightfall: **sub noctem**

at once: **simul**

at one blow: **uno ictu**

at one's own peril: **suo periculo**

at our own risk: **nostro periculo**

at pleasure: **a bene placito** or **ad libitum**

at present: **hodie**

at that time: **id temporis**

at the agreed hour: **ad horam compositam**

at the beginning: **ad initium** or **initio** or **sub initio**

at the beginning of the year: **initio anni**

at the critical moment: **in ipso periculi discrimine**

at the end of the book: **in extremo libro**

at the foot of the mountain: **infimus mons**

at the man: **ad hominem**

at the marriage: **ad ostium ecclesiae**

at the mercy of fate: **ut fata trahunt**

at the opportune time: **in tempore opportuno**

at the outbreak of war: **in limine belli**

at the place: **ad locum**

at the point of death: **in articulo mortis** or **in extremis**

at the present time: **in praesenti**

at the public expense: **sumptibus publicis** or **sumptu publico**

at the right moment: **in tempore**

at the right time: **justo tempore**

at the same time: **simul** or **uno tempore**

at the suit of: **ad sectam**

at the turning point: **in discrimine rerum**

at the very instant: **in tempore ipso**

at this place: **ad hunc locum**

at this time: **hoc tempore**

at this word: **ad hanc vocem**

at what price fame?: **quanti fama?**

at will: **ad arbitrium**

at your instigation: **impulsu tuo**

attentive: **auritus**

augur: **auspex** or **haruspex**

B

backwards: **retro**

backwards and forwards: **sursum deorsum**

bad conscience: **conscientia mala**

bad money: **nummi adulterini**

bald: **calvus**

banquet: **convivium**

barefoot: **pedibus nudis**

bastard child: **filius populi**

battlefield: **locus pugnae**

beast of burden: **jumentum**

because he fears: **quia timet**

before: **ante** or **pro**

before all things: **ante omnia**

before childbirth: **ante partum**

before daybreak: **ante lucem**

before death: **ante mortem**

before its time: **ante tempus**

before meals: **ante cibum**

before noon: **ante meridiem** or **ante meridianus**

before the court: **in facie curiae**

before the judge: **sub judice**

before the war: **ante bellum**

beggar: **mendicus**

beginning: **genesis**

behind: **a tergo**

Behold the Lamb of God!: **Ecce Agnus Dei**

Behold the Man!: **Ecce Homo**

below: **infra**

beneath one's dignity: **infra dignitatem**

beside oneself: **mente captus** or **sui impotens**

beside the point: **nihil ad rem**

best friend: **alter ego**

between: **inter**

between a rock and a hard place: **a fronte praecipitium a tergo lupi**

between hope and fear: **inter spem et metum**

between the hammer and the anvil: **inter malleum et incudem**

between two reigns: **interregnum**

between us: **inter nos**

beware of danger: **in cauda venenum**

beware of dog: **cave canem**

beyond: **ultra**

beyond measure: **extra modum**

beyond one's power: **ultra vires** or **supra vires**

beyond the legal limit: **ultra licitum**

beyond the value: **ultra valorem**

beyond the walls: **extra muros**

Big Dipper: **Ursa Major**

bird: **avis**

birthday: **dies natalis** or **genitalis dies**

bishop: **episcopus**

bit by bit: **frustillatim**

blacksmith: **faber ferrarius**

blameless: **rectus in curia**

blank slate: **tabula rasa**

bless you!: **benedicite!**

blessed are the peacemakers: **beati pacifici**

blessed are the poor in spirit: **beati pauperes spiritu**

blood: **sanguis**

blood relative: **consanguinitas**

bodily strength: **vires corporis**

body: **corpus**

body of Christ: **Corpus Christi**

body of law: **corpus juris**

body of the crime: **corpus delicti**

boiling water: **aqua bulliens**

bond of marriage: **vinculum matrimonii**

book: **codex** or **liber**

bookseller: **bibliopola**

bookworm: **helluo librorum**

born: **natus**

born to glory: **natus ad gloriam**

both: **ambo**

bottom of the sea: **imum mare**

braggert: **homo gloriosus**

brain: **cerebrum**

bread: **panis**

breakfast: **ientaculum**

bridge: **pons**

bringing back: **redux**

British peace: **Pax Britannica**

brother: **frater**

bull: **taurus**

burden of proof: **onus probandi**

buried: **sepultus**

busy: **occupatus**

butterfly: **papilio**

buyer: **emptor**

by a leap: **per saltum**

by accident: **per accidens** or **per infortunium**

by birth: **natu**

by chance: **per accidens**

by command: **iussu** or **jussu**

by common consent: **communi consensu**

by courage and faith: **animo et fide**

by craft: **per dolum**

by day: **interdius**

by degrees: **gradatim** or **tractim**

by design: **ex proposito**

by divine right: **jure divino**

by fair means or foul: **per fas et nefas**

by families: **per stirpes**

by favor: **de gratia**

by force: **manu forti**

by heart: **ex memoria** or **memoriter**

by implication: **implicite**

by invitation: **invitatu**

by its own motion: **suo motu**

by its own power: **proprio vigore**

by itself: **per se**

by Jove: **per Jovem**
by land: **pedibus**
by law: **jure**
by marital law: **jure mariti**
by means of: **per**
by moonlight: **ad lunam**
by mouth: **per os**
by my advice: **me auctore**
by my fault: **mea culpa**
by night: **noctu** or **nocturnus**
by no means: **nullo modo** or **nullo pacto**
by oneself: **solus**
by one's own prowess: **suo Marte**
by one's peers: **per pares**
by order: **iussu** or **jussu**
by permission: **permissu**
by perservering: **perserverando**
by proxy: **per procurationem**
by reason of domicile: **ratione domicilii**
by reason of soil: **ratione soli**
by retaliation: **per vices**
by right: **de jure** or **jure**
by right of blood: **jure sanguinis**
by right of crown: **jure coronae**
by right of relationship: **jure propinquitatis**
by right, not by gift: **jure non dono**
by sea and by land: **per mare per terram**
by special favor: **speciali gratia**
by that very fact: **ipso facto**
by the court: **per curiam**
by the day: **per diem**
by the entire court: **per totam curiam**
by the gift of God: **ex dono Dei**
by the favor of God: **Deo favente**
by the grace of God: **Dei gratia**
by the hundred: **per centum**
by the judge: **per eundem**
by the law itself: **ipso jure**
by the light of day: **de claro die**

by the living voice: **per vivam vocem**
by the month: **per mensem** or **per mese**
by the roots: **radicitus**
by the straight road: **per vias rectas**
by the thousand: **per mille**
by the way: **obiter**
by the way of sorrows: **per viam dolorosam**
by the wayside: **in itinere**
by the will of the people: **jure humano**
by this sign conquer: **in hoc signo vinces**
by threats: **per minas**
by virtue of one's office: **ex officio**
by way of: **per viam**
by what means?: **quo modo?** or **quomodo?**
by what right?: **quo jure?**
by which: **per quod**
by word of mouth: **ore tenus**
by your leave: **pace tua**
bygone years: **praeteriti anni**

C

calendar of events: **fasti**
cancellation of debts: **novae tabulae**
canon law: **jus canonicum**
cardinal point: **cardo duplex**
cast of characters: **dramatis personae**
cattle market: **forum bovarium** or **boarium**
cause it to be done: **fieri facias**
celebrity: **vir insignis**
celestial mysteries: **arcana caelestia**
censor of morals: **censor morum**
century: **centum anni**
children's paradise: **limbus puerorum**
Christian: **Christianus**
church: **ecclesia**
circular reasoning: **circulus vitiosus**
citizen of the world: **mundanus**

City of God: **Civitas Dei**

city center: **media urbs**

civil law: **jus civile**

civil war: **bellum civile** or **bellum domesticum** or **bellum intestinum**

close by: **juxta**

close formation: **phalanx**

coffin: **sarcophagus**

coined money: **aes signatum**

coined silver: **argentum signatum**

college: **collegium**

comic genius: **vis comica**

comity of nations: **comitas inter gentes**

common bread: **panis cibarius**

common folk: **plebs**

common good: **bonum publicum** or **commune bonum**

common law: **jus commune** or **lex non scripta**

common rabble: **faex populi** or **profanum vulgus**

commonwealth: **res publica** or **respublica**

communion of the saints: **communio sanctorum**

community: **communitas**

companion volume: **vade mecum**

compare: **confer**

comparison: **parabola**

compassion: **misericordia**

completely: **funditus**

compulsory: **in invitum**

concerning: **in re** or **re**

conditions of peace: **legis pacis**

confidentially: **sub rosa**

confused: **in nubibus**

connectedness: **nexus**

consider the outcome: **finem respice**

constellation: **astrum**

contemplation of flight: **meditatio fugae**

contract: **pactum**

contradiction in terms: **contradictio in adjecto**

contrary to good manners: **contra bonos mores**

contrary to nature: **opposuit natura**

conversely: **vice versa**

corpse: **cadaver**

corrections: **corrigenda**

costly: **magno pretio**

cottage: **casa**

court action: **querela**

crab: **cancer**

credits: **accepta**

creed: **credo**

crescent moon: **crescens luna** or **luna crescens**

crime: **delictum**

criminal act: **actus reus**

crocodile tears: **lacrimae simulatae**

cross: **crux**

crown: **corona**

cure-all: **panacea**

cursing: **maledictum**

custodian of morals: **custos morum**

customs: **mores**

D

daily: **in dies**

daily bread: **victus cotidianus**

dandy: **homo elegans**

dare to be wise: **aude sapere** or **sapere aude**

daughter: **filia**

dawn: **aurora**

Day of Judgment: **Dies Irae**

day is breaking: **lucescit**

day's journey: **iter unius diei**

daybreak: **diluculum**

daytime: **dies**

dead: **ad patres** or **mortuus**

dead men tell no tales: **mortui non mordant**

dead of the night: **concubia nocte** or **intempesta nox**

debt: **aes alienum** or **debitum** or **res alienae**

deceased: **demortuus**

decided case: **res judicata**

decree: **edictum**

deed: **factum**

deeds not words: **facta non verba**

deep calls unto deep: **abyssus abyssum invocat**

deep silence: **altum silentium** or **silentium altum**

defendant being absent: **absente reo**

Defender of the Faith: **fidei defensor**

defense of one's life conduct: **apologia pro vita sua**

definitely: **in terminis**

deification: **apotheosis**

delight of battle: **gaudium certaminis**

den of iniquity: **colluvies vitiorum**

deputy: **locum tenens**

deservedly: **pro meritis**

desire: **libido**

desirous of praise: **laudis cupidus**

dessert: **mensa secunda** or **secunda mensa**

devil: **diabolus**

Devil's advocate: **advocatus diaboli**

diametrically opposite: **toto caelo**

diary: **adversaria** or **commentarii diurni**

dictum: **ipse dixit**

died: **obiit**

died without issue: **obiit sine prole**

different kind: **alieni generis**

digression: **excursus**

diplomatic agreement: **pacta conventa**

directly: **per vias rectas**

divide and rule: **divide et impera**

divination: **divinatus**

divine food: **ambrosia**

divine law: **jus divinum**

divine soul: **anima divina**

dizziness: **vertigo**

do not admit: **ne admittas**

do unto another as to thyself: **alteri sic tibi**

dog in a manger: **canis in praesepi**

door to door: **ostiatim**

double: **duplex**

double jeopardy: **non bis in idem**

downstream: **secundo flumine**

dozen: **duodecim**

draught: **haustus**

drop by drop: **guttatim**

drops: **guttae**

drunkard: **homo ebriosus**

during absence: **durante absentia**

during dinner: **inter cenam**

during hostilities: **flagrante bello**

during life: **durante vita**

during the trial: **lite pendente**

E

each day: **per diem**

ear: **auris**

early in the morning: **multo mane**

earth: **terra**

Earthly City: **Civitas Terrena**

earthquake: **terrae motus**

easily the first: **facile princeps**

ebb and flow: **accessus et recessus**

echo: **vocis imago**

eclipse of the sun: **labores solis**

egg: **ovum**

eldest child: **maximus natu**

empty threat: **brutum fulmen**

enemy: **hospes hostis**

enough: **satis**

equal: **par**

equal parts: **partes aequales**

equal to the task: **par oneri**

equally: **juxta**

equally at fault: **in pari delicto**

equals with equals: **pares cum paribus**

error: **erratum**

especially: **in primis**

essentially: **per essentiam**

eternal darkness: **tenebrae aeternae**

eulogy: **laudatio funebris**

Evening Star: **Hesperus**

evening of life: **vita occidens**

everlasting: **aere perennius**

everlasting glory: **sempiterna gloria**

every hour: **omni hora** or **quaque hora**

every morning: **quaque mane**

every night: **omni nocte**

every other day: **alternis diebus**

every other year: **alternis annis**

everyone: **nemo non**

everything: **nihil non**

everywhere: **ubique**

evil: **malum**

evil omen: **omen infaustum** or **omen sinistrum**

evil person: **homo nefarius**

evolution: **rerum progressio**

exactly: **verbatim et literatim**

exceedingly: **sane quam**

excellent!: **bene!**

excessive: **immodicus**

exempt: **immunis**

eye: **oculus**

eyewash: **collyrium**

F

fable: **fabella**

face to face: **coram**

faith alone: **sola fide**

faithful to the end: **ad finem fidelis**

faithfully: **fideliter**

fallacy of cause and effect: **post hoc ergo propter hoc**

false modesty: **malus pudor**

false reading: **falsa lectio**

farce: **fabula**

farewell: **bene vale** or **vale** or **valete**

farewell forever: **aeternum vale**

farthest point: **nil ultra**

father: **pater**

favorable omen: **omen faustum**

fellowship: **communitas**

festival: **dies festus**

fig: **ficus**

finally: **ad finem**

finishing point: **terminus ad quem**

fire: **ignis**

firm of purpose: **propositi tenax**

first: **primo**

first act: **actus primus**

first among equals: **prima inter pares**

first among his equals: **primus inter pares**

first come, first served: **prior tempore, prior jure**

first impression: **prima facie**

first light: **prima lux**

first mover: **primum mobile**

first name: **praenomen**

fish: **piscis**

fish market: **forum piscarium** or **piscatorium**

Five Ways: **Quinque Viae**

flood: **diluvium**

flourished: **floruit**

flowing free: **fusus crines**

fluid: **fluidus**

following: **in sequens**

food for Acheron: **Acheruntis pabulum**

food of the soul: **pabulum animi**

fool: **homo stultus**

foot-washing: **pedilavium**

for a few days: **ad paucos dies**

for a memorial: **pro memoria**

for a short time: **ad exiguum tempus**

for a time: **in tempus**

for all time: **ad vitam aeternam** or **in omne tempus**

for an indefinite period: **in incertum**

for and against: **pro et contra**

for better or for worse: **de bono et malo**

for bravery: **fortitudini**

for each individual: **per capita**

for each month: **per mensem**

for example: **exempli gratia**

for glory: **ad gloriam**

for instance: **exempli causa** or **verbi causa**

for life: **ad vitam**

for many years: **ad multus annos**

for my part: **pro mea parte**

for my sake: **mea gratia**

for now: **pro nunc**

for political reasons: **rei publicae causa**

for reference: **ad referendum**

for sure: **pro certo**

for the first time: **primitus**

for the future: **in futurum** or **in posterum**

for the last time: **ad postremum**

for the moment: **in praesens** or **pro tempore**

for the most part: **maximam partem**

for the present: **de praesenti** or **impraesentiarum** or **in praesentia**

for the present time: **in praesens tempus**

for the public good: **pro bono publico**

for the sake of gain: **lucri causa**

for the sake of honor: **honoris causa**

for the sake of piety: **pietatis causa**

for the sake of the joke: **joci causa**

for the second time: **iterum**

for the third time: **tertium**

for the time being: **pro tempore**

for the winter: **hibernus**

forbidden: **impermissus**

forefathers: **patres**

forever: **ad infinitum** or **ad perpetuitatem** or **in aeternum** or **in perpetuum**

forever and ever: **in saecula saeculorum**

formerly: **quondam**

fortunate fault: **felix culpa**

fortune favors the bold: **audentes fortuna juvet** or **audaces fortuna juvet**

fortune favors the strong: **fortes fortuna [ad]juvat**

forward and backward: **per recto et recto**

four times: **quater**

four times a day: **quater in die** or **quater die**

freak of nature: **lusus naturae**

free time: **otium**

free will: **liberum arbitrium**

friend and foe: **aequi iniqui**

friend of the court: **amicus curiae**

friendship without deceit: **amicitia sine fraude**

from: **ab**

from a distance: **e longinquo** or **ex longinquo**

from anger: **ab irato**

from bed and board: **mensa et toro**

from beginning to end: **ab ovo usque ad mala**

from boyhood: **a pueris** or **a puero**

from cause to effect: **a priori**

from childhood: **a teneris annis** or **ab incunabulis**

from day to day: **de die in diem** or **diem ex die** or **in dies singulos**

from door to door: **ostiatim**

from effect to cause: **a posteriori**

from every perspective: **omni ex parte**

from head to toe: **a capite ad calcem**

from home: **domo**

from one to all: **ab uno ad omnes**

from possibility to reality: **a posse ad esse**

from table and bed: **a mensa et toro**

from tender years: **a teneris annis**

from that day: **a die**

from the absurd: **ab absurdo**

from the beginning: **a principio** or **ab initio** or **ab origine** or **ab ovo**

from the beginning of time: **ab aeterno**

from the bonds of marriage: **a vinculo matrimonii**

from the bottom: **funditus**

from the bottom of the heart: **ab imo pectore** or **imo pectore**

from the date: **a datu**

from the first: **a primo**

from the founding of the city: **ab urbe condita**

from the greatest to the least: **a maximis ad minima**

from the heart: **ex animo**

from the high mountain: **de monte alto**

from the inconvenience involved: **ab inconvenienti**

from the inside: **intus**

from the lesser to the greater: **a minori ad majus**

from the library of: **ex libris** or **e libris**

from the outside: **ab extra**

from the side: **a latere**

from the spear a crown: **a cuspide corona**

from which: **a quo**

from within: **ab intra**

from words to blows: **a verbis ad verbera**

from youth: **a teneris annis**

gap: **lacuna**

gentle reader: **lector benevole**

give: **da**

Glory be to God Most High: **Gloria in Excelsis Deo**

Glory be to the Father: **Gloria Patri**

glory: **gloria**

go in peace: **vade in pacem**

goat: **capricornus**

God be with you: **Deus vobiscum**

God forbid!: **quod abominor!** or **quod avertat Deus!**

God is the greatest good: **Deus est summum bonum**

God save the king: **salvum fac regem, O Domine**

God save the queen: **salvam fac reginam, O Domine**

God willing: **Deo volente** or **volente Deo**

god: **deus**

God's speed!: **salve!**

goddess: **dea**

going step by step: **gradarius**

gold: **aurum**

good: **bene**

good conscience: **conscientia recta**

good deeds: **bene facta**

good fortune: **fortuna prospera** or **fortuna secunda**

good luck: **bene vale vobis** or **macte!**

good-will: **benevolentia**

goods: **bona**

goose bumps: **cutis anserina**

Gospel: **evangelium**

gout: **dolor artuum**

grace alone: **sola gratia**

gradually: **minutatim**

Grant Us Peace: **Dona Nobis Pacem**

grass: **herba**

gratitude: **gratus animus**

gravity: **nutus et pondus**

Great Mother: **Magna Mater**

great good: **magnum bonum**

great unwashed: **ignobile vulgus**

great year: **annus magnus**

greatly: **magno opere**

Greetings!: **Salutem dicit!** or **ave**

gross negligence: **culpa lata**

guardian deity: **genius loci**

guest: **hospes**

guild: **conlegium**

guilty person: **homo reus**

guily intent: **mens rea**

H

habitually: **de more**

Hail!: **ave!**

Hail Mary: **Ave Maria**

half: **semis**

half a pint: **hemina**

hallucination: **aegri somnia**

handful: **manipulus**

happily: **feliciter**

happiness: **beata vita** or **vita beata**

hare: **lepus**

harmony: **concordia**

having resigned from office: **functus officio**

he is hit: **habet!** or **hoc habet!**

he owes nothing: **nihil debet**

he says nothing: **nihil dicit** or **nil dicit**

head: **caput**

healing power: **vis medicatrix**

healing power of nature: **vis medicatrix naturae**

heart: **cor**

heartbroken: **animo fractus**

height of glory: **summa gloria**

held in trust: **in commendam**

hello!: **heus** or **hui**

here!: **adsum**

here and everywhere: **hic et ubique**

here and now: **hic et nunc**

here and there: **passim** or **sic passim**

here begins: **incipit**

here lies: **hic iacet** or **hic jacet**

here lies buried: **hic iacet sepultus** or **hic sepultus**

here lies . . . : **hic situs est . . .**

heroine: **virago**

heyday: **flos aetatis**

hidden: **occultus**

High Mass: **Missa solemnis**

high priest: **Pontifex Maximus**

high treason: **laesa majestas**

highest evil: **extremum malorum**

highest good: **extremum bonorum** or **summum bonum**

highest law: **summum jus**

highest point: **ne plus ultra**

hither and thither: **huc et illuc** or **ultro et citro**

Holy Roman Empire: **Sacrum Romanum Imperium**

holy deeds: **acta sanctorum**

holy of holies: **sanctum sanctorum**

holy place: **fanum**

homeless: **homo sine censu**

honorable mention: **accessit**

honorary: **honoris gratia**

hope: **spes**

horn of plenty: **cornu copiae**

horse: **equus**

horse track: **hippodromos**

hot: **calidus**

hour: **hora**

hourly: **in horas**

House of Lords: **Domus Procerum**

house: **domicilium** or **domus**

house-arrest: **custodia libera**

household: **familia**

how do you do?: **quid agis?**

human being: **homo**

human body: **corpus humanum**

human soul: **anima humana**

humanity: **humanitas**

hundred: **centum**

husband: **vir**

husband and wife: **vir et uxor**

I

I: **ego**

I absolve: **absolvo**

I am a man: **homo sum**

I am ashamed: **pudet me**

I came, I saw, I conquered: **veni, vidi, vici**

I have sinned: **peccavi**

I hope in the Cross: **in cruce spero**

I know not what: **nescio quid**

I love as I find: **amo ut invenio**

I myself: **ego ipse**

I think I can: **posse videor**

I think, therefore I am: **cogito ergo sum**

I'm sorry: **me paenitet**

if necessary: **si opus sit**

ignorance of the law does not excuse: **ignorantia juris non excusat**

Iliad of woes: **Ilias malorum**

ill-will: **malevolentia**

illegal: **inlicitus**

illegally: **contra leges**

illegitimate son: **filius nullius** or **nullius filius**

image of God: **imago Dei**

imbecile: **impos animi**

immediately: **ilicet**

immoral life: **vita turpis**

impartial judge: **judex incorruptus**

impasse: **pari ratione**

implicit trust: **uberrima fides**

important witness: **testis gravis**

in a bad sense: **in malum partem** or **sensu malo**

in a broad sense: **lato sensu**

in a domestic court: **in foro domestico**

in a dream: **in somnis** or **per somnum**

in a folio volume: **in folio**

in a friendly way: **amiciter** or **via amicabili**

in a good sense: **sensu bono**

in a heap: **in cumulo**

in a nutshell: **in nuce**

in a safe place: **in tuto esse**

in a series: **seriatim**

in a single bound: **per saltum** or **uno saltu**

in a state of doubt: **in tenebris**

in a state of nature: **in naturalibus**

in a straight line: **ad lineam** or **ad perpendiculum** or **in directum**

in a strict sense: **stricto sensu**

in a test tube: **in vitro**

in a vacuum: **in vacuo** or **vacuo**

in a word: **uno verbo**

in absence: **in absentia**

in all directions: **in omnes partes**

in all respects: **in omnibus**

in all things love: **in omnibus caritas**

in an analogous case: **in pari materia**

in an equal cause: **in pari causa**

in an evil manner: **malo modo**

in an instant: **puncto temporis**

in an opposite direction: **in contrarium**

in an orderly manner: **secundum ordinem**

in an outward direction: **ad extra**

in another place: **in alio loco**

in another way: **alio pacto**

in bad faith: **mala fide**

in being: **in esse**

in body: **in corpore**

in both cases: **in utraque re**

in brief: **ne multa**

in Christ's name: **in Christi nomine**

in close order: **grege facto**

in confidence: **sub rosa**

in confusion: **nec caput nec pedes**

in contemplation of flight: **in meditatione fugae**

in contempt of court: **in contumaciam**

in darkness: **in tenebris**

in default: **in mora**

in different ways: **alius aliter**

in doubt: **in ambiguo** or **in dubio**

in droves: **gregatim**

in due time: **ad tempus**

in each month: **in singulos menses**

in episcopal robes: **in pontificalibus**

in equilibrium: **in equilibrio**

in error: **frustra**

in everlasting remembrance: **memoria in aeterna**

in every respect: **omnibus rebus**

in fact: **de facto**

in few words: **paucis verbis**

in French: **Gallice**

in full: **in pleno**

in full court: **in banco**

in full leaf: **comata silva**

in full measure: **pleno modio**

in fun: **per ludibrium**

in general: **ad summam**

in happier times: **melioribus annis**

in his own way: **more suo**

in ill-will: **in invidiam**

in intention and fact: **animo et facto**

in inverse order: **inverso ordine**

in Italian: **Italice**

in its place: **in situ**

in its proper place: **suo loco**

in itself: **in se** or **per se**

in jest: **per jocum**

in kind: **in genere**

in like manner: **similiter**

in many respects: **in rebus multis**

in many ways: **multimodis**

in memory: **in memoriam**

in mourning: **atra cura**

in my absence: **me absente**

in my judgment: **meo judicio**

in my lifetime: **me vivo**

in my opinion: **me judice**

in my own way: **more meo**

in name only: **verbo**

in one place: **in unum**

in one's own person: **in propria persona**

in one's own right: **suo jure**

in open court: **in curia**

in opposition: **ex adverso**

in part: **ex parte**

in passing: **obiter**

in peace: **in pace**

in perpetual remembrance: **in perpetuam rei memoriam**

in person: **in persona**

in plain words: **nudis verbis**

in pledge: **in vadio**

in prison: **in carcerem** or **in custodiam**

in private: **in privato**

in private life: **privatim**

in prospect: **in prospectu**

in public: **in propatulo** or **in publico**

in public view: **in oculis civium**

in readiness: **in promptu**

in reality: **in actu**

in reserve: **in pectore**

in respect of: **intuitu**

in secret: **in pectore** or **januis clausis**

in short: **ad summam**

in silence: **sub silentio**

in smoke: **in fumo**

in so many words: **in totidem verbis** or **totidem verbis**

in sport: **per ludibrium**

in substance: **in corpore**

in the abstract: **in abstracto**

in the back: **in dorso**

in the beginning: **in limine** or **in principio**

in the clouds: **in nubibus**

in the course of the year: **anno vertente**

in the court of conscience: **in foro conscientiae**

in the custody of the law: **in custodia legis**

in the egg: **in ovo**

in the end: **tandem denique**

in the English fashion: **more Anglico**

in the evening: **vesperi**

in the first place: **ante omnia** or **imprimis**

in the following month: **proximo** or **proximo mense**

in the future: **in futuro**

in the Golden Age: **in illo tempore**

in the highest: **in excelsis**

in the Irish fashion: **more Hibernico**

in the Italian manner: **Italice**

in the Latin manner: **Latine**

in the living organism: **in vivo**

in the meantime: **ad interim** or **per interim**

in the middle: **in medio**

in the midst of the work: **opere in medio**

in the midst of things: **in mediis rebus**

in the mind: **in intellectu**

in the name of: **in nomine**

in the name of the Father, the Son, and the Holy Spirit: **in nomine Patris et Filii et Spiritus Sancti**

in the name of the Lord: **in nomine Domini**

in the nature of things: **in rerum natura**

in the nick of time: **in ipso articulo temporis**

in the notes: **in notis**

in the nude: **in naturalibus**

in the open air: **sub dio** or **sub divo** or **sub Jove**

in the original state: **in statu quo**

in the past year: **praeterito anno**

in the place: **loco**

in the place cited: **in loco citato** or **loco citato**

in the place mentioned above: **ubi supra**

in the place of a parent: **in loco parentis**

in the proper place: **in loco**

in the rear: **a tergo**

in the same place: **ibidem**

in the silence of night: **silentio noctis**

in the south: **in meridiem**

in the usual manner: **more solito**

in the very act: **in actu**

in the very act of crime: **in flagrante delicto**

in the very words: **ipsissimis verbis**

in the womb: **in utero** or **in ventre**

in the work cited: **opere citato**

in the year of our Lord: **anno Domini**

in the year of the reign: **anno regni**

in the year of the world since the creation: **anno mundi**

in this direction: **horsum**

in this month: **hoc mense**

in this place: **hoc loco**

in this sense: **hoc sensu**

in this year: **hoc anno**

in time of war: **in bello**

in transit: **in transitu**

in truth: **re vera** or **revera**

in turn: **in vicem** or **in vices**

in unison: **in concordia vocum**

in use: **in usu**

in vain: **frustra** or **in cassum**

in various directions: **alius alio**

in whatever manner: **quovis modo**

in witness: **in testimonium**

in your judgment: **te judice**

indirectly: **per ambages**

indiscriminately: **per saturam**

indispensible condition: **causa sine qua non** or **conditio sine qua non** or **sine qua non**

indisputably: **sine controversia**

individuality: **propria natura**

individually: **viritim**

inherently evil: **mala in se**

inherited property: **patrimonium**

inland: **mediterraneus**

innate goodness: **naturae bonitas**

innermost thoughts: **penetralia mentis**

insanity: **dementia**

inside: **intra**

instead of: **ad vicem**

intelligible world: **mundus intelligibilis**

intentionally: **de industria**

intermarriage: **connubium**

internal witness: **testimonium internum**

international law: **jus gentium**

interwoven: **intertextus**

into the heart of the matter: **in medias res**

intrinsically: **per se**

invalid law: **lex irrita est**
inward teacher: **magister internus**
inwards: **intro**
iron: **ferrum**
island: **insula**
it does not follow: **non sequitur**
it happens: **usu venit**
it has been proven: **probatum est**
it is all over: **actum est**
it is day: **lucet**
it is done: **factum est**
it is finished: **consummatum est**
it is fraud to conceal fraud: **fraus est celare fraudem**
it is lawful: **fas est**
it is legal: **licet**
it is pointless: **nihil attinet**
it is proper: **oportet**
it is rumored: **fama est**
it is so: **ita res est** or **ita est**
it is the third hour: **tertia hora est**
it is useful: **res expedit**
it seems: **videtur**
itch for writing: **cacoëthes scribendi**
jealousy: **zelotypus**

J

Jew: **Iudaeus**
jointly: **in solidum** or **in solido**
journal: **adversaria**
judge: **judex**
judgment of God: **Dei judicium** or **judicium Dei**

K

keen wit: **sal Atticum**
kinetic energy: **vis viva**
king: **rex**
king of kings: **rex regum**

king's peace: **pax regis**
kiss of peace: **osculum pacis**
know thyself: **nosce te ipsum** or **nosce teipsum**
knowledge is power: **scientia est potentia**
known: **cognitus**

L

laboratory: **officina**
laboratory of nations: **officina gentium**
Lamb of God: **Agnus Dei**
lapse of memory: **lapsus memoriae**
last farewell: **ultimum vale**
last of the heirs: **ultimus haeres**
last of the kings: **ultimus regum**
last year: **priore anno**
late at night: **multa de nocte** or **multa nocte**
late night study: **lucubratus**
law: **lex** or **jus**
law of consanguinity: **jus sanguinis**
law of nations: **jus gentium**
law of retaliation: **lex talionis**
law of the land: **lex terrae**
law of the place: **lex loci**
law of the soil: **jus soli**
law of the sword: **jus gladii**
lawless: **inlex**
lawlessness: **leges nullae**
leader of the pack: **dux gregis**
leaf: **folium**
leap-year: **annus bisextus**
learned: **literatus** or **litteratus**
learned class: **literati** or **litterati**
least: **minimus**
leave well enough alone: **actum ne agas**
left: **sinister**
left eye: **oculus sinister**
left-hand page (the backside): **folio verso**
left-hand page of a book: **verso folio**
legal detention: **habeas corpus**

legal right: **jus**

leisure: **otium**

length-wise: **in longitudinem**

lest ye forget: **ne obliviscaris**

let it be so!: **fiat**

let me know: **fac sciam**

let the buyer beware: **caveat emptor**

let there be light: **fiat lux**

let us be joyful (while we are young): **gaudeamus igitur (juvenes dum sumus)**

letter: **epistula**

letter of the law: **strictum jus**

liberally: **quantum libet**

liberty: **libertas**

library: **bibliotheca**

life: **vita**

life span: **vitae summa**

lifelike: **ad vivum**

light: **lux**

light of faith: **lumen fidei**

light of grace: **lumen gratiae**

light of nature: **lumen naturale**

light of the world: **lux mundi**

like father, like son: **patris est filius** or **qualis pater, talis filius**

likeness of God: **similitudo Dei**

likewise: **item** or **itidem**

limb by limb: **membratim**

lion: **leo**

liquid: **fluidus**

literally: **ad litteram** or **ad verbum** or **e verbo** or **literatim** or **litteratim** or **pro verbo**

Little Dipper: **Ursa Minor**

little by little: **unciatim**

live for today: **vive hodie**

loan: **pecunia mutua**

long conversation: **multus sermo**

long live the king: **vivat rex**

long live the king and queen: **vivant rex et regina**

long live the queen: **vivat regina**

long live the republic: **vivat respublica**

look for this: **hoc quaere**

loophole: **fenestra**

Lord have mercy: **Kyrie eleison**

Lord's Day: **dies dominicus**

Lord's Prayer: **Paternoster** or **Pater Noster**

Lord's Supper: **Cena Domini**

loss: **damnum**

lost: **adiratus**

love: **amor** or **caritas**

love begets love: **amor gignit amorem**

love conquers all things: **amor vincit omnia** or **omnia vincit amor**

love of country: **amor patriae**

love of money: **amor nummi**

love of money is a root to all evil: **radix omnium malorum est cupiditas**

love of one's neighbor: **amor proximi**

love of self: **amor sui**

love potion: **philtrum**

love sick: **aeger amore** or **aegra amans**

lovers' quarrels: **amantium irae**

Low Mass: **Missa bassa**

lower class: **proletarius**

lucky and unlucky days: **fasti et nefasti dies**

lucky day: **dies faustus**

lukewarm: **tepidus**

lunar eclipse: **defectio lunae**

lunch: **prandium**

M

made of pottery: **fictilis**

magical: **Hecatean**

magician: **magus**

maiden: **virgo**

majority: **major pars**

make it so: **fieri facias**

Maker of the World: **Orbis Factor**

malpractice: **mala praxis**

man: **homo** or **vir**

man is a wolf to man: **homo homini lupus** or **lupus est homo homini**

man is the measure of all things: **homo mensura**

man of letters: **homo doctus** or **vir literatus** or **vir litteratus**

man of the people: **homo plebeius**

manner of living: **modus vivendi**

many times: **multis partibus**

many-headed snake: **Hydra**

market: **emporium**

married: **nupta**

Mass: **Missa**

Mass of the faithful: **Missa fidelium**

master: **magister**

master of ceremonies: **magister ceremoniarum**

masterpiece: **magnum opus** or **opus magnum**

may it flourish: **floreat**

may the omen augur no evil: **absit omen**

meanwhile: **interim**

memorandum: **notandum**

men of straw: **faeneus homines**

mercantile law: **lex mercatoria** or **mercatorum**

mercury: **argentum vivum**

mere assertion: **gratis dictum**

mere word: **flatus vocis**

meritorious: **bonae notae**

middle of the road: **media via** or **via media**

middle way: **media via** or **via media**

middling: **mediocris**

midnight: **media nox**

milk: **lac**

Milky Way: **lacteus orbis** or **via Lactea**

mine and thine: **meum et tuum**

minister of the Word of God: **Verbi Dei Minister**

miscarriage of justice: **judicium perversum**

misfortune: **fortuna adversa** or **infelicitas** or **res adversae**

mix: **misce**

mob: **mobile vulgus**

mode of operating: **modus operandi**

money does not smell: **pecunia non olet**

month: **mensis**

monthly: **menstruus** or **per mensem**

moon: **luna** or **noctiluca**

moonlight: **lunae lumen**

more lasting than bronze: **aere perennius**

more than usual: **plus solito**

morning star: **lucifer**

most excellent: **optime**

mother: **mater**

mountain: **mons**

mountain air: **afflatus montium**

much in little: **multa paucis** or **multum in parvo**

much later: **multo post**

much obliged: **bene facis**

murder: **homicidium**

music of the spheres: **vox stellarum**

mutual consent: **assensio mentium** or **mutuus consensus**

mutually: **inter nos**

mystical union: **unio mystica**

mythical creature: **chimaera**

N

naked body: **nudatum corpus**

naked truth: **nuda veritas**

name having been changed: **mutato nomine**

namely: **scilicet** or **videlicet**

narrow-minded: **animus angustus**

national hero: **pater patriae**

native soil: **natale solum**

natural advantages: **naturae bona**

natural intelligence: **lumen naturale**

natural law: **jus naturae**

natural world: **rerum natura**

nature abhors a vacuum: **natura abhorret a vacuo**

near: **circa**

near at hand: **inibi**

necessary changes being made: **mutatis mutandis**

necessity is the mother of invention: **mater artium necessitas**

necessity knows no law: **necessitas non habet legem**

needle: **acus**

negative vote: **non placet**

neither: **neuter**

neither delay nor rest: **nec more nec requies**

neither desire nor fear: **nec cupias nec metuas**

neither head nor foot: **nec caput nec pedes**

new king, new law: **novus rex, nova lex**

new moon: **nova luna**

night: **nox**

nightlong: **pernox**

no: **non**

no contest: **nolo contendere**

no offense intended: **absit invidia**

no one else: **nemo alius**

no sooner said than done: **dictum ac factum**

noble class: **optimates**

non agreement: **res discrepat**

nonexistence: **non esse**

nonsense!: **fabulae!**

noon: **meridies**

North Pole: **polus glacialis**

north wind: **Boreas**

not a doubt: **haud dubie**

not in the least: **nihil omnino**

not of sound mind: **non compos mentis**

not particularly: **non ita**

not permitted: **non licet**

not pleasing: **non libet**

not sacred: **profanus**

not too much: **ne nimium**

note well: **nota bene**

nothing: **nihil**

nothing new under the sun: **nihil sub sole novum**

notwithstanding: **non obstante**

notwithstanding these things: **his non obstantibus**

now: **nunc**

now and always: **et nunc et semper**

now and later: **alius alias**

now and then: **interdum**

now or never: **nunc aut nunquam**

O

O Come, All Ye Faithful: **Adeste Fideles**

of his own right: **proprio jure**

of low birth: **filius terrae**

of one mind or spirit: **unanimus**

of one's own accord: **ex proprio motu** or **motu proprio**

of that age: **id aetatis**

of the faith: **de fide**

of the lower world: **infernus**

of the people: **plebeius**

off the record: **obiter dictum**

officially: **ex cathedra**

oil: **oleum**

old age: **fessa aetas**

older child: **major natu**

on a level surface: **in plano**

on alert: **arrectus auribus**

on deposit: **in deposito**

on equal terms: **ex aequo** or **in aequo**

on foot: **pedibus**

on hand: **in manibus**

on my account: **mea de causa** or **meo nomine**

on my behalf: **nomine meo**

on my word of honor: **fide mea**

on purpose: **ex industria**

on the back: **in dorso**

on the contrary: **e contrario** or **ex contrario** or **per contra**

on the ground: **humi**

on the left: **a sinistra**

on the other hand: **e contra**

on the right: **a dextra**

on the spot: **ilico**

on the spur of the moment: **ex tempore** or **temporis causa**

on the way: **in transitu** or **obiter**

on the whole: **ad summam** or **ex toto** or **in toto**

on tiptoe: **suspenso gradu**

once for all: **semel pro semper**

one by one: **membratim**

one of a kind: **sui generis**

one of two: **alteruter**

one or two: **unus et alter**

one quarter: **quarta pars**

one thing after another: **aliud ex alio**

one witness is no witness: **testis unus, testis nullus**

one-sided: **iniquus**

only-begotten: **unigena**

opposite: **contra**

optical illusion: **deceptio visus**

orally: **viva voce**

oratory: **ars dicendi**

origins: **primordium**

our light comes from God: **a Deo lux nostra**

our people: **nostri**

out of court: **ex curia**

out of date: **obsoletus**

out of sight, out of mind: **absens haeres non erit**

out of the depths: **de profundis**

out of tune: **absonus**

over: **super**

over a glass: **inter pocula**

P

pain: **dolor**

pain of judgment: **poena sensus**

pain of the damned: **poena damni**

painless: **sine dolore**

painted by: **pinxit**

painter: **pictor**

pair of scales: **libra**

pair of scissors: **forfex**

pair of tongs: **forceps**

pale Death: **pallida mors**

pale with rage: **pallidus irae**

palimpsest: **codex rescriptus**

panel of jurors: **judicis**

papal encyclical: **bulla**

part for the whole: **pars pro toto**

partially: **per studium**

partnership: **consortium**

party: **convivium**

passion for writing: **furor scribendi**

patriot: **civis bonus**

Peace of God: **Pax Dei**

Peace of the Church: **Pax Ecclesiae**

peace: **pax**

peace be with you: **pax vobiscum**

peace in war: **pax in bello**

pearls before swine: **margaritas ante porcos**

pending: **in fieri**

pending lawsuit: **lis pendens**

pending the suit: **pendente lite**

perennials: **semper florens**

perfectly: **ad unguem** or **in unguem**

perforce: **nolens volens**

perpendicularly: **ad lineam**

perpetual motion: **mobile perpetuum** or **perpetuum mobile**

person of full legal rights: **legalis homo**

petition: **libellus**

philosopher's stone: **lapis philosophorum**

physician, heal thyself: **medice, cura te ipsum**

pilgrimage: **peregrinatio sacra**

pint: **octarius**

pious fraud: **fraus pia**

place of the seal: **locus sigilli**

please: **amabo te** or **amabo** or **si placet**

poetic genius: **vis poetica**

poetic inspiration: **furor poeticus**

poetic license: **licentia vatum**

point for point: **punctatim**

point of time: **punctum temporis**

political revolution: **novae res**

posse: **posse comitatus**

postscript: **postscriptum**

potentially: **in posse** or **in potentia**

poverty: **impotentia**

power: **vis**

power of inertia: **vis inertiae**

pray for the soul of . . . : **orate pro anima**

pray for us: **ora pro nobis**

prepared for all things: **in omnia paratus**

prepared for either event: **in utrumque paratus**

prepared for the worst: **ad utrumque paratus**

presence of mind: **praesentia animi**

pretty: **bellus**

prevenient grace: **gratia praeveniens**

priest: **pontifex**

principle elements: **principia rerum**

private life: **vita privata**

private person: **vir privatus**

privately: **privatim** or **sub silentio**

pro and con: **in utramque partem**

probable: **veri similis**

procedural law: **ordinandi lex**

prodigy: **niger cycnus** or **rara avis**

prohibition: **interdictum**

promise of protection: **fides publica**

promoter of the faith: **promotor fidei**

property: **bona**

proportionally: **pro rata**

providential intervention: **deus ex machina**

public affairs: **negotia publica**

public archives: **tabulae publicae**

public enemy: **inimicus**

public inscription: **aes publicum**

public land: **ager publicus**

public life: **respublica forum**

public opinion: **vulgi opinio**

public place: **locus communis**

public square: **forum**

pure act: **actus purus**

puzzle: **crux**

Q

Queen of Heaven: **Regina Caeli**

queen: **regina**

quota: **numerus clausus**

R

race track: **hippodromos**

rain clouds: **cumulus nimbus**

rainbow: **arcus pluvius**

ram: **aries**

raw: **incoctus**

read between the lines: **sub audi**

ready for battle: **in procinctu**

really?: **ita?**

rear guard: **agmen novissimum** or **agmen extremum**

received text: **textus receptus**

reciprocally: **inter se**

recitation: **recitatio**

recluse: **homo solitarius**

records: **annales**

red-handed: **flagrante delicto**

redundant act: **actum agere**

reference volume: **vade mecum**

regarding: **re**

regent: **interrex**
rejoice in God: **Jubilate Deo**
reluctantly: **gravatim**
renown: **ad astra**
repeatedly: **identidem** or **toties quoties**
republic: **res publica** or **respublica**
rest in peace: **requiescat in pace**
restored to life: **redivivus**
reverse side: **verso** or **verso folio**
résumé: **curriculum vitae** or **vitae curriculum**
riddle: **aenigma**
right: **jus**
right eye: **oculus dexter**
right hand: **dextra**
right of pledge: **jus pignoris**
right of possession: **jus possessionis**
right of property: **jus proprietatis**
right of royalty: **jus regium**
right of the first night: **jus primae noctis**
right of the widow: **jus relicti**
right-hand page (the front side): **folio recto**
right-hand page of a book: **recto** or **recto folio**
robber: **raptor**
Roman mile: **mille passuum**
Roman peace: **Pax Romana**
room for doubt: **ambigendi locus**
rub well: **tere bene**
rumor: **fama clamosa**
runner-up: **proxime accessit**
rural: **paganus**

S

said and done: **dictum factum**
salient point: **punctum saliens**
salt seasons everything: **sal sapit omnia**
salvation is by the Cross: **a cruce salus**
same old thing: **crambe repetita**
scandal: **fama clamosa**

scene of the crime: **locus criminis** or **locus delicti**
scholar: **vir doctus**
science: **scientia**
scorpion: **scorpio**
scripture alone: **sola scriptura**
sculptured by: **sculpsit**
seasoning: **condimentum**
second self: **alter idem**
second to none: **nulli secundus**
secret teaching: **disciplina arcana**
secretarial matters: **ab epistulis**
see: **vide**
see above: **vide supra**
see after this: **vide post**
see before: **vide ante**
see below: **vide infra**
see the above comment: **vide ut supra**
seize the day: **carpe diem**
self-confidence: **fiducia sui**
sense of duty: **officium**
sensible world: **mundus sensibilis**
sensual pleasures: **voluptates corporis**
sentimental value: **pretium affectionis**
series of calamities: **Ilias malorum**
seriousness: **gravitas**
severely wounded: **graviter ictus**
sex drive: **libido**
shade: **umbra**
shake: **agita**
short cut: **via compendiaria**
siblings: **fratres**
sick: **aeger**
sickly: **infirmus**
sideways: **in obliquum**
siege machines: **moles belli**
sieve: **cribrum**
silent: **tacitus**
silent actor: **persona muta**
silver: **argentum**
sincerely: **bona fide**
sinew of proof: **nervus probandi**
sinew of things: **nervus rerum**

sing unto the Lord: **cantate Domino**

sister: **soror**

sketch: **adumbratio**

sleep on it: **in nocte consilium**

sleepless: **ex somnis** or **insomnis**

slip of the pen: **lapsus calami**

slip of the tongue: **lapsus linguae**

smell of profit: **odor lucri**

snake in the grass: **anguis in herba**

so far: **pro tanto**

so help me God!: **medius fidius!**

so ordered: **ordinatum est**

social life: **vitae societas**

solar eclipse: **defectio solis**

sole heir: **heres ex asse**

solid earth: **terra firma**

someone significant: **aliquid**

something significant: **aliquid**

son: **filius**

son of the earth: **terrae filius**

soon: **mox**

sorcery: **ars magica**

sorrow: **dolor**

soul: **anima** or **animus**

sound of mind: **compos mentis**

sounding alike: **idem sonans**

source of evils: **fons malorum**

source of life: **vivendi causa**

south: **australis**

southward: **ad meridiem**

southwest wind: **ventus Africus**

speak of the devil: **lupus in fabula**

speech impediment: **haesitantia linguae**

speechless: **bos in lingua**

spirit: **numen**

spirit of the law: **mens legis** or **sententia legis** or **voluntas legis**

spirits of the dead: **manes**

spoken in Latin: **Latine dictum**

sponsorship: **aegis**

spontaneously: **de proprio motu** or **proprio motu**

spoonful: **cochleare**

spouse: **conjunx** or **conjux**

SPQR (the Senate and the People of Rome): **Senatus Populusque Romanus**

Spring: **ver**

spring water: **aqua fontana**

star: **astrum**

stark naked: **in puris naturalibus**

starting point: **terminus a quo**

state secrets: **arcana imperii**

statute law: **lex scripta**

step by step: **gradatim** or **per gradus**

still water runs deep: **aqua profunda est quieta**

stone: **lapis** or **saxum**

straight ahead: **recta via**

straight line: **recta linea**

stranger: **hospes hostis**

strength: **vis**

struck by lightning: **fulmine ictus**

such as it is: **talis qualis**

suicide: **felo-de-se**

sum of all things: **summa summarum**

summarily: **acervatim**

Summer: **aestas**

sunflower: **heliotropium**

sunny: **apricus**

superior force: **vis major**

supreme achievement: **spolia opima**

supreme jurisdiction: **jus gladii**

surname: **cognomen**

syphilis: **lues venerea**

T

table salt: **sal culinarius**

take courage!: **macte animo!**

take notice: **nota bene**

task-master: **operis exactor**

tasteless: **sine sapore**

teacher: **magister**

tear of Christ: **lacrima Christi**

tell me: **fac ut sciam**

temperate zone: **orbis medius**

temporarily: **in tempus** or **pro tempore**

Ten Commandments: **Decalogus**

tendency to find fault: **cacoëthes carpendi**

tendency to talk: **cacoëthes loquendi**

thank you: **benigne dicis** or **gratias tibi ago**

thankfulness: **animus gratus**

thankless: **ingratus**

thanks be to God: **Dei gratias** or **Deo gratias**

thanks to me: **opera mea**

that and that alone: **id demum**

that is: **id est**

that is to say: **id est**

the cure is worse than the disease: **aegrescit medendo**

the die is cast: **alea jacta est** or **jacta est alea** or **jacta alea est**

the end: **explicit** or **finis**

the finding of the jury: **sententiae judicum**

the following: **sequens**

the following things: **sequentia**

the many: **multi**

the master has spoken it: **magister dixit**

the play is over: **acta est fabula**

the question is settled: **res confecta est**

the same: **idem**

the same as: **idem quod**

the time for play: **tempus ludendi**

the Virgin: **Virgo**

the whole: **totum**

there is need: **opus est**

therefore: **ergo**

they leave the stage: **exeunt**

thigh: **femur**

third choice: **tertium quid**

this day: **hodie**

this do: **hoc age**

this for that: **quid pro quo**

this is my body: **hoc est corpus meum**

this pleases me: **hoc mihi placet**

thoughtful of the future: **prudens futuri**

thread by thread: **filatim**

three times: **ter**

three times a day: **ter in die**

thrice holy: **Tersanctus** or **Trisagion**

through carelessness: **per incuriam**

throughout: **passim**

thumb's down: **pollice verso**

thus: **sic**

time: **tempus**

time flies: **tempus fugit**

time reveals all things: **tempus omnia revelat**

time reveals the truth: **veritatem dies aperit**

tit for tat: **par pari refero** or **quid pro quo**

to: **ad**

to a great extent: **magna ex parte**

to a higher degree: **in majus**

to and fro: **ultro citroque**

to call into question: **in dubium vocare**

to descend into the lower world: **ad inferos descendere**

to die: **abiit ad plures** or **ad majores**

to each his/her own: **cuique suum** or **suum cuique**

to err is human: **errare humanum est** or **hominis est errare** or **humanum est errare**

to feed the flame: **alere flammam**

to give thanks: **gratias agere**

to go by foot: **iter pedestre**

to go by land: **iter terrestre**

to hang by a thread: **pendere filo**

to infinity: **in infinitum**

to live for the moment: **in horam vivere**

to live for today: **in diem vivere**

to my house: **ad me**

to one's advantage: **in rem**

to one's taste: **ad gustum**

to remain on stage: **manet**

to rush to arms: **ad arma concurrere**

to swear an oath: **facere sacramentum**

to take a turn for the better: **in melius mutari**

to that extent: **pro tanto**

to the best of one's ability: **pro sua parte** or **pro virili parte**

to the center of the road: **ad filum viae**

to the center of the stream: **ad filum aquae**

to the extreme: **ad extremum**

to the gentle reader: **lectori benevolo**

to the greater glory of God: **ad majorem Dei gloriam**

to the highest authority: **ad limina apostolorum** or **ad limina**

to the highest point: **ad summum**

to the last: **ad ultimum**

to the light of day: **superas ad auras**

to the matter: **ad rem**

to the people: **ad populum**

to the place: **ad locum**

to the point of disgust: **usque ad nauseum** or **ad nauseam**

to the point of extermination: **ad internecionem**

to the same degree: **ad eundem gradum**

to the same point: **ad idem**

to this: **ad hoc**

to what end?: **cui bono?**

to your disadvantage: **incommodo tuo**

toastmaster: **arbiter bibendi**

today: **hodie**

tomorrow: **cras**

tomorrow evening: **cras vespere**

tomorrow morning: **cras mane**

tomorrow night: **cras nocte**

tongue: **lingua**

tonight: **hoc nocte**

touch of bitterness: **amari aliquid**

tragic farce: **flebile ludibrium**

travel weary: **fessus de via**

traveling day and night: **itinera diurna nocturnaque**

trial by ordeal: **Dei judicium**

triple brass defense: **aes triplex**

truism: **dictum**

trust God: **crede Deo**

trust not to appearances: **ne fronti crede**

truth: **veritas**

truth conquers all things: **vincit omnia veritas**

truth will prevail: **veritas praevalebit**

turn of phrase: **genus dicendi**

turning point: **magni momenti**

twice a day: **bis in die**

twice as much: **alterum tantum**

twilight: **crepusculum**

twins: **gemini**

two: **duo**

two pairs: **bis bina**

U

unabridged: **in extenso**

unaided: **sine auxilio**

unanimously: **ad unum omnes** or **per totam curiam** or **una voce** or **uno animo** or **uno consensu** or **uno ore**

unbeaten: **invictus**

unbelief: **impietas**

unborn: **nondum natus**

unburied: **inhumatus** or **insepultus** or **intumulatus**

unchanged: **status quo**

uncle: **avunculus** or **patruus**

unconstitutional: **non legitimus**

unconventionally wise: **abnormis sapiens**

uncooked: **incoctus**

under: **sub**

under arms: **in armis**

under bad auspices: **malis avibus**

under my direction: **me duce**

under penalty: **sub poena**

under the influence of wine: **sub vino**

under the protection of the law: **in gremio legis**

under the skin: **intercus**

under this title: **hoc titulo**

underground: **subterraneus**

undeveloped: **in ovo**

undomesticated: **ferae naturae**

unfaithful: **infidelis**

union is strength: **vis unita fortior**

unique: **sui generis**

universal consent: **consensus omnium**

universal peace: **pax orbis terrarum**

universally: **in universum**

universe: **mundi universitas**

unknown: **ignotus**

unknown land: **terra incognita**

unknown painter: **pictor ignotus**

unknown person: **quidam**

unlucky: **infaustus**

unlucky day: **dies infaustus** or **nefasti dies**

unmarried: **innuba** or **innupta**

unprepared: **illotis manibus**

unprovoked: **non laccessitus**

unpublished: **nondum editus**

unrestrained: **impotens sui**

unsatisfactorily: **minus bene**

unsolicited: **sponte sua** or **sua sponte**

unthankful: **male gratus**

until late at night: **ad multam noctem**

until late in the day: **ad multum diem**

unwelcome person: **persona non grata**

unwillingly: **ab invito**

up and down: **sursum deorsum**

up the mountain: **in adversum montem**

up to: **ad**

up to this point: **hactenus**

uphill: **adverso colle** or **adversus collem**

upside down: **inversus**

upstart: **novus homo**

useful: **ex usu**

useless: **inutilis**

V

valid law: **lex rata est**

vanguard: **agmen primum**

variant reading: **varia lectio**

vegetable market: **forum holitorium**

venal throng: **grex venalium**

very little: **minimum**

very much: **impendio**

vestal virgin: **virgo vestalis**

veteran: **emeritus**

vexing question: **quaestio vexata**

victim: **hostia**

virtuous life: **vita honesta**

vital force: **vis vitae**

vital principle: **nisus formativus**

voice of one crying in the desert: **vox clamantis in deserto**

voice of the people: **vox populi**

W

war-cry: **clamor bellicus**

war horse: **equus bellator**

warning: **caveat**

watch and pray: **vigilate et orate**

water: **aqua**

water-carrier: **aquarius**

way of sorrows: **Via Dolorosa**

We praise Thee, O God: **Te Deum, Laudamus**

we cannot: **non possumus**

we have a pope!: **habemus papam!**

weariness of life: **taedium vitae**

weary traveler: **fessus viator**

weightiness: **gravitas**

well-being: **bene esse**

well-read: **literatus** or **litteratus**

western: **Hesperius**

westward: **ad occasum** or **ad occidentem**

what does this mean?: **quid hoc sibi vult?**

what is to be done?: **quid faciendum?**

what is truth?: **quid est veritas?**

what now?: **quid nunc?**

what time is it?: **hora quota est?**

what's new?: **quid novi?**

whenever necessary: **pro re nata**

where are you going?: **quo tendis?**

where in the world?: **ubi gentium?**

wherever the book opens: **ad aperturam libri**

wherever you like: **qualibet**

which is: **quod est**

which is the same: **quae est eadem**

which see (pl.): **quae vide**

which see (sing.): **quod vide**

while feasting: **inter epulas**

while still day: **de die**

while still night: **de nocte**

while unmarried: **dum sola**

whirlpool: **vortex**

whisper: **vox clandestina**

whither goest thou?: **quo vadis?**

why do you laugh?: **quid rides?**

why not?: **quid ni?**

wife: **uxor**

wild: **ferus**

will of heaven: **numen divinum**

willy-nilly: **nolens volens**

winter solstice: **bruma**

wisdom: **sapientia**

with: **cum**

with a grain of salt: **cum grano salis**

with advancing years: **aetate progrediente**

with advantage: **ob rem**

with all one's might: **totis viribus** or **viribus totis**

with ease: **de plano**

with envy: **aegris oculis**

with equal pace: **pari passu**

with evil intent: **malo animo**

with favorable omens: **faustis ominibus**

with few words: **paucis verbis**

with full right: **optimo jure** or **pleno jure**

with good reason: **non sine causa**

with great loss (of life): **magno cum detrimento**

with great praise: **magna cum laude**

with greater force: **a fortiori**

with highest honors: **summa cum laude**

with limitations: **secundum quid**

with many tears: **magno cum fletu** or **multis cum lacrimis**

with my pleasure: **me libente**

with praise: **cum laude**

with regard to rank: **salvo ordine**

with the left hand: **sinistra manu**

with the stream: **flumine secundo**

with the teeth: **mordicus**

with the utmost accuracy: **verbatim et literatim et punctatim**

with this proviso: **hac lege**

with tossled hair: **passis crinibus**

with unequal steps: **haud passibus aequis**

with united strength: **viribus unitis**

with unwashed hands: **illotis manibus**

with what intent?: **quo animo?**

within: **intra**

within range: **intra jactum**

within the walls: **intra muros**

without: **sine**

without a blow: **sine ictu**

without anger: **sine ira**

without any danger: **sine omni periculo**

without care: **sine cura**

without charge: **pro bono publico**

without cost: **gratis** or **gratuitus**

without date: **sine anno**

without deceit: **sine fraude**

without delay: **sine mora**

without doubt: **sine dubio**

without envy: **sine invidia**

without hatred: **sine odio**

without help: **sine ope**

without issue: **sine prole**

without jesting: **sine joco**

without legitimate issue: **sine legitima prole**

without male issue: **sine mascula prole**

without objection: **nihil obstat**

without offending modesty: **salvo pudore**

without partiality: **pari passu**

without place: **sine loco**

without prejudice: **salvo jure** or **sine praejudicio**

without pretense: **sine fuco**

without reservation: **simpliciter**

without smell: **inolens**

without stain: **sine maculis**

without strength: **sine nervis**

without surviving issue: **sine prole supersite**

without this: **absque hoc**

without violating sense: **salvo sensu**

witness to a will: **obsignator**

woman: **femina**

wonderful year: **annus mirabilis**

word for word: **ad verbum** or **de verbo**

wordy: **verbosus**

work of art: **opus**

world: **mundus** or **orbis terrae** or **orbis terrarum**

world of images: **mundus imaginalis**

world soul: **anima mundi**

worse: **peior** or **pejor**

worst: **pessimus**

worthy of note: **notatu dignum**

wow!: **hui**

wrath of god: **ira deorum**

writer's cramp: **chorea scriptorum**

written by: **scripsit**

Y

year: **annus**

year from now: **ad annum**

yearlong: **perennis**

yes: **certo** or **etiam** or **ita**

yesterday: **heri** or **hesternus**

yield not to misfortunes: **nec cede malis**

younger: **junior** or **minor natu**

youth: **bona aetas**

Z

Zodiac: **orbis signifer**